ABSOLUTE
CONFUSION

THE BARNA REPORT VOLUME 3 1993-94

ABSOLUTE CONFUSION

HOW OUR MORAL AND SPIRITUAL FOUNDATIONS ARE ERODING IN THIS AGE OF CHANGE

GEORGE BARNA
AUTHOR OF THE FROG IN THE KETTLE

Regal Books
A Division of Gospel Light
Ventura, California, U.S.A.

Published by Regal Books
A Division of Gospel Light
Ventura, CA 93006
Printed in U.S.A.

Scripture quotations in this publication are taken from the following versions:

CEV—Contemporary English Version, Holy Bible for Today's Family. © 1991 by American Bible Society.
Scripture quotations marked *NIV* are from the HOLY BIBLE, NEW INTERNATIONAL VERSION®. NIV®. Copyright © 1973, 1978, 1984 by International Bible Society. Used by permission of Zondervan Publishing House. All rights reserved.

ISSN 1063-1437
ISBN 0-8307-1641-6

1 2 3 4 5 6 7 8 9 10 11 12 13 14 / 01 00 99 98 97 96 95 94 93

Rights for publishing this book in other languages are contracted by Gospel Literature International (GLINT). GLINT also provides technical help for the adaptation, translation, and publishing of Bible study resources and books in scores of languages worldwide. For further information, contact GLINT, Post Office Box 4060, Ontario, California, 91761-1003, U.S.A., or the publisher.

CONTENTS

Acknowledgments

The following people were gracious and supportive as I worked to develop this book. With one exception, they are listed in alphabetical order.

My colleagues at the Barna Research Group have once again accepted a greater level of responsibility during my absence to enable this book to see the light of day. They helped develop and collect the data, and have prayed for me during this time. Thanks go to Cindy Coats, Gwen Ingram, Vibeke Klocke, George Maupin, Paul Rottler and Telford Work for their role in this project.

My colleagues at Gospel Light Publications have again come through as world-class partners in this team effort. This project is one of the more demanding ones produced by Regal Books. I continue to pray that the efforts of the Regal team produce significant results for God's Kingdom. Having full knowledge that I am unintentionally leaving out many whose work deserves recognition, let me at least acknowledge those with whom I have worked most closely: Bill Denzel, Terry Donnelly, Kyle Duncan, Barbara Fisher, Bill Greig Jr., Bill Greig III, Nola Grunden, Gloria Moss, Dennis Somers and Virginia Woodard.

Don Wildmon, of the American Family Association, graciously consented to allow us to use some of the data from a study his organization commissioned in 1992. Thank you, Don, for permission to use the information and for your continued efforts to be a faithful servant of God. May 1993 and the coming years bring you great health and abundant blessings.

Finally, my greatest appreciation is extended to my wife and daughter. Nancy endured yet another manuscript being written under crunch conditions, giving up her husband for several days of author's seclusion. Samantha surrendered daddy for several days and nights when he probably should have been playing with stuffed animals and building blocks instead. I trust that God will reward these precious women for their sacrifice in the creation of this resource for the Church.

INTRODUCTION

Perhaps my favorite Bible verse is found in 1 Chronicles 12. In that chapter, we have a recitation of all the people with whom King David surrounded himself after his predecessor, Saul, died. We read a listing of tribe after tribe of mighty warriors David brought to his side to protect and extend his kingdom. In all, we are introduced to more than 340,000 mighty men and warriors upon whom David and Israel would depend for security.

But tucked in the middle of the passage is a single verse that cannot be overlooked if we are to understand leadership and how God intends to care for His people. Verse 32 of chapter 12 talks about the men of Issachar, who are described "as men who understood the times and knew what Israel should do."

David, as wise as he was, knew very well that his own wisdom, just as that of any person, was corruptible and fallible. He therefore strove to surround himself with people who could bring additional insights and perspective to bear on his own decision making. He was not so arrogant to believe he alone knew all that needed to be known to make great choices on behalf of his people. He hired a team of wise advisors to help lead the people.

In the same way, Joshua demonstrated his understanding of the importance of information as a leader of God's people. In Joshua chapter 2, and again at various points during his tenure, the Bible tells us that Joshua sent spies into the land of the enemy to determine who they were and what they were up to. In essence, Joshua was conducting research—striving to know all he could about his competition and his work environment to arrive at a more informed, intelligent strategy for moving forward. Instead of relying upon instinct, prayer and experience alone, he integrated what he learned from his researchers into his mental decision-making matrix. And he made better decisions as a result.

This book is geared to provide you with some of the same types of insights that David, Joshua and other great leaders of God's people require when they make key decisions or reflect on the possibilities for building God's Kingdom. My intent in writing this book is to help you better understand the times so that you, too, might have a clearer sense of what God is calling you, as one of His chosen servants, to do in this day.

FOLLOW THE PAPER TRAIL

You may not be aware that this is the third annual *Barna Report*. When we began the series, we were hoping that there would be sufficient interest among church leaders in discovering the attitudes, opinions, values, beliefs and lifestyles of today's people to justify the two major national surveys that comprise the data base for each year's report.

In this volume, as in the past, you will read about a wide variety of thoughts and behaviors of the American people. Some of the news is encouraging. Some is, shall we say, challenging. I hope that as you read the findings of our research, you will be able to relate these realities to your own life and ministry to become a more effective servant of the God who has called you to His service.

This book contains mostly unique information—that is, data on matters that have not been examined in prior reports. A few "tracking" questions are included—matters such as church attendance or how many adults are Christians—which have been asked in past years and allow us to track the changes evident in those areas. When the insights gleaned from this report are combined with those of the past two years, you can attain a fairly comprehensive body of knowledge regarding the mind and heart of the American people—both those inside and outside of the Christian Church.

A USER-FRIENDLY LAYOUT

We have created this book in a way that, hopefully, is easy for you to use. In the front sections, each chapter provides commentary on what our surveys discovered, along with some graphics designed to portray some of the key findings.

The closing portion of each chapter provides A Personal Challenge designed to stimulate your thinking and gives helpful suggestions on how you might translate the information into practical ministry activities.

In the back portion of the book, we have provided the cross-tabulated data tables from our surveys for each of the survey questions commented on within the book. For each question, the answers of the aggregate sample of 1,000+ people are displayed, as well as the responses of each of 40 subgroups of the population. Each page of these data tables provides both the total number of people from a subgroup who answered that question, as well as the proportion of people from that segment who chose each of the designated answers.

Having access to these data tables, you can look up the responses to a question to satisfy your curiosity or professional interests, or to explore the responses of a particular subgroup that might not have been featured in the commentary in the appropriate chapter.

A word of comfort, though: If you wish to avoid tackling the data tables, you won't miss much. The text of the book has been designed to call your attention to all of the most significant research findings. You need not wade through the data tables unless you are so inclined.

The back portion of the book contains other appendices, too. One of those describes the data collection methods we used to obtain this information. It also includes information regarding some of the subgroup definitions we utilized and a discussion of sampling error.

Before You Dive In

Allow me to add a final thought before you begin to explore the condition of America, as conveyed in these pages.

The data discussed in this book is in no way an attempt to minimize God's power or authority. Surveys and other resources are merely tools to help us better understand the environment He has placed us in for ministry. God, alone, is sovereign and may do whatever He pleases, whenever He pleases, survey results and other tools notwithstanding.

I pray that you will find ways to use this information that will enlighten you and challenge you, that will spark creative ideas and enhance existing notions and efforts to serve God more significantly. God does not judge us on the basis of our effectiveness, but on the basis of how pure our hearts are before Him. Hopefully, armed with the information contained within this book, you will be motivated to be an obedient, intelligent and joyful minister of God's truth to a world that is searching for truth, meaning and joy.

An Overview of The Barna Report 1993-94

For most Americans, the search for meaning in life continues. Despite our technological sophistication and political savvy, millions of adults are desperately seeking the keys that will unlock the secrets to achieve significance in life and bring them greater fulfillment. As a nation, we are exploring many avenues. Comparatively few have arrived at what is deemed to be a reasonable or satisfying conclusion.

In this, the third annual *Barna Report,* you will discover some new, sometimes unnerving truths about the American people. The challenge you face is how to convert such insight into life-changing action for the glory of God.

STORM CLOUDS ARE BREWING

Most Americans realize that there is extreme racial and ethnic tension in the country today. One of the growing concerns on the minds of the American people is if and how our leaders will address this societal menace. The issue is made all the more urgent by the perception that racial prejudice and tension are growing in magnitude. Sadly, few adults would be surprised by an outbreak of race riots and ethnic battles across the nation. What makes this even sadder is that these indignities are both predictable and avoidable.

Such issues are but a harbinger of the turmoil and agony that await us in the days ahead. This, too, is predictable, given the crumbling moral foundation of the nation. No longer do Americans evaluate a social circumstance and make an informed decision on the basis of an underlying philosophy of life or coherent worldview. Rather, we make our decisions on the basis of situational ethics and convenience.

People's views regarding how to handle homosexuality within the military serve as a clear example of how utilitarian we have become in our decision making. When asked to share their feelings about the permissability of having homosexuals serve in the military, adults exhibited utter confusion on the issue. The answers they gave depended upon the context within which the question was posed, alternatively viewing the core issue as that of morality, freedom or productivity.

Put differently, this means that manipulating public opinion on such volatile matters may be surprisingly easy. This is attributable to the lack of clarity of most people regarding truth and values. Our convictions, unfortunately, are sometimes not even skin deep.

The fact that most adults describe themselves as "mostly conservative" on matters of finance and the economy, domestic and social policies, and international and foreign policy is of little apparent consequence when it comes to their actual views on major social issues or related to personal behavior. The same type of political gridlock that characterized the Bush years is likely to reoccur during the current Clinton tenure. Why? Because Mr. Clinton's penchant for rule-by-consensus cannot be effective when the electorate (and, by extension, their elected representatives) is unable to articulate a consistent, well-conceived basis for growth and change.

At the very least, we may anticipate continued disenchantment with public leadership during the coming days. This is based on people's competing self-interests—the desire for a better quality of life, heightened personal fulfillment, significant relationships—but an unwillingness to sacrifice, to make long-term commitments, or to trust other people or institutions.

Where Is the Church?

Religion, although an enduring interest of Americans, remains oddly incapable of influencing the lives of a large number of people. Growing evidence shows, too, that the traditional foundations of our spiritual character—such as church attendance, involvement in small groups, and Bible reading—are on the decline. Our study also showed that it is increasingly less common for people to describe themselves by traditional religious labels such as Protestant, Catholic or Jewish. In short, the foundations of America's faith are crumbling.

Is this a serious condition? I think it is. Consider what we have learned over the last three years, as reported in these studies.

- Most Americans reject the notion of absolute truth.
- A growing proportion of people, now up to one-third of the population, do not believe in the God described in the Bible, but have other notions of who (or what) God is or means.
- Most adults do not believe that Satan is a real being.
- Most people believe that it does not matter what god you pray to because every deity is ultimately the same deity, shrouded in different names and attributes by humankind.
- A minority of Americans have a personal relationship with Jesus Christ.
- Nearly two out of three adults contend that the choice of one religious faith over another is irrelevant because all faiths teach the same basic lessons about life.
- Americans are nearly evenly divided regarding whether or not Christ was perfect; almost half of the public believe that Jesus made mistakes while He was on earth.

These revelations paint a portrait of a people who are not aggressively pursuing a deeper relationship with the God of Israel. This study discovers much about the prayer life of Americans. But one could easily conclude that, unlike David, who is described as being a person after God's own heart, Americans are more absorbed with other tangible, cultural concerns than how to know, love and serve a God that they do not really perceive to be holy, righteous and deserving of their worship and service.

Our decision to ignore or disobey God is not consistently intentional. As so many of the elements of our lives, our faith is in a constant state of transition. What we believe, how we practice our faith and how our beliefs become integrated into our lives changes almost daily. Thus, it is not impossible for the Church to have a profound, positive influence upon this nation. However, the longer we wait, the tougher it will become.

BEWARE THE MEDIA

Generalizations are dangerous, and that pertains to our characterization of the media. Most Americans maintain that the media are subjective in interpreting and reporting events and information, and contend that the media typically reflect a liberal bias in their reporting. But we must remember that there are some honorable and helpful journalists and media outlets. The difficulty is knowing how to tell those who are performing a valid public service apart from those promoting a particular agenda.

Slowly but surely, Americans have developed a significant distrust for the media. Television, in particular, raises the ire of many adults; at the same time we devote unconscionable amounts of our free time viewing televised productions.

Our study estimates that during the past year the typical adult spent the equivalent of two entire months watching television programming. Americans do this in spite of the fact that they consider most television programming not very enjoyable. At the same time that we commit four precious hours a day to watching the tube, we also criticize TV for showing too much violence, using too much foul language and depicting too much explicit sexual activity.

Christians cannot point the finger at other people, claiming that the Christian community has had little or no part in the development of this situation. The truth is that Christians are virtually indistinguishable from other adults in their media consumption habits. Our study indicates that the mother lode of immoral programming—MTV—is just as popular among Christians as non-Christians.

THE FINAL ANALYSIS

Is there something to be gleaned from this research? I believe that even the most informed and astute analyst of our culture will gain some new insights into today's American by reading this book. Depending on your personal ideology and purpose in life, the picture that emerges may not be a pretty one. As we strive to make a difference with our lives, knowledge of the environment in which we are called to have influence cannot help but enhance our efforts.

If, as a Christian (and especially if you serve as a leader within a church) you need a reason to get involved in the chastening and renewing of our society, consider this information your call to action.

RENEWED HOPE IN THE MIDST OF SEVERE CHALLENGES

CHAPTER HIGHLIGHTS

- Most Americans are experiencing a renaissance of hope for the future. Many believe that President Clinton will restore the American Dream and help America regain its progress. Baby boomers and baby busters are especially hopeful that things might be turned around in short order.
- Evangelicals are generally at odds with the prevailing enthusiasm about the days to come. Not supportive of Bill Clinton during his presidential candidacy, they are also leery about what the future holds for America now that the former Arkansas governor leads the nation.
- Although churches and families are thought to be losing influence in our society, people believe that the media and journalists are rapidly gaining influence in the national agenda.
- Americans realize that there is extreme racial and ethnic tension in the country today. They perceive that tension to be growing. Few would be surprised by an outbreak of race riots and ethnic battles across the nation.
- People are confused by major social issues that have a moral component as their underpinning. The issue regarding allowing homosexuals in the military is a prime example. Our attitudes are inconsistent, leading to a confusing set of signals we send concerning how we wish this matter to be handled.

WHAT WE DISCOVERED

Americans have typically been an optimistic people. Backed by a long history of accomplishment that has revolutionized global lifestyles and thinking, modern Americans innately believe that they can accomplish just about anything that is important, if they set their minds to it.

The late '80s and early '90s, however, ushered in an uncharacteristic era of malaise and self-doubt. It should not come as much of a surprise, of course.

Consider all the crises, failures and disappointments wrought by the warped or unrealistic standards and expectations embodied by the '80s. Materialism was tried but found lacking. Religion was expected to clarify our purpose and values, but it generally did not. Sexual experimentation and promiscuity proved incapable of satiating our sexual and emotional appetites. The best efforts of government failed to solve our emotional, spiritual and physical problems. The continual restructuring of the traditional family has caused much consternation, but produced little productive response.

After years of stalled progress toward satisfying our true needs, millions of Americans let down their guard and temporarily lost their sense of hope and optimism about the future. Past glories, including recent ones such as scientific breakthroughs (e.g., the moon landing, the Saturn discoveries), medical cures for debilitating diseases, harnessing digital technology through computers, and victory in the Cold War, proved to be inadequate victories. Americans entered a dark period in which all of life seemed to be fast-track aimlessness, having minimal hope of making a lasting difference or of enjoying the process.

Many say, "It all just moves too fast, takes too much energy, and for not much real benefit. Sometimes I ask myself if it's all worth it. The scary part is that sometimes I don't know." This outlook, not unusual for many adults in their 20s and 30s, reflects the growing sense of anomie and despair felt by Americans during the last 5 years, in particular.

The mid-'90s, however, appear to be moving people in a new, more hopeful and confident direction. Perhaps it is simply the early euphoria ushered in by Bill Clinton's election. Maybe it has to do with signs that the economy is poised for a comeback. Some might attribute it to the continued spiritual quest of millions of Americans. It may be related to the growing sense of comfort with being a central player in the global village. Whatever the reason—and it is more likely a combination of reasons than any single reality—Americans are becoming more upbeat about the days ahead.

Signs of Optimism

Consider, for instance, two-thirds of the nation (63%) contend that things will be better for them five years from now, compared to current conditions. This represents an increase in optimism; less than half of the population made the same bold claim in 1991.

What makes this vision most heartening is that it is our younger adults—the baby boomers and baby busters—who have the greatest expectations regarding the future.[1] America lagged during the last half-decade largely because our young adults had lost their energy and enthusiasm about the future. Now, however, three-quarters of the under-50 crowd is looking forward to better days ahead; by comparison, only half of those 47-65 years of age and just 4 out of every 10 senior citizens maintain such optimism about the future.

"I think we've been through some tough times," explained a thoughtful 26-year-old from the Midwest. "But there seems to be a new spirit among people. Some say it can't get worse, it can only get better. But I think most people genuinely feel that with a lot of the negativism behind us now, we can start to build a more appealing and realistic future. And believing that is probably half the battle."

Intriguingly, it is the Protestant masses who are less excited about what they see coming. Catholics are twice as likely as Protestants to strongly agree that the future will be better than the present. Born-again Christians are no more likely than non-Christians to view the future positively. The more theologically and politically conservative, religiously active adults—commonly referred to as "evangelicals"—see a less promising future than do other segments of society. Barely half of the evangelicals interviewed (55%) expect things to be better five years from now.[2]

Many people who are expecting better days to come are awaiting great things from President Clinton. In January 1993, just as the new president was about to assume his duties as the nation's chief executive, almost 6 out of 10 adults (57%) agreed that the new president will have "a strong, positive effect on the condition of America in general during the next 4 years." It has been more than a decade—since Ronald Reagan's victory in 1980—since the public has had such high expectations of a president.

Some danger exists in such reasoning, of course. The data indicate that the loftiest expectations are held by America's disenfranchised: adults from low-income households, blacks and Hispanics. Having felt ignored by the system for many years, the hopes of the downscale public have been aroused. Failure by the president to deliver on the multitude of promises made about the new societal landscape could leave permanent scars and develop unassailable obstacles for future leaders and generations. For the moment, though, hope has been restored for many who believe that government can bring meaningful solutions to the nation and that President Clinton embodies those needed reforms.

The rosy outlook regarding the new administration is not shared by either Republicans or evangelicals, though. A majority of the Republicans (58%) and evangelicals (62%) interviewed indicated that they do

---

Evangelicals Did Not Support President Clinton on Election Day
(N=993 registered voters, voted 11/92)

People group	Candidate voted for: Clinton	Bush	Perot
All voters*	43%	38%	19%

People group	Candidate voted for: Clinton	Bush	Perot
Christians	43	47	10
Non-Christians	47	32	20
Evangelicals	20	72	8
Protestants	39	47	14
Catholics	46	35	19

*The final vote count for all voters is based upon actual election results, not survey data. The self-reported vote choice of survey respondents was nearly identical to the final outcome. Among survey respondents who reported a voting choice, 45% claimed they voted for Clinton, 38% for Bush, 17% for Perot.

---

not anticipate a positive outcome from President Clinton's tenure. Only 25% of the evangelicals expect good things to result from the Clinton era. Interestingly, born-again Christians were twice as likely as the evangelical segment to expect positive results from the Clinton administration.

It might be worth noting, too, that Mr. Clinton drew his support on election day from a broad coalition of voters, but fared especially well with the politically disenfranchised. He gained only 20% of the vote of evangelicals, while Mr. Bush pulled 72% of the evangelical support. Once again there was a significant divide between the behavior of the born-again constituency and the evangelical bloc. Among born-again Christians, 47% supported Mr. Bush, 43% chose Mr. Clinton. (Ross Perot, the third-party candidate who garnered 19% of the vote nationally, collected just 10% of the born-again vote.)

Life Is Good

Most Americans are hopeful about the future, but they are also generally pleased with the way life is going these days. Six out of 10 adults strongly agreed that life is very satisfying for them. Almost 9 out of 10 (86%) agreed either strongly or somewhat with that sentiment. Despite the chaos and rapid change that characterizes the lives of most people, they manage to navigate through the twists and turns of daily life and arrive at a level of pleasure that makes it all worthwhile.

Hidden in the reams of data we collected are some indications that life is tougher for some than others. For instance, boomers and busters were slightly less likely than their elders to paint an upbeat view of life. Single adults were less excited about life than were their married counterparts. Minority adults were significantly less enthusiastic about life than were whites.

The most clear-cut influence on life satisfaction was religious involvement. Born-again Christians placed higher on the life satisfaction scale than did non-Christians. Evangelicals were a notch higher on that scale than were born-again Christians (see Figure 1.1). In the same manner, adults who commonly attend church services were more likely to be very satisfied with life than were adults who avoid church activities.

The more actively involved in personal religious activity a person was (such as Bible reading, prayer, lay leadership in church work), the more likely that person was to view life as being satisfying. Thus, although a person's lifestyle may not be overtly affected by their religious beliefs in many instances, the data show that those who participate most actively in the Christian faith have a greater sense of satisfaction and fulfillment in life.

Far from Perfect

Although most Americans find life satisfying and are hopeful about the future, maintaining confidence in the things yet to unfold is not simple. Our research noted that nearly two out of three adults (62%) believe that life is too complex these days. This sentiment was most commonly expressed by women, senior citizens, parents of young children, the least affluent and evangelicals.

It was not uncommon for us to hear people express thoughts such as those of a young working mother who is active in her church and in community volunteer work.

"It's an exciting time to be alive, because there are so many new opportunities and so much is happening. But it just tires you out. Who can keep up with it all? As the world keeps getting more complicated and bigger, I feel like I keep getting more superficial and smaller—like I'm in touch with a shrinking part of the world. Sometimes I worry that by the time my kids are in junior high, I won't be able to keep up with what they know and what they're learning. And being a working mom is a real juggling act, but one of necessity for us. There are just no easy solutions anymore, no time when you can let go for a breather just to recoup. Yeah, life is exciting these days, but it's draining and a bit overwhelming, too."

Indeed, education seems to be one of the means to cope with the increasingly complexities of life. People who had some college background were less likely to see the world as being too complex; those who had a high school education or less were more concerned about complexity.

CHANGE AGENTS

Change sometimes results in feelings of futility brought on by the sense that things are beyond our control, or maybe out of control altogether. Change is uncomfortable for most people, though it is a central part of our daily experience. That most Americans remain

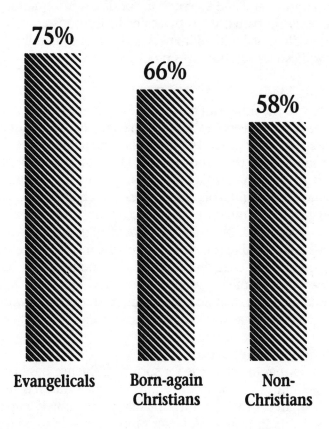

Life Is More Satisfying for
Christians than for Non-Christians
Percent who strongly agree that
"life is very satisfying for you."

75%

66%

58%

Evangelicals

**Born-again
Christians**

**Non-
Christians**

Figure 1.1

Source: Barna Research Group, Ltd. 1993

pleased with the present and are optimistic about the future, in spite of a level of anxiety about the complications of modern life, is no small miracle.

This positive spin on reality might partially be explained by noting that people perceive the balance of influence to have changed in definable ways during the last five years (see Figure 1.2). In a world that is changing rapidly and profoundly, Americans believe that the social institutions and agents that influence our thinking and behavior are being dramatically realigned. This is of major importance because the ways we cope with our changing world are directly related to how we come to understand and accept that world. The information and associated values imparted to us by major institutions and structures of American life shape our willingness and ability to handle change and the new lifestyles such changes produce.

The Mass Media
According to the American people, one of the big winners in the repositioning of influencers has been the mass media. Six out of 10 respondents told us that journalists and media personalities have more influence today than they did 5 years ago; only 1 out of every 8 respondents said the media have less influence these days. (Views on the nature of that influence are discussed in chapter 7.)

The growth in influence was especially noticeable to adults under 50—the very generations that have grown up under the dominance of the mass media and that have embraced the media as a central part of their generational character. Among the boomers and busters, the influence of the media was said to have increased rather than decreased by better than an 8 to 1 margin—more than twice the margin reflected in the answers of older Americans.

The U.S. Supreme Court
Another winner in the battle for societal influence has been the U.S. Supreme Court. Overall, 30% of adults said the Court has gained influence compared to its standing of five years ago; 17% perceived a decrease in its influence. (A larger proportion—44%—said the influence of the Court has remained unchanged during this time frame.) The two subgroups that were more likely to see the influence of the Court expanding were those with opposing views: registered Democrats and Baptists.

Influence Changes over Time
(N=1004)
Level of influence
compared to 5 years ago

Influence agent	More	Same	Less
Journalists and media personalities	58%	26%	12%
U.S. Supreme Court	30	44	17
Churches	21	40	33
Political parties	21	35	38
Marriage	18	35	41

The Church's Influence

The Church's loss of influence was most prolificly believed among people in the 47-65 age bracket; those on the upper half of the income continuum; residents of the western states; people registered to vote as Republicans or who were independent of party affiliation; Catholics and evangelicals. Despite the death siren sounded by many in regard to the urban church, note that people who live in cities and those who are from minority populations were less likely than others to say that churches have lost influence during the last five years.

Political Parties

Perceptions of the political parties were the most volatile. Whites were twice as likely to say parties had lost influence as to contend they had increased their influence. However, blacks were evenly split on the matter, and Hispanics were more inclined to believe that parties are gaining, rather than losing, influence. In like manner, people 28 or older were much more likely to cite a loss of influence for parties than to posit a gain, but among the baby busters there was no such perception.

How can such discrepancies between people groups be explained? Partly by realizing that the groups that have experienced the greatest increase in attention by the parties themselves—the recent pandering to youth and ethnic subcultures, especially by the Democratic Party—are merely reflecting favorable reactions to that heightened attention.

Marriage

Perspectives related to marriage also showed a wide range of opinion. No people groups were more inclined to say that marriage has gained rather than lost ground in the last five years. But the data point out that the range extends from the views of the most affluent, who essentially view marriage as having held steady in influence since 1987, to those of senior citizens, who claim marriage has lost ground rather than gained influence by a five-to-one margin. A majority of evangelicals also portrayed marriage as having less influence than it used to.

Who has lost ground as a change agent in our society? According to the public, churches wield less influence today than they did five years earlier; political parties have lost some of their clout; and marriage, as a social institution influencing our thinking and lifestyles, was described as the biggest loser in the influence arena.

DOES THE SYSTEM WORK?

Remember the activists of the '60s who challenged America to dismantle the system and replace the establishment with entirely new structures for governing?

Those people were the heart of the baby-boom generation. Now in positions of influence and affluence in our culture, it is interesting to discover that two-thirds of the boomers assert that "our system of government is not perfect, but it works pretty well." Young adults (those under 47) are no less likely than are older adults to compliment the system; although they are less intense in their support. Although just 21% of the younger generations strongly agree that the system works well, 31% of the older adults strongly agree.

One group in the '60s that forcefully proclaimed its dissatisfaction with the prevailing power structure was the black community. The levels of dissatisfaction persist even today. Blacks are only half as likely as other Americans to strongly agree that the system works well: just 14% concur. No other people group we studied reflected such disappointment with our government system.

Clearly, a stumbling block exists in the lack of consensus on political vision. The ideological distinctions that emerged during the

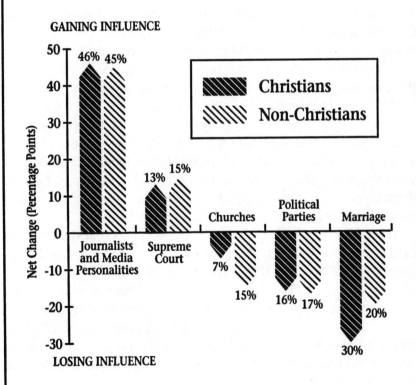

Look Who Is Gaining – and Losing – Influence

Net difference in the proportion of adults who believe the entity is gaining or losing influence in our society compared to five years ago

GAINING INFLUENCE

Net Change (Percentage Points)

50 —
46% 45%
40 —

[] Christians
[] Non-Christians

30 —

20 —

13% 15%
10 —

Churches

Political Parties

Marriage

0 —

Journalists and Media Personalities

Supreme Court

7%

-10 —

15% 16% 17%

-20 —

20%

-30 —

30%

LOSING INFLUENCE

Figure 1.2

Source: Barna Research Group, Ltd. 1993

1992 presidential campaign reflect a growing sense of separation between competing factions in the country. Seven out of 10 adults (71%) said that "the division between political liberals and conservatives is preventing the government from working effectively." This viewpoint was most aggressively championed by baby busters (76%); residents of the southern states (75%); Republicans (75%); Protestants (75%); Baptists (86%); born-again Christians (75%); and evangelicals (82%). Notice the polarizing relationship between politics and religious views.

Urban Distress Is Coming

As our research has been suggesting for several years, racial tension in America is on the rise. Things may be as tense today as at any other time in the past 50 years. Urban unrest is a distinct possibility, if not probability, during the remaining years of this century.

Government leaders may not be moving to address or acknowledge the issue, but the existence of racial and ethnic animosity is no secret to the American people. Nine out of 10 Americans (88%) agree that there is "a lot of anger and hostility between the different ethnic and racial groups in America" (see Figure 1.3). The minority groups themselves are most intense in their feelings about this state of affairs. Not surprisingly, it is also the areas of the nation where the unrest is most likely to explode—the Northeast, the West, and urban areas—where people's assessment of the problem is most severe.

Three-quarters of all Americans (76%) contend that the cross-cultural hostility exists and is also growing in its intensity. Again, the seriousness of the situation is underscored by members of minority populations, especially blacks and Hispanics. Baby busters, who are prone to greater cultural sensitivity, are the generation most likely to perceive the racial and ethnic tensions to be growing. Those in the 47-65 age segment (who, not coincidentally, comprise the majority of major public officeholders) are the least likely to sense a growing hostility between races and ethnic groups.

The data clearly exhibit a relationship between affluence and perspective on this matter. That is, the more education people have, and the higher their income, the less likely they are to sense that racial tension in America is growing.

Most Americans, Regardless of Their Background, Believe There Is a Lot of Anger Between Different Racial and Ethnic Groups

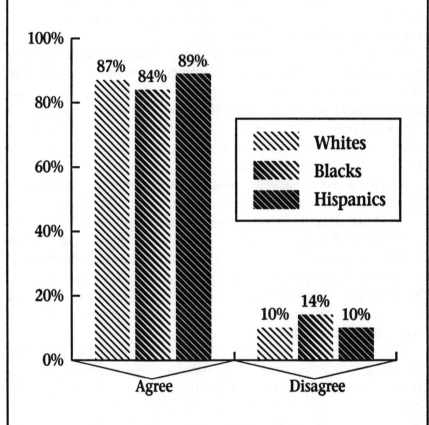

Figure 1.3

Source: Barna Research Group, Ltd. 1993

Wars on Other Fronts

The racial and ethnic battles that are approaching represent serious challenges to our system and its leaders, as well as to our culture at large, but there are other challenges that Americans clearly acknowledge.

The Traditional Family

The American family, for instance, has always stood as a central foundation in our nation's development. On the basis of the love, trust and stability provided by the traditional family, America has been able to move forward while nations lacking such a bedrock of stability and continuity have struggled to keep pace.

During the '90s, we know that records are being shattered regarding the numbers of people who are going through divorces; having children without being married; living together and having sexual relationships outside of marriage; and creating unisexual family units.[3] The traditional family itself, as a concept underlying the American experiment, has been redefined during the last 10 years so that "family" no longer means what it used to.[4]

Yet, in spite of our adventurousness regarding family arrangements and intimate personal relationships, 7 out of 10 adults claim that "if the traditional family unit falls apart, the stability of American society will collapse" (see Figure 1.4). The most vocal proponents of this perspective are women; adults 47 or older; married people; southerners; Protestants; born-again Christians; and evangelicals. Just as important are those segments that have the least concern about the collapse of the traditional family: single adults; blacks; Hispanics; and people who have no church affiliation.

The intensity of advocacy for the traditional family by the evangelical bloc is astounding. Eighty-one percent of the evangelicals strongly agreed that the loss of the traditional family will spell the doom of our society. No other people group we studied comes close to mirroring this level of concern for the traditional family. Because they represent just a small proportion of the aggregate population (12%), their voice on this issue may not gain the attention that the depth of their conviction might seem to warrant.

If the Traditional Family Unit Falls Apart, People Believe Our Society Will Collapse

Levels of agreement

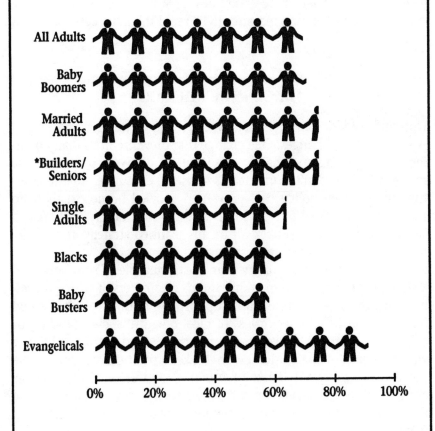

Figure 1.4

* Builders = People Born 1928-1945
Source: Barna Research Group, Ltd. 1993

Abortion

A related issue is abortion. This battle has been waged in the courts, in the streets and in the media for more than two decades. However, ever since the *Roe vs. Wade* decision was rendered, Americans are apparently tired of this issue.

Almost 6 out of 10 adults (58%) stated that the abortion issue "gets more attention than it deserves." This view was especially common among blacks, Hispanics and the unchurched. Evangelicals stood out as the sole subgroup that was not likely to see the issue getting more than its fair share of attention: 40% agreed that it gets more attention than it deserves, but 53% disagreed. Even among born-again Christians, a majority (54%) said the issue gets too much attention.

GAYS IN THE MILITARY

During President Clinton's first weeks in office he initiated several sweeping policy changes. One change that drew fire from many quarters was his command that homosexuals be allowed to serve in the military. Clinton's initial intent was to use an executive order to overturn the existing policy that prevented avowed homosexuals from serving in the armed forces. However, the public outcry that ensued caused the president to back off on his planned strategy and implement a less far-reaching proposal instead.

The issue of homosexuality is an ideal example of how confused the American people are in taking stands on matters of ethics, morality and values. Most Americans support the notions of liberty and justice for all people, regardless of race, religion, social standing or other qualifications. However, when it comes to defining and living with the realities of a worldview that takes a position on some of the more complex social issues of our day, confusion and paralysis abound. How to perceive and respond to homosexuals in light of their desire to serve America in the military is one such challenging issue.

Consider the competing interests people must weigh. There is the issue of liberty and freedom. Most Americans believe that sexual orientation is a private matter. The survey showed that 8 out of 10

The Dividing Line Is Clear

Segments Supporting
Homosexuals in the Military:

Women   Hispanics
Busters   Democrats
Builders   Catholics
Singles   Unchurched
Blacks   Non-Christians

- - - - - - - - - - - - - - - - - - -

Segments Rejecting
Homosexuals in the Military:

Men   Rural Residents
Boomers   Republicans
Seniors   Protestants
Marrieds   Churched
Parents of Kids Under 18   Born-again Christians
Whites   Evangelicals

Figure 1.5

Source: Barna Research Group, Ltd. 1993

Americans (81%) contend that "whether a person is a homosexual or not is a private matter that is nobody else's business." The most avid proponents of this viewpoint were women, college graduates, Hispanics, Democrats, non-Christians, the unchurched, and people living in the Northeast and West. The one segment we studied that jumped out as diametrically opposed to this perspective was evangelicals. Among them, 35% strongly disagreed with this sentiment, more than 3 times the incidence of such opinion among the rest of the public.

Most adults argue that a person's sexual orientation should not infringe upon the rights to enjoy any of the opportunities afforded to other Americans. Thus, 57% of all Americans agreed that "acknowledged homosexuals should not be prohibited from serving in the military solely because of their sexual orientation." The younger the person, the stronger was the inclination to agree with this perspective. Blacks and Hispanics were more likely than whites to agree, as were urban residents, those living in the Northeast and West, Democrats and the unchurched. The people least supportive of this concept were evangelicals, Republicans and Baptists (see Figure 1.5).

It is perhaps worthy of note: Although the general position is that homosexuality is a private matter of which nobody should be informed, when such information is available, the minds of a proportion of the population *are* swayed, nevertheless. In this case, we see that the aggregate support for homosexuals enjoying all manner of freedoms and rights dropped from 81% to 57%.

But such an issue raises more than just matters pertaining to liberty; it raises issues related to morality, too. Currently, a majority of Americans (55%) claim that homosexual activity is immoral. This belief was most common among men (60%); senior citizens (67%); people without any college education (64%); Republicans (63%); Baptists (75%); born-again Christians (70%); and evangelicals (92%). One clear pattern is that the more affluent or educated people become, the less likely they are to label homosexuality immoral.

The issue also raises questions regarding efficacy. Most adults (58%) concurred that having homosexuals in the military would make it more difficult for some heterosexual soldiers to concentrate on their job duties. Two-thirds of all men agreed that this would happen. Above average proportions of southerners (63%), Republicans (72%), born-again Christians (65%), Baptists (66%) and evangelicals (78%) foresaw such a problem.

Very few Americans believe that allowing homosexuals in the military will make our armed forces more effective in combat. Overall, just one out of every seven adults supported such a notion. About half of all respondents strongly disagreed with this idea. For certain people groups, such as men, people 47 or older, whites, married adults, Protestants, Christians and evangelicals, more than half expressed strong disagreement that homosexuals in the military would strengthen our combat effectiveness.

Personal issues are raised by this matter, too. Would you, personally, want to serve in the military beside avowed homosexuals? A plurality of adults said no: 49% said they would not want to do so; 42% said they would be willing to serve with homosexuals. The remaining 9% did not know how they felt on this matter. Once again, men, who comprise the primary military labor pool, were considerably more adamant against allowing homosexuals in the military than were women: 58% stated they would not want to serve with homosexuals; 40% of the women concurred. Evangelicals remained the most consensually resistant to such an idea: 78% agreed that they would not want to be forced to serve with homosexuals.

Perhaps we discovered the key to understanding the American psyche on such delicate and complex matters. Two-thirds of all adults said that our government should have the right to deny admission to the military for homosexuals *if there is proof that their presence would jeopardize the effectiveness of the armed forces in times of combat.*

In other words, what is most important, perhaps, is the issue of self-interest. Homosexuals can have rights and make social gains as long as they do not undermine our ability to lead a fulfilling, safe, successful life. Once the tendencies of others get in the way of such a pursuit, neither their rights nor their needs are as important as our own. The bottom line, then, is how the ultimate decision affects our personal lives and needs. The larger philosophical or structural issues melt away when faced with the realities of personal sacrifice.

The most widely reported type of perspective is what Americans tell us they desire in a policy. On this matter, the confusion abounds. The public is evenly split about what the government should do as a general policy. Forty-seven percent told us they would prefer that the government maintain the policy that does not allow acknowledged homosexuals to serve in the armed forces; 44% said they would reject that policy.

The Government Should Have the Right to Deny Homosexuals Admission to the Military if There Is Proof Their Presence Would Jeopardize Combat Effectiveness
(N=1205)

People group	Agree	Disagree	Don't Know
All adults	68%	23%	8%
Whites	71	20	8
Blacks	66	27	7
Hispanics	56	44	*
Northeast	58	24	7
Midwest/South	70	21	9
West	53	29	7
Democrats	61	32	7
Republicans	78	15	7
Protestants	75	17	8
Catholics	66	29	5
Evangelicals	91	4	5

Why is there such confusion? Largely because people are forced to make an important decision on the basis of a set of underlying values and beliefs that do not yet exist. Lacking a coherent, holistic world-view, most Americans have no basis for comprehending the far-reaching implications of such policy dictates, nor do they feel comfortable imagining such changes. Consequently, in taking a stand on such important issues of the day, people make decisions on the basis of vague, generic impressions and unconnected notions of justice, liberty, righteousness and efficacy.

So if you watch the public opinion polls and population surveys and seem to detect a considerable degree of inconsistency in how people react to issues, opportunities and ideas, it may be a reflection of the superficial perspectives that most of us possess in key matters such as operational values and belief systems.

A PERSONAL CHALLENGE

Many people have a tendency to trust in our government and other human institutions to provide the answers to our toughest challenges and crises in life. This raises the danger of false hope. As the euphoria over the Clinton election subsides and the effect of his policy initiatives settles, are we simply expecting too much from our flawed institutions? Where do you put *your* trust for meaningful answers to the daily challenges and obstacles you face?

This is a particularly important question for evangelicals. The natural inclination of some might be to recede into the background while President Clinton and his supporters pursue different directions through vision and policy. Can evangelicals resist the tendencies to become isolated and to withhold their assistance during a time when their influence is important in shaping values, attitudes and policies that will affect the lives of millions of people?

Indeed, if the present conditions point to the imminence of urban dissension, is there a way foresighted thinkers and change agents can undermine the imminent? It starts, of course, with leaders exhorting people to take matters into their own hands, initiating meaningful dialogue and other bridges designed to overcome the difficulties inherent in class differences, racial misunderstandings and unrealistic expectations. Each American must assume his or her share of the responsibility for calming the national heart. And, as in so many crisis situations, time *is* of the essence.

Influencing the attitudes of others who may be different from ourselves requires some fundamental reconsideration of our values and our perspectives on the very meaning of life itself. What can be done to enable people to arrive at a coherent worldview that will better allow them to make intelligent, consistent decisions? One of the difficulties of leading people today is the absence of a sense of purpose in life, and how people's values and beliefs can fit together into an intelligible life philosophy that informs their decisions. Until people can see the big picture of reality in their minds, the small, day-to-day decisions they make will frequently be contradictory and self-defeating. What types of programs, training or encouragement can be provided to lead people down a path of deeper thought and more strategic decision making?

Notes

1. Baby boomers are the people born between 1946 and 1964. The largest generation in our nation's history, there are approximately 79 million boomers in America today. The baby busters are the generation that succeeded the boomers, born between 1965 to 1983. There are currently about 68 million busters—the second-largest generation in America's annals. For more insight into the busters, a truly unique and struggling generation, see *The Invisible Generation: Baby Busters*, George Barna, (Glendale, CA: Barna Research Group Books, 1992).

2. Evangelicals are defined in this research as people who meet specific criteria regarding religious beliefs and religious practice. The definition is described in detail in Appendix 1 (Definitions) of this book. Realize that various researchers and religious analysts define the term in different ways, and thus may use the same terminology to refer to an entirely different group of people.

3. For the most recent statistics on these behavioral patterns, see *The Future of the American Family*, George Barna, (Chicago, IL: Moody Press, 1993).

4. A majority of Americans now define family to be any group of people who care about you, or about whom you care. The traditional definition of family—people related by marriage, birth or adoption—has become a secondary perspective. For a further description of this research, see chapter 2 of *The Future of the American Family*, cited in note 3.

CHAPTER 2

CLINTON'S VICTORY DID NOT ERASE CONSERVATIVE VIEWS

CHAPTER HIGHLIGHTS

- By an overwhelming margin, Americans consider themselves to be "mostly conservative" on matters of finance and the economy; domestic and social policies; and international and foreign policy.
- A majority of Americans adults (60%) disagree that "freedom means being able to do anything you want to do." Notice, however, that nearly 4 out of 10 adults buy this perspective.
- Most Americans have an identity crisis, juggling different associations they claim they consciously represent. The most common entities we claim to represent are America and Jesus Christ. Parents, ethnic heritage, and church or synagogue were less commonly represented.
- Most people base key life decisions on "situational ethics." About one-fifth of all adults identified the Bible as their basis for moral and ethical judgments.
- Adults are evenly divided on the meaning of the term "family values"; half of the population is "not sure what it means anymore." Even so, most adults claim that the expression has a positive, favorable meaning for them.
- One out of three Americans believes that you cannot trust anyone other than family and close friends these days.

WHAT WE DISCOVERED

Shortly after Bill Clinton was elected president, many political analysts began hailing his victory as evidence of a return to liberal political leanings among Americans. A common interpretation of the Clinton triumph was that Americans, fed up after a dozen years of "cold-hearted, self-serving" leadership by two Republican presidents, were ready and willing to sacrifice their personal interests in favor of the greater social good.

These analysts have painted a portrait of a new American culture in which the people's desire to serve others and to develop a sense of community will be unleashed, like the genie escaping the bottle after being pent up for many years. This perspective proclaims that America in the last years of the millennium will be a more thoughtful, loving and accepting nation.

There certainly has been no lack of anecdotal evidence that people are looking forward to the Clinton era.

"He stands for a new way of taking care of people, of looking out for the common man," proclaimed one happy voter from the Plains states who cast his ballot for the former Arkansas governor.

"The Reagan experiment failed" was the analysis of a young computer engineer from Texas. "At the time, it made sense. But look what has happened. We turned into a nation of hardened, selfish, short-sighted greed-mongers. We assumed that if we could just keep generating new growth everything would fall into place. We couldn't and it didn't. And now there is a price to be paid. The American people have again demonstrated their wisdom by cutting the flawed experiment short, so we can restore our confidence in the system, in each other, and live healthier lives."

For several months, the mass media collected personal testimony after personal testimony, and weaved them into a tapestry that seemed to reflect the heart design of the nation. Combined with the sense of euphoria that bubbled over among boomers, who finally had one of their own in control, the emerging story was that this was an emotional, if not spiritual, turning point for the nation.

IDEOLOGICAL CONFLICT

A major difficulty with this provocative tale is that it conflicts with the prevailing values, ideologies and expectations of the American public. The Clinton connection to the baby boom notwithstanding, the pulse of the electorate indicates that the Clinton administration and its proponents will have a tough time convincing the American people that personal sacrifice, liberal policy initiatives and a new era of politics and social action are the proper and appropriate course to pursue.

Economy and Public Finance

On no single issue area were the Clinton and Bush campaigns more divided than the economy and public finance. The Clinton campaign gained momentum largely because George Bush was blamed for the tattered state of the economy and because the incumbent president failed to forcefully promote significant economic initiatives. Nevertheless, Americans by a *four-to-one margin described themselves as "mostly conservative" on matters pertaining to finances and the economy* (see Figure 2.1).

Nearly half of the registered voters we interviewed (47%) said they were mostly conservative on such issues; only 12% described themselves as "mostly liberal"; the remaining 37% said they were somewhere in between. This self-description is, of course, in vivid contrast to the types of policies and programs that the newly elected president views as his mandate for government and social change.

Several people groups that were overwhelmingly supportive of President Clinton—most notably the baby busters, blacks, voters in the Northeast and registered Democrats—were considerably more likely to define themselves as mostly liberal on economic matters. However, *even a substantial plurality of these people groups reject the "mostly liberal" label to define their personal views on finance and economics.* At the same time, some of the segments of the electorate that were most supportive of President Bush (e.g., the most affluent, suburbanites, registered Republicans, and evangelicals) were most likely to describe themselves as mostly conservative on economic issues.

How can the Clinton victory be explained in light of his liberal agenda and the public's decidedly conservative leanings in this critical issue arena?

"I voted for Clinton because he represented change," explained one middle-aged woman from the South, sounding the familiar theme of the president's campaign. "I planned to vote for Bush again, but he never gave me a good enough reason to do so. I'm not that excited about Clinton's economic proposals, but at least he seemed interested enough in the state of the economy to come up with some new ideas on what to do."

Was it the content of Clinton's plans that motivated support, or simply his thrust to do something different? "For me, personally, the idea of just remaining calm and standing firm didn't sit well. When I look at my own financial power these days, I cannot afford to stand firm. Something has to change. Bush didn't seem to understand that."

Domestic and Social Policies

On domestic and social policies, adults were also more likely to describe themselves as mostly conservative than mostly liberal by nearly a two-to-one margin (35% to 20%). Baby busters, Hispanics, Democrats, non-Christians and unchurched adults were most likely to accept the liberal label. Conservative thinking was most frequently adopted by those who were 47 or older (i.e., the pre-boomers, or "builders"), Republicans, Christians and evangelicals. Evangelicals were nearly twice as likely as the population-at-large to say they were mostly conservative on issues related to domestic and social policy.

International and Foreign Policy

The conservative bent won out also in the arena of international and foreign policy, this time by a three-to-one margin (39% versus 12%). Once again, the baby busters were at ideological odds with their elders, emerging as being nearly twice as likely as older adults to label themselves mostly liberal in such affairs. And, again, evangelicals emerged as the segment most likely to embrace the mostly conservative perspective on such issues.

Public Morality and Responsibility

Despite the radical changes happening in people's lifestyles and perspectives, a majority of Americans maintain traces of a traditional viewpoint on public morality and responsibility. One example of this is that most adults (60%) disagree with the notion, "freedom means being able to do anything you want to do." This is an enticing idea that has gained a virtual monopoly in the entertainment media's depiction of the healthy, successful life in modern America. But most Americans still believe that we must be responsible in our decision making and daily actions.

A Conservative People with a Liberal President?

Percent of adults who call themselves "mostly conservative" compared to those who are "mostly liberal" in matters of:

Economy and Public Finance

Liberal: 12% Conservative: 47%

Domestic and Social Policy

Liberal: 20% Conservative: 35%

International and Foreign Policy

Liberal: 12% Conservative: 39%

Figure 2.1

Source: Barna Research Group, Ltd. 1993

Freedom without accountability is merely anarchy. Although we embrace the general public freedoms we have as Americans, we have not yet come to the point where most people adopt an "anything goes" philosophy of life. (The fact that 40% *have* done so, however, raises other interesting, if not frightening, questions about the direction in which we may be moving.)

Is there truly a popular mandate for a liberal political agenda in America in the mid-'90s? If so, it may be defined by personal values systems and other lifestyle choices, rather than a sweeping desire to usher in a new series of liberal policies and social programs. The public appears to be reflecting an attitude of greater interest in the plight of the downtrodden, without truly accepting the need for higher taxes, "progressive" laws and policies, and new social programs geared to reform our society to address their needs in a different manner.

WHAT WE STAND FOR

Our ideological leanings are at least partly reflected by what we believe we stand for as individuals. We may be emotionally or psychologically attached to many different entities, but what we view ourselves as representing, indicate a lot about what we truly value in life.

We asked people how often, if ever, they consciously think of themselves as a representative of each of five entities. The answers reveal that we deem ourselves to be (1) Americans first; (2) Christians second; (3) family members third. All else trails behind in importance. But the data also underscore that although we juggle various identities, we embrace no single identity that we always keep foremost in our minds.

United States
Notice, for instance, that the identity we are most likely to maintain— that of being a representative of the United States—is a perception that less than one-third of all adults (31%) say they "always" bear in mind. In total, less than half of the adult public answer "always" or "often" when asked if they consciously consider themselves to be a representative of the United States. This thinking was most common among senior citizens (59% said they think of themselves this way always or often); Hispanics (58%); people living in the Midwest (52%);

and Baptists (54%). Such a mind-set was least likely among blacks (36%); residents of the Northeast (37%); and people not registered to vote (36%).

Jesus Christ

One-quarter of all adults say they always think of themselves as a representative of Jesus Christ. Slightly more than 4 out of every 10 adults (44%) claim they view themselves as representatives of Christ always or often. Perhaps surprisingly, 2 out of 10 non-Christians always view themselves as representatives of Christ; as do 1 out of every 8 people who have no church affiliation.

Some significant differences were revealed between people groups in "always" seeing themselves as Jesus' representatives (see Figure 2.2). Women were much more likely than men to claim this characteristic (33% versus 20%). Blacks were twice as likely as nonblacks to claim this perspective (47% versus 24%). People in the upper-income ranges were less likely to take on this identity (22%) than were people earning less than $40,000 (31%).

People living in the Northeast (21%), in the Mountain States and western states (13%), were far less likely to see themselves as representatives of Jesus Christ than were people from the central (30%) and southern regions (37%). Other segments that scored unusually high in this matter were people in rural areas (33%); Republicans (34%); Protestants (35%); Baptists (45%); born-again Christians (38%); and evangelicals (50%). Standing out as unexpectedly low on the scale were Catholics (20%).

Family

Relatively few adults say they always consciously represent their parents (23%), and a similar proportion (20%) claimed they often think of themselves in this way. The people most likely to assume this perspective are those from middle- and lower-income households; blacks and Hispanics; residents of the South; and people living in rural areas. These groups are among the shrinking number of population segments who have been most adamant in maintaining traditional views, including ideas on family and personal responsibilities.

Barely one-fifth of the adult public consciously consider themselves to always represent ethnic heritage, and an additional 15% often consider this characteristic. Not surprisingly, blacks were the most likely to maintain such feelings; 48% say they always represent their ethnic heritage. That was double the proportion among Hispanics (25%) and three times the percentage among whites (15%).

Church or Synagogue

Just one out of every seven adults claims to always think of themselves as a representative of their church or synagogue. This was nearly twice as common among women as among men; twice as likely among adults 47 or older as among younger adults; twice as likely among people in the Midwest and South as among residents of the Northeast and West; twice as likely in urban and rural areas as among suburbanites; twice as common among Protestants as Catholics; and twice as likely among born-again Christians as among other adults. Evangelicals (30%) were twice as likely as the national average to adopt this persona.

Vague Perspective of Identity

In short, Americans fill a plethora of roles during the typical day, and react to each new circumstance on the basis of many role models and a wealth of relationships and moral intentions. Sometimes they may consciously realize that their actions reflect on people or associations with which they have been affiliated; just as often, they act in total ignorance of such considerations.

Given the broad base of experiences and affiliations of most Americans, combined with a culture that extols the virtues of independence and self-determination, it is increasingly difficult for adults to crystallize a consistent perspective of who they are and whom, if anybody, they represent. The pressures are no less severe for Christians, regardless of their level of commitment to their faith, than for others of different faiths.

MORALS, ETHICS AND INFLUENCE AGENTS

People grow into their personality and life perspectives largely on the basis of external influences. Often, the agents we wish to have the greatest influence on us are different from those we realize, in actuality, influence us the most. Our research on who influences children found such a discrepancy.

What Types of People Always – and Never – Think of Themselves as Representatives of Jesus Christ?

Always

Evangelicals (50%)
Blacks (47%)
Born-again Christians (38%)
Southerners (37%)
Protestants (35%)
Senior Citizens (35%)
Republicans (34%)
Women (33%)
Rural Residents (33%)
Income Under $40,000 (31%)

Never

Unchurched People (45%)
Westerners (35%)
Non-Christians (25%)
Income Over $60,000 (29%)
People 47-65 (24%)
College Graduates (22%)
Men (21%)
Single Adults (21%)

Figure 2.2

Source: Barna Research Group, Ltd. 1993

Parents' Influence on Children

Nearly all parents of young children said they felt it was their responsibility and privilege as parents to have the greatest influence on their children. However, only a small proportion of them said they believed they had the greatest influence on the thinking and behavior of their offspring. Surprisingly, parents did not rate themselves as the most prolific influence upon their own children.[1]

"I'd like to say that my kids really look up to me as the fountain of all wisdom, and the source of their inspiration and decisions," laughed a mother of three who lives in the Northeast. Her smile faded quickly, though, as she considered the rejoinder to that thought.

She grew serious and added, "But the truth is I know that my input is often overruled by the ideas planted in their minds by their friends, by television and by their teachers. It's pretty discouraging sometimes, hearing what they choose to do and why. I sometimes think it's almost out of control, that my influence is so small I can't even impact them."

Daily Decisions

What about the moral and ethical decisions adults must make every day? When asked to identify the basis of those decisions we constantly make, the responses suggest that most people engage in what social scientists term "situational ethics"—making moral and ethical decisions on the basis of what would work best at the time, in a given situation, or upon the basis of what seemed to work suitably in the past. This type of decision-making perspective characterized the actions of a majority of Americans (57%). Another 13% based their decisions upon "the common wisdom." The remaining alternatives were basing such responses upon the Bible (21%) or upon the advice of friends and family (6%) (see Figure 2.3).

The Bible. Who bases their moral and ethical decisions upon the Bible these days? As you might have anticipated, evangelicals were on the top of the scale: 69% claimed the Scriptures as their primary authority for such decisions. No other segment of the population had anything close to a majority that chose the Bible as their dominant authority in these matters. However, the survey showed that women were much more likely than men to do so (25% to 15%); residents of the South were most likely, regionally, to turn to the Bible (31%); Protestants were nearly four times more likely than Catholics to

The Basis of Our Ethical Decisions

- Advice of Family, Friends 6%
- Let Whatever Happens Happen 8%
- Common Wisdom 12%
- Past Experience 28%
- Other 13%
- Available Choices and Their Likely Outcomes 13%
- The Bible 20%

Figure 2.3

Source: Barna Research Group, Ltd. 1993

assume this approach (30% versus 8%); and born-again Christians were three times as likely as other adults to rely upon the Bible for guidance in these decisions.

Religion. Nevertheless, in identifying what has produced the greatest degree of influence upon a person's views and beliefs about life, in general, the importance of one's religion is magnified. Our survey discovered that when adults were asked which of 5 specified sources of influence had most influenced their views and beliefs about life, religious views was the most popular influence, cited by 41% of the public. The closest rival influence was the attitudes and opinions of family and friends, listed by 32%. None of the other influences—government laws and regulations (7%); information and suggestions from the media (5%); and the views of public leaders (2%)—were named by more than 1 out of every 10 people (see Figure 2.4).

Religious views were most likely to be identified as the primary influence by women (51%); parents of young children (49%); blacks (51%); people from the South (48%) and Midwest (46%); Republicans (54%); Protestants (52%); born-again Christians (58%); and evangelicals (78%). Religious input was least influential among baby busters (26%); the unchurched (22%); and non-Christians (30%).

Indeed, regarding contemporary moral and ethical standards, most adults acknowledge that those standards have taken a beating in recent years. Just 10% of the adult population strongly agreed with the statement "the moral and ethical standards of Americans these days are as high as ever." Another 12% agreed somewhat. The vast majority of the population (75%) disagreed with this sentiment (see Figure 2.5). Disagreement was particularly prevalent among evangelicals (93%) and born-again Christians (82%).

FAMILY VALUES AND PUBLIC POSTURING

Because electoral politics relies so heavily upon sound bites, images and emotional issues, important issues and circumstances sometimes become trivialized for the benefit of a candidate or movement. In the past two years, the expression "family values" has become just such a matter. Recognizing that the vast majority of Americans say that family is very important to them, and that their lifestyles, beliefs and values all relate intimately to their notions and experiences of family,

Religion is a Bigger Influence in Adults' Lives than Many Other Forces

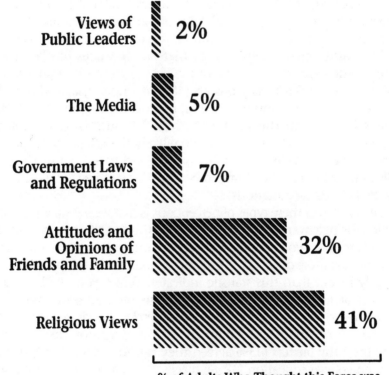

Views of
Public Leaders   2%

The Media   5%

Government Laws
and Regulations   7%

Attitudes and
Opinions of
Friends and Family   32%

Religious Views   41%

% of Adults Who Thought this Force was
Influencial in their Lives.

Figure 2.4

Source: Barna Research Group, Ltd. 1993

public leaders have latched on to the notion of promoting family values. Over the course of the 1992 campaign season, however, it became clear that one person's family values are another's moral and ethical conundrums.

Our survey showed that adults are evenly divided about the clarity of the term "family values." Half of the adult population agreed that the phrase "has been used in so many ways, you're not sure what it means anymore." The other half disagreed, indicating that they have a clear sense of what the term means in public usage.

Despite the confusion that the term "family values" raises for many, a majority (56%) claim that the expression has a positive, favorable meaning for them. A considerable proportion of people (38%) disagree, insinuating that family values has acquired a tainted image.

The parties most likely to state that family values has become a problematic term include some of the people groups that possess liberal political leanings: baby busters (48% of whom disagreed that the phrase has positive connotations); upper-income persons (51%); Hispanics (56%); and the unchurched (50%). Surprisingly, though, Democrats (39%) were not much more likely than Republicans (32%) to reject the phrase. Also shocking was the fact that 4 out of 10 evangelicals (39%) found the phrase to be something other than positive or favorable in its connotations.

The upshot of these types of perceptions is that we are slowly becoming increasingly wary of other people. One-third of all Americans (32%) now claim that "you cannot trust anyone other than your family and close friends these days"—and our studies found that the proportion is actually higher than this statistic indicates. Why?, you ask. Because a number of respondents disagreed with this proposition due to their view that *they cannot even trust their family or close friends anymore!*

The people groups that exhibited the least degree of trust in others were the baby busters (43% agreed they cannot trust others); people with no college education (42%); blacks (45%); and people not registered to vote (41%).

Our lack of confidence in other human beings is reaching epidemic proportions. It is not suprising that Americans are among the most isolated, friendless people on earth. Given the things we value (i.e., our possessions, our time, our achievements), relationships with people can only stand in the way of maximizing our potential in regard to those elements.

Our Ethical Standards Are Slipping

Response to the statement, "The ethical and moral standards of Americans these days are just as high as ever."

Somewhat Agree 12%

Somewhat Disagree 25%

Strongly Agree 10%

Don't Know 3%

Strongly Disagree 50%

COOKIES

Figure 2.5

Source: Barna Research Group, Ltd. 1993

At the same time, it is important to recognize that although we might chastise adults for feeling so skeptical toward other people, there is likely some basis for retaining such skepticism; the fear of being taken advantage of by others is not simply the unfounded trepidation of the paranoid. The current condition certainly raises questions—and significant opportunities—regarding the difference a relationship with Christ ought to make in our own involvement in the lives of people who neither know Christ nor have much reason for confidence in the potential of people and relationships.

A PERSONAL CHALLENGE

Have we bought into the media-driven notion that the 1992 election reflects a ground swell of public opinion supportive of liberal policy and program initiatives and lifestyles? If so, we ought to correct the misperception and recognize that most Americans remain fundamentally opposed to liberal alternatives to our current economic, political and international conditions and policies.

Caving in to liberal agendas, out of a sense of being in the minority, is neither necessary nor democratically healthy. As you consider the future of your community, your region and your country, what are some of the issues on which you might take the tough stand, dissenting from the prevalent view of the current administration or other activist groups?

During this time of political posturing and repositioning, it would be healthy for Americans to get back to some of the most basic concepts of the meaning and foundation of our democracy. Western Europe, Eastern Europe, the Middle East and portions of Africa are struggling through realignment and a redefinition of the basic truths and propositions that will serve as their fundamental views of life. Thus, Americans, too, would be wise to reconsider the very meaning of pivotal concepts such as justice, community and freedom.

Freedom cannot be taken to mean "liberty without responsibility" or "actions without consequences," as millions of Americans are tacitly assuming. If the church and its people are to have an enduring influence upon this nation, we must stand for certain, unchanging truths and realities. By deciphering the true meaning and implications of Christ's death and resurrection, we can better assist all people in confronting the privileges and responsibilities of democratic freedom in our nation. By radically eradicating our eternal bondage to sin, while clarifying our duties and obligations as world Christians, we may light the way to a superior experience and understanding of human freedom based on spiritual truths and insights.

In that light, have you thought about how satisfactorily you represent the One who provided you with such freedoms, opportunities and responsibilities? Research from various disciplines has underscored the fact that people learn best when they see a behavior or perspective modeled by another human being.

As an "ambassador for Christ," how consciously and conscientiously do you model His values, His purposes and His heart to a skeptical but observing world? Most committed Christians fail to consistently view themselves as His representatives. Perhaps recognizing that we are both called to be His reflection in this world, and that the world watches us more closely than we may realize, will better enable us to shape our thinking and behavior to conform to His calling on our lives.

If we take on a more Christ-like demeanor in all aspects of our existence, perhaps the tendency to embrace situational ethics would be replaced by a biblical standard for decision making. The evidence must be clear that our society has fallen prey to serious ethical and moral decline at least partially because of the absence of a sense of the proper foundation for ethical choices.

Are you prepared to integrate Scripture into the decisions you make every day, backing your choices with a logical, defensible biblical understanding of the choice that Christ would have made in that same situation? Making decisions on the basis of what is easy (the path of least resistance), what is societally acceptable or in vogue (the path of cultural relativism), or as a result of a snap judgment (the path of emotional inertia) rarely results in sound choices.

Note
1. George Barna, *The Future of the American Family* (Chicago, IL: Moody Press, 1993), pp. 98,99.

CHAPTER 3
PARTICIPATING IN THE COMMUNITY OF FAITH

CHAPTER HIGHLIGHTS

- Just under half of all adults (45%) claimed to have attended a church service, other than for a special event (such as a funeral or wedding), during the prior week. This represents a small decline from the levels of the previous two years.
- One out of four adults volunteered free time during the week prior to the survey to help a church. That ratio remains consistent with previous measures.
- One out of three adults had read from the Bible, other than during services at a church or synagogue, during the week before the survey. Reported Bible reading during a "typical week" was down; less than half of the adult population now claim to read the Bible on a weekly basis.
- Our survey revealed that just 2% claimed to have read from the Book of Mormon during the week in question.
- Last year, 13% said they served in a position of leadership within a church. This year, the figure dipped to 9%. In addition, 1 out of 10 adults stated that they teach a Sunday School or Christian-education class.
- One out of four adults was involved in a small group in 1991 and again in 1992. The most recent figures, generated at the beginning of 1993, show a substantial decline to just 16%. In addition, 6% participate in a recovery group or 12-step group associated with a local church.

- Nearly one-quarter of the adult public (22%) had not attended any religious services in the past six months. Among them, people were more than twice as likely to attend a church service if invited by a friend or family member than to attend a small-group Bible study if invited by a friend or family member.

What We Discovered

During the past two years, significant natural and human events have challenged our thinking and our sense of security in life. Consider, for instance, within a 24-month period Americans were exposed to the following life-changing events:

- The war in the Persian Gulf;
- The multi-billion dollar destruction of Hurricane Andrew;
- The collapse and subsequent turbulence of the Soviet Union and Eastern bloc nations;
- The deterioration of the European Economic Community;
- The political defeat of George Bush and Reagonomics;
- The spread of AIDS to heterosexuals, as manifested by basketball star Magic Johnson;
- The steady deterioration of the American economy.

Any one of these conditions could, in itself, have precipitated major change in the lives of millions of people. The effect of so many significant events occurring within such a constricted time span has caused tens of millions of Americans to reexamine their fundamental belief systems and their goals for the future in light of the unpredictability and seeming transience of today's world.

Religion has continued to play an important role in the questioning and explorations of our population. During this time, many are seeking a more internally consistent and meaningful view of the world and life itself. Searching the basic propositions of major faiths, such as Christianity, has played a pivotal role in this journey.

But have the American people really changed their behavioral patterns much, in terms of their religious activities and beliefs, especially during the past year?

The Week in Religion

During the week before our interviews were conducted, we learned that large numbers of people participated in various religious activities.

Church attendance. Just under half of all adults (45%) claimed to have attended a church service, other than for a special event (such as a funeral or wedding) during the prior week (see Figure 3.1). This means that roughly 85 million adults attended such a service on any given Sunday. The profile of those most likely to attend includes women; people 47 or older; married adults; people living in the South and Midwest; born-again Christians; and evangelicals.

Volunteer work. Half as many adults (24%) said they had also volunteered some of their free time during the prior week to help a church. The same segments of the population as were most likely to attend a church service emerged as more likely than others to have volunteered their time, too.

Bible reading. Reading from the Bible, other than during services at a church or synagogue, was engaged in by one-third of the adult public (34%) (see Figure 3.2). The same segments who attend church proved to be the most likely to read the Bible. Also worthy of note were a few segments that were clearly less likely than others to engage in Scripture reading: those in the highest income brackets; residents of the Northeast; Catholics; and those who live in the suburbs.

Book of Mormon. The Book of Mormon has received greater public exposure during the last few years, thanks to aggressive television advertising campaigns and broader placement in the rooms of several large hotel chains, but few Americans typically read the Book of Mormon. The survey revealed that just 2% claimed to have done so in the week in question. Although the data are far from conclusive, the indications are that Hispanics and residents of the western states (including, but not limited to, Utah) were most likely to read from the Book of Mormon.

Consistent Practice
Some of these levels of activity reflect a large number of people engaging in religious practices, but realize that the statistics represent virtually no change from the levels of the past several years. The spiritual search that appears to be happening in our society today is taking place largely in the minds and hearts of people, rather than in the buildings of churches.

If any change has occurred, it appears that people's "public" faith is perhaps on the decline. Notice, for instance, that church attendance has remained static for the last eight years, perhaps dipping slightly over the past couple of years. Volunteerism at churches has remained unchanged.[1] Bible reading, too, remains on par with recent past measurements.

Attendance at Church Services in the Past Week

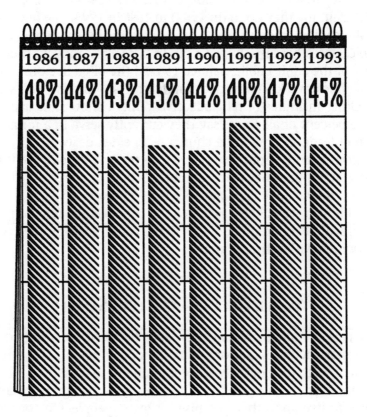

1986	1987	1988	1989	1990	1991	1992	1993
48%	44%	43%	45%	44%	49%	47%	45%

Figure 3.1

Source: Barna Research Group, Ltd. 1993

Even if we change the time frame for our measurements to understand how often such religious activities transpire in a typical month,
the curve remains flat. For instance, we discovered that 4 out of 10
adults claimed they attended religious services 4 or more times each
month; 1 out of 4 adults do so 3 times or less often each month; and
3 out of 10 adults never attend. This is almost identical to the figures
derived from our studies in 1991 and 1992.[2]

Regarding Bible reading, a slight drop-off has occurred in people's
tendency to read from the Bible during a typical week, dipping from
53% claiming they do so (in 1992) to 46% in 1993. The frequency of
Bible reading among those who read from the Scriptures during a
typical week has also slipped a bit. In last year's study we found that
19% of the adult public claimed to read the Bible five or more days
in a typical week. That proportion fell to 14% in this year's study.

Other measures of religious involvement show similar patterns.
Nine percent of all adults say they currently serve in a formal position of leadership within a church (e.g., elder, deacon, staff), which
is down slightly from last year's 13% mark. One out of 10 adults
(10%) states that they teach a Sunday School or Christian-education
class at their church (similar to 8% in 1992). Notice, too, that women
are almost twice as likely as men to fill this teaching function, which
is particularly interesting in light of the current debate about the role
of women within the Church.

SMALL GROUPS—GETTING SMALLER

The rage in church-growth circles lately has been the rush to develop
an infrastructure based on a small-group program. Good reasons
abound, both theologically and communally, to do so.

However, the current study indicates that small groups may have
failed to live up to their promise for many people. One out of four
adults was involved in a small group in 1991 and in 1992. The most
recent figures show a decline to just 16% who are involved in a small
group that meets for Bible study, prayer or Christian fellowship,
other than a Sunday School class (see Figure 3.3). In addition, 6%
meet in a nontraditional small-group setting—a recovery group or
12-step group associated with a local church. Allowing for overlap

Bible Reading During the Week, Outside of Church, Is Declining

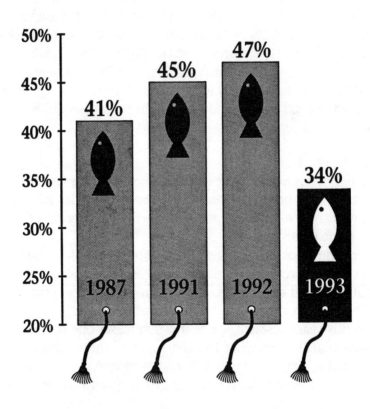

Figure 3.2

Source: Barna Research Group, Ltd. 1993

between these segments, though, we still find a small drop in participation, to 21% overall.

This decline in small-group involvement has occurred equally among men and women. However, the decline is considerable among the boomers (those 28-46 years old) and the builders (adults 47-65). Among boomers, participation levels dropped from 22% to 14%. Among the builders, the decline was even more precipitous: from 37% to 16%. Other segments that have departed from small groups in noteworthy numbers during the past year are those with the lowest levels of formal education and residents of the South.

The growth of 12-step and recovery groups has been hailed by some as one of the most significant recent breakthroughs within church circles. The 6% of adults currently involved in a church-related group of this type represent some 10-12 million adults who are seeking help from the church in this way. Demographically, these groups are most popular among senior citizens (12% of whom are involved); blacks (16%); and born-again Christians (10% of whom attend, three times the prevalence of non-Christians).

Bearing Fruit

Evangelism has been a topic of controversy over the last decade, as a variety of new programs, perspectives and theologies related to the motivation for evangelism and the practice of spreading the gospel have come under scrutiny.

One thing has not changed much, though: people's willingness to speak with others about their religious beliefs. In any given month, about one-third of all adults share their religious beliefs with other adults who they think have a different set of beliefs.

In this year's research, we found that about one out of every six adults—that is, somewhat less than half of those who share their faith during the year—stated that at least one person with whom they had shared their faith had changed views and accepted the same beliefs as those of the evangelist. This type of "success" was most commonly realized by baby busters; people with middle or lower incomes; blacks; people in the South; born-again Christians; and evangelicals. Evangelicals had double the "conversion" rate of the population at-large (31%).[3]

Involvement in Small Groups Declined in the Past Year

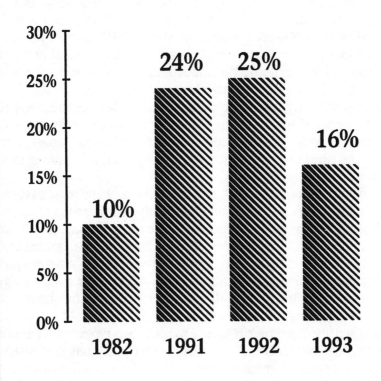

Figure 3.3

Source: Barna Research Group, Ltd. 1993

THE UNCHURCHED AMERICAN

Although the proportion of adults who attended church services in a given week remained consistent with past levels, the two surveys revealed that nearly one-quarter of the adult public (22%) had not attended any religious services in the past six months (see Figure 3.4).

The people who do not attend religious services in a typical month had a guarded openness to alter that behavioral pattern. Overall, only 1 out of every 14 adults who do not attend church services said they would definitely do so if a friend or family member who attends a Christian church in their area invited the nonattender to accompany them to the church. A large proportion (42%) said they would probably attend, but our past examination of people's follow-up on such offers, when their interest is lukewarm, shows that less than 1 in 3 of those adults would actually do so. Overall, we project that about 20% of all adults who currently do not attend religious services would accompany a friend or family member upon invitation.

Demographically, the unchurched adults who are most apt to attend a service if invited include women (twice as likely as men); baby busters; people in the middle- and upper-income ranges; residents of the Northeast. The segments most opposed to changing their pattern were the senior citizens.

The data point out that unchurched adults would be more likely to attend a church service with a friend or family member than to attend a Bible study group, if invited to such a gathering. In total, just 4% of the unchurched said they would definitely attend a small group, and a mere 12% stated that they would probably do so. These figures project to less than 10% of all unchurched adults attending a Bible study group if invited—less than half the efficiency rate that might be expected by inviting people to a church service.

The intensity of people's response to these two types of invitations varies considerably. Only 17% said they would "definitely not" attend the church service to which they were invited; more than twice that total (43%) said they would "definitely not" attend a small group, in spite of an invitation to do so.

Why the discrepancy in interest levels? These studies did not delve into the motivations and concerns of unchurched respondents. However, other studies we have conducted intimate that the dominant distinctions relate to the greater level of anonymity afforded by the

Millions of Adults Still Remain Unchurched – but the Proportion Is Declining

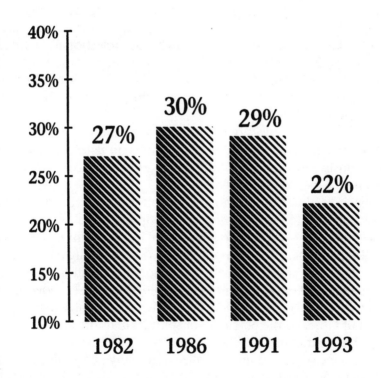

Figure 3.4

Source: Barna Research Group, Ltd. 1993

church service. The assumption is that a person can observe the activities during a church service, but might be expected to say or know something in the smaller group. The unchurched also have a greater sense of discomfort being around and interacting with a small group of religious people, as opposed to blending in among a larger group of adults who attend a church service.

A PERSONAL CHALLENGE

If anything, during this time of wondering about the place of religion in people's lives, adults seem less likely to actively engage in corporate religious experiences. We have more Protestant churches, per capita, than we had a decade ago. We have a glut of professionally trained, Protestant ministers. We currently raise more money for ministry than ever in history. We have developed an extensive network of Christian media to reach people with messages about the gospel and the work of the local church.

Yet, the evidence points out that millions of adults are still baffled about the true purpose and value of the Christian faith. Consequently, they consistently and stubbornly resist efforts to become involved in the life of a local church.

Discussions about the number of people who engage in church-based activities often obscure the more important reality associated with such behavior—what *difference* did the involvement make in the life of the participant? As you reflect on your own religious journey and involvement, consider what you, personally, might do to ensure that your spiritual development is not defined merely by how much time you devote to religious endeavors, or what spiritual activities you pursue, but rather by the potential for spiritual maturity and Christian growth that your efforts facilitate.

At the same time, you might realize that many people live outside the domain of the church world. Many, if not all, of those people would profit from exposure to what good churches and their people have to offer.

Can you conceptualize or implement, through your own personal relationships with unchurched or nonbelieving people and through the course of your ongoing church involvement, ways that make the life of the church more attractive and transforming for those who venture in from the outside? Building the church family is more than simply a career challenge for pastors and their staff. Every Christian has the privilege and responsibility of making Christianity sufficiently real and practical so that every adult will find true, deep value in the church's offerings.

One means of making the church relevant in the lives of those who have rejected it is to establish significant relationships with those people. Consciously prepare for a time when you might have an opportunity to expose them to the benefits that Christianity, through an outward-looking, Christ-centered, people-sensitive church has to offer. Engaging with the unchurched on their turf is sometimes scary, sometimes uncomfortable. However, if your church is sensitive to the needs and backgrounds of your unchurched friends, what better gift could you ever provide them than the chance to know Christ personally and share in the eternal grace available by God through His Son?

But this opportunity presents a serious challenge: Is your church prepared to address the needs and struggles of your unchurched friends? Instituting the changes required to arrive at an affirmative reply to that question is, in itself, a dynamic ministry option worthy of your commitment. It is important to get involved in ministry for the sake of those who need to know Christ but have been shielded from Him by bad past experiences with churches. Many of the unchurched are ignorant of the realities of the Church and the Christian faith, and have a lack of opportunities to explore the claims of Christ. As you get involved in the life of a church, these and myriad other possible reasons will provide you with a sense of fulfillment that cannot be replicated by other means.

Notes
1. For comparative data, see *The Barna Report 1992-93: America Renews Its Search for God*, George Barna (Ventura, CA: Regal Books, 1992), pp.89-97.
2. Ibid.
3. The terms "success" and "conversion" are used cautiously here. It is my understanding of Scripture that when a person embraces Jesus Christ as Savior, although we may play a role in the process, we cannot take the

credit for the conversion; only God, through the supernatural working of His Holy Spirit, can actually cause such a change of heart. One of the enduring difficulties in the American Church is the perception that a person who obediently and intelligently shares his or her faith with another person, but does not see that person accept Christ as Savior, has been a failure. Conversely, people who share their faith with nonbelievers and witness a conversion are labeled "successful" evangelists. The Church would be a healthier place if it could liberate people from the burden of affecting a conversion. The Church needs to redefine successful evangelism to be that which is done with a good heart, in obedience to God's calling, using whatever resources are available to skillfully and prayerfully tell people about Christ and the grace He offers.

CHAPTER 4 THE CONTENT OF OUR FAITH

CHAPTER HIGHLIGHTS

- Two out of every three adults claim that religion is "very important" to them. Combined with those who say religion is at least somewhat important to them, more than four out of five adults claim that religion is personally important.
- It is increasingly less common for people to describe themselves by traditional religious labels such as Protestant, Catholic or Jewish. Currently, only 2 out of 5 consider themselves to be Protestant; 3 out of 10 describe themselves as Catholic; and just 1% called themselves Jewish.
- Three-quarters of all adults believe there are spiritual forces that we cannot see but that affect the material world in which we live. Baby boomers are among the most prolific in accepting the unseen world.
- Nearly two out of three adults contend that "it does not matter what religious faith you follow because all faiths teach similar lessons about life."
- Two-thirds of adults say they believe that God is the all-powerful, all-knowing Creator of the universe who rules the world today.
- Almost 9 out of 10 Americans (86%), regardless of their view of God, believe that God hears and has the power to answer people's prayers.
- Americans are nearly evenly divided on whether or not Christ was

perfect. Although 47% say He was perfect, 44% argue that while He was on earth He made mistakes.

- Ultimately, almost three-fourths of our adult population (71%) expect Jesus to return some day. More than four out of five adults believe that God will judge people individually. Yet, only 36% might be categorized, according to their beliefs about salvation, as born-again Christians.

WHAT WE DISCOVERED

We have discovered much about people's religious beliefs during the last few years. God is many things to many people and increasingly is not perceived the same as He was by past generations of Americans. Jesus remains a pivotal, historical figure, but to a large segment of our population He had His fair share of faults and failures during His earthly tenure. The Church itself is often critiqued by the public for some of its flaws and failings.

Yet, religion remains a matter of fascination and significance to most Americans. Just what is it that we believe?

WHAT MATTERS TO YOU?

A large majority of Americans contend that religion is important in their lives. Two-thirds of all adults (65%) claim that religion is "very important" to them (see Figure 4.1). An additional one-fifth say it is at least somewhat important to them. Overall, 84% claim that religion holds a place of importance in their lives. The people most likely to cite religion as being very important include women (75%); senior citizens (84%); blacks (77%); residents of the South (75%); churched adults (74%); and born-again Christians (85%). On the other side of the coin, the segments least likely to view religion as important in their lives are people in the West, unchurched adults and non-Christians.

As high as that proportion might seem, however, it represents a decline from the feelings of Americans about religion one year earlier. Over the past decade, we have seen some volatility in people's beliefs about the importance of religion in their lives. In 1991, 59% cited religion as very important. In 1992, in the wake of the Gulf War, publicity about the spread of AIDS, and other major crisis events as described in chapter 3, religion zoomed up to 69%. This year's slow drift back to prior levels is not unexpected, given the reduced sense of worldwide anxiety that Americans are experiencing, and our even further entrenched feelings of self-reliance and control.

Said one respondent, "For a while there I really thought 'gee, maybe the end of the world is approaching.' Everything was just so out of control, so despairing, I figured it must be just about over. I spent time thinking about my family, my career; I even prayed some. But things have settled down again. It's a lot more comfortable now, even though the world is still a bit crazy."

WHAT IS YOUR LABEL?

Traditional church affiliations are becoming less significant to people. Notice, for instance, that the proportion of adults who describe themselves as Protestant, Catholic or Jewish continues to decline. Currently, only 41% consider themselves as Protestant (although more than 60% associate with Protestant churches); 28% describe themselves as Catholic; and just 1% called themselves Jewish. Less than a decade ago, we typically found that about 6 out of 10 adults portrayed themselves as "Protestant"; today, the proportion is 4 out of 10 (see Figure 4.2).

This shift can easily be traced to the perspectives of younger adults. If you compare the self-descriptions of senior citizens and baby busters, the contrast is quite startling. Among seniors, 67% say they are Protestant; only 8% assign themselves to an "other" faith group, beyond Protestant, Catholic, Jewish or atheist. Among busters, however, just 19% call themselves Protestants, and double that proportion (38%) say they are affiliated with some "other" faith group. The pattern shows that the younger people are, the more likely they are to associate with the "other faith" category; the older they are, the more likely they are to relate to the Protestant grouping.

When pressed to explain why they reject the label "Protestant," young people give various explanations. One common response is "I just don't think of myself as a Protestant. That seems so old-fashioned. I believe in Christianity, I attend a Presbyterian church, I read the Bible. What does that have to do with being Protestant? I'm not even sure if that's a religion, a church group, or some other category."

For many young Americans, their lack of history knowledge and their distance from many of the traditions of prior generations serve as a barrier to embrace some of the labels we normally associate with their behavior and belief patterns.

Another point of fascination deals with the gravitation of young adults to the Catholic label. Although busters are not especially prolific in Catholic churches on any given weekend, the Catholic church is

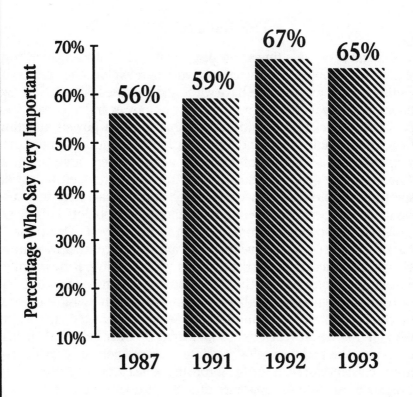

Religion Is Very Important to Most Americans

Percentage Who Say Very Important

56%	59%	67%	65%
1987	1991	1992	1993

Figure 4.1

Source: Barna Research Group, Ltd. 1993

described as the spiritual home of 38% of these young adults. This is a substantial increase from the levels measured during the prior several years. This sudden jump in inclination may have more to do with the current religious experimentation and church-hopping of busters than with their determination to permanently align themselves with the Catholic community.

Also of interest is the finding that a majority of blacks (54%) said they were associated with a faith group other than the three traditional groups.

THE BIG PICTURE

In difficult economic times and periods of social turbulence, history shows that people are attracted to media that explore the unknown. During the last five years we have witnessed increased sales of New Age books. We have witnessed the popularity of movies and television specials that depict bizarre and inexplicable spiritual powers affecting lives, and spreading fame and fortune accorded to musical groups that sing praises to all manner of unseen universal powers, from Satan, to "the great tree god," to Jesus Christ. Americans are open to a wide spectrum of spiritual perspectives today, and they are investing substantial resources in discovering more about these potential realities.

Given this spending record, it may not surprise you to learn that 3 out of 4 adults (77%) believe there are spiritual forces that we cannot see but that affect the material world in which we live. Baby boomers are a leading force behind this acceptance of the unseen world: 6 out of 10 are strongly convinced of the existence of such invisible powers; by comparison, only one-third of our senior citizens (i.e., the adults who are the "most religious" as measured by their beliefs, their religious practices and their self-stated interest in religion) strongly believe in the existence of such forces. Surprisingly, just 2 out of 3 born-again Christians buy into the existence of such spiritual forces.

What may be more surprising, though, is the application of such thinking to people's spiritual worldview. Captivated by the intrigue, adventure and personal potential represented by spiritual truths and mysteries, most people exhibit an alarming näiveté about the divergent religious faiths in the marketplace. Two-thirds of all adults (62%) agree that "it does not matter what religious faith you follow because

Fewer Adults Call Themselves "Protestant" These Days

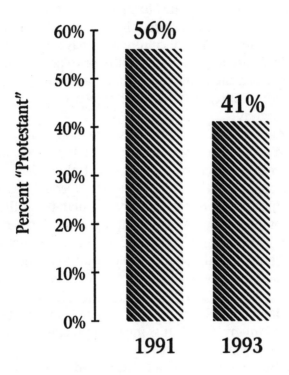

Figure 4.2

Source: Barna Research Group, Ltd. 1993

all faiths teach similar lessons about life." This viewpoint is widely shared, but it is especially prevalent among Hispanics (81%). A majority of both Catholics (76%) and Protestants (52%) accept this perspective as true. Two out of five born-again Christians buy into this view as well (see Figure 4.3).

How is this possible? It might be explained by research that points out that Americans now have wide exposure to a variety of religious faiths, but gain very superficial insight into any given faith. Thus, people's analysis of any particular religious group emerges as strikingly similar to that applied to any other religious group. This embodies a series of philosophies or truths geared to enable a person to lead a happier, more successful life without undermining the ability of others to do the same. In our life-on-the-run culture, who has time to dig deeper to flesh out the idiosyncrasies of each faith, or to determine which is and is not valid as a life foundation? More importantly, from the view of adults, why bother since they all appear to offer the same basic assistance anyway?

The interchangeability of religious faiths corresponds with people's beliefs that when people pray they all pray to the same gods, no matter what names or other labels are associated with those deities.[1]

"In the end, only one religion is right. As imperfect people, we don't have the information or the capacity to untangle all the man-made trappings of religion and to figure out which religion is right. In fact, there probably is not a single, right religion. The important thing is not which religion you buy into, but that you accept the fact that there is a spiritual dimension to life, and you immerse yourself in it somehow. Mohammed, Buddha, Jesus Christ, they all teach the same things; they all stand for a higher plane of personal development and sensitivity." So say many Americans, including literally millions of people whose chosen faith is Christianity.

This sense of the uniformity of all faiths is made a little more perplexing by the fact that a majority of Americans (60%) continue to believe that the Bible is totally accurate in all it teaches. But upon deeper examination, again we find that most adults take this position without making a strong commitment to the veracity of Scripture. Once we delve into specific teachings drawn from the Bible and ask people if those teachings represent absolute truth or simply a useful proposition worthy of a person's consideration, the belief that the

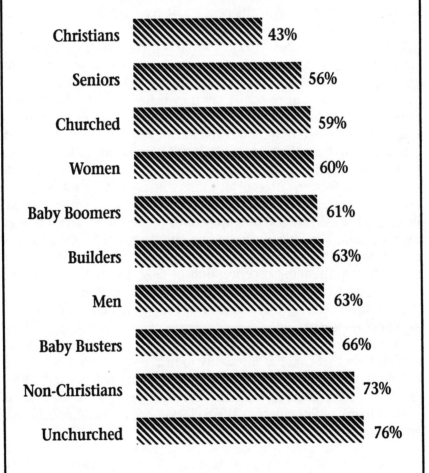

Most People Concur:
"All Religious Faiths Teach the
Same Lessons About Life."

Group	Percentage
Christians	43%
Seniors	56%
Churched	59%
Women	60%
Baby Boomers	61%
Builders	63%
Men	63%
Baby Busters	66%
Non-Christians	73%
Unchurched	76%

Figure 4.3

Source: Barna Research Group, Ltd. 1993

Bible is wholly accurate can be seen to be a thin veneer coating a deeper reserve of doubt, compromise, uncertainty and ambivalence.

WHO IS YOUR GOD?

When God displayed His true character for humankind, through His encounters with the patriarchs of Israel, through handing down the Ten Commandments, and through His promises to Israel through the covenant He formed with His people, He left little ambiguity about who He is. Today, the concept of belief in God remains solid in most people's lives; 90% believe in God. What is more revealing, though, is how we construe "god." One out of three Americans believes in a conception of God that conflicts with the biblical portrait of the Father.

Sixty-eight percent of adults say they believe that God is the all-powerful, all-knowing Creator of the universe who rules the world today. People living in the South and Midwest, women, Hispanics and senior citizens have the highest likelihood of believing in such a God.

Education seems to draw people away from an orthodox Christian view of God. Three-quarters of all adults who did not have any formal education beyond high school believe in the God of Israel, as He described Himself, but less than two-thirds of those who have a college degree concur. Similarly, the cosmopolitan lifestyle either facilitates or attracts nontraditional views of God. Although three-quarters of rural residents buy the biblical conception of God, less than two out of three people living in cities and suburbs accept that view.

It is also revealing that one out of four churched adults have a nonbiblical view of God.

Almost 9 out of 10 Americans (86%), regardless of their view of God, believe that God has the ability to hear people's prayers and the power to answer them. Those people groups that reflect the greatest certainty of this include women (80% strongly agree, compared to 62% of men); senior citizens (81%); blacks (90%); southerners (83%); and Protestants (82%).

PASSING JUDGMENT ON JESUS

Past research has shown that more than four out of five Americans believe that Jesus Christ was a historical figure. The debate begins once you start to define who He was, what He did, and His ultimate significance in the scope of human history.

Given the fact that not quite 4 out of 10 adults may be described as born-again believers, it is quite telling to realize that more than 8 out of 10 adults (85%) believe that Jesus was crucified, died and resurrected *and is spiritually alive today.*

To recognize that half of all the people who accept the biblical account of Jesus' death, resurrection and eternal life nevertheless have not sought any type of serious, permanent relationship with Him is rather astonishing. This must raise some questions both about our culture and the ways the American church fosters its faith within the context of this culture. As well, a majority of unchurched adults (64%) and non-Christians (77%) assert that He died, rose and exists today.

Perhaps part of the reluctance of many Americans to pursue an ongoing relationship with Christ is that millions of people believe His character is not what the Bible portrays it to be. For instance, adults are divided on the matter of Jesus' perfection: 44% agree that He made mistakes, 47% disagree and 9% could not decide (see Figure 4.4). Certainly, if Jesus had made mistakes, it would challenge His deity and authority over the world, and undermine the value of a relationship with Him. At the same time, a majority of the people who assert that He made mistakes also claim that the Bible is accurate in all that it teaches. This is yet another example of the spiritual inconsistency and biblical illiteracy of our nation.

Among several subgroups of the population, a majority believe that Jesus was mistake-prone. Baby busters (56%); those with incomes exceeding $60,000 annually (56%); residents of the Northeast (52%); and western states (58%). The unchurched (57%) and non-Christians (56%) lead the way. Among the major religious groups, Catholics (53%) are the most likely to believe that Jesus sometimes made mistakes.

Of course, to some of these people, for Jesus to make errors in His decisions and behavior would be perfectly rational since they view Him as being human during His earthly ministry. Overall, four out of five Americans (82%) acknowledge that He was as much human as we are. The indications are, though, that many people confuse the humanity of Christ with the imperfection of the rest of the human race.

Ultimately, almost three-fourths of our adult population (71%) expect Jesus to return someday. Of particular note is the finding that although barely two-thirds of the white (69%) and Hispanic (66%) populations are awaiting the return of Christ, 89% of all blacks anticipate His return.

WHERE DO WE GO FROM HERE?

The matter of life after death has captured people's fancy generation after generation. What becomes of people after they pass away raises an important question of very personal significance. It is the significance of the question that makes the lukewarm pursuit of Christ so astounding.

Most people believe that there will be a judgment time for all people. Overall, 85% concur that "eventually all people will be judged by God." Given the divergent views of God and the meaning of eternal salvation, this point of belief may not hold the power that a traditional Christian view would provide.

Once again, several population segments appear to be less likely to accept the notion of the impending judgment by God. Compared to others, people who have a college degree, people living in the West, city residents, the unchurched and non-Christians are the least likely to support the concept of heavenly judgment.

One of the more alarming perspectives of people, because it conflicts so clearly with biblical teaching, is that a majority of adults believe that "if a person is generally good, or does enough good things for others during life, they will earn a place in Heaven." More than half of all adults (57%) accept this to be true; 1 out of 3 people reject the notion (34%); and 1 out of 10 people (9%) do not take a position on this matter.

Although the Bible plainly exhorts people to rely upon Christ for their salvation, and to demonstrate that new life found in Him by serving others by doing good deeds, many Americans separate the two streams of activity and make the matter more exclusive. It is the focus upon personal deeds as the means to salvation that has brought a surge of young people to the Catholic church. Combine an aggressive promotion of social ministry as a means to an eternal end with an activist mind-set and belief that hope for the future lies in human

Jesus Perfect? Not According to Many Americans...

"Jesus sometimes made mistakes."

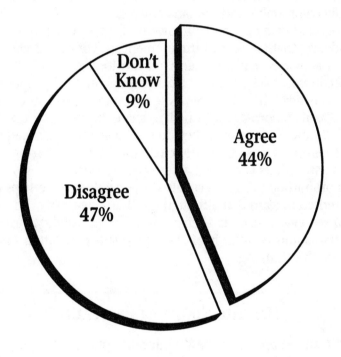

Don't Know 9%

Agree 44%

Disagree 47%

Figure 4.4

Source: Barna Research Group, Ltd. 1993

efforts to save creation, and the result is millions of young adults aligning themselves with Catholicism.

Look at the segments of the population that are most prone to accept the "do good, earn heaven" view. Baby busters (64%); Hispanics (72%); adults from the Northeast (69%); Catholics (84%); and non-Christians (67%) head the list. Several million Catholics embrace the "salvation by faith alone" doctrine. However, they are clearly in the minority.

Indeed, in modern America, the theology of salvation by faith in God, as proven by a lifetime of good works, is more comfortable than any faith that emphasizes faith in Christ alone. Why? Because such a faith is more self-determined, personally controlled, tangible, emotionally comfortable and human-centered.

Judgment by a holy and all-powerful God is all the more ominous considering that one out of three Americans contend there are some human activities that not even God can forgive. People from lower socioeconomic backgrounds, blacks and unchurched people are most likely to believe this. However, note that one out of four evangelicals and 27% of all born-again Christians share this viewpoint.

Most Americans assume they do not have any type of responsibility for telling others about their religious beliefs. Sharing religious beliefs with others is deemed a personal responsibility by 45%, but a larger proportion (52%) reject this as a person's duty. Perhaps you will be surprised to learn that although less than one-third of all Catholics (31%) see evangelism as their personal responsibility, just 56% of Protestants and two-thirds of the born-again population (68%) also embrace this thinking.

HAS THE KINGDOM PLATEAUED?

In 1991, there appeared to be a significant upturn in the proportion of born-again Christians in America, as measured in our January 1992 study. The proportion had hovered around the 32-35% range for the preceding decade; however, the figure jumped to 40% in the 1992 study.

Our 1993 measure indicates that there has been a minor decline in the proportion of born-again Christians, returning to the prior levels that had been achieved. Currently, using our normal means of estimation, 36% of the adult population might be described as born again because they say they have made a "personal commitment to Jesus Christ that is still important in their life today" *and* they believe that when they die they will go to heaven because they have confessed their sins and have accepted Jesus Christ as their Savior.[2]

A Demographic Profile of "Born-again" Adults
(N=435)

Population segment	Proportion that can be classified as born again*
All adults	36%
Men	31%
Women	41%
Baby busters (18-27)	26%
Baby boomers (28-46)	38%
Builders (47-65)	40%
Seniors (66 or older)	36%
Whites	37%
Blacks	46%
Hispanics	20%
Northeast	19%
South/Southwest	50%
Central	40%
West/Mountain	29%
Urban	36%
Suburban	27%
Rural	40%
Protestant	55%
Catholic	18%

*"Born again" is defined as adults who say they have made a personal commitment to Jesus Christ that is still important in their lives today *and* believe that when they die they will go to heaven because they have confessed their sins and accepted Jesus Christ as their Savior. The term "born again" was not used in this screening process.

Notice three important realities about the proportion of adults who say they have made a personal commitment to Jesus Christ that is still important in their lives today. First, a large majority of adults (66%) claim they have made such a commitment. Second, that proportion has not changed in the last five years. Third, these figures indicate that almost half of all the people who have made such a commitment are relying upon something other than their faith in Christ as their means to eternal salvation. The most common perspectives on eternity held by those people is that they simply do not know what will happen to them after they die, or they believe that as long as they do good works, it is a combination of their faith and works that will earn God's favor for them.

THE HOT BUTTONS

A number of questions facing the Christian church in America have caused heated debate lately.

Women's Role in the Church
One of those has to do with the role of women in the Church. Our previous studies have shown that most people believe women are just as capable as men are in most areas of activity, and that many women have tremendous leadership skills. But the discussion over the role of women as leaders in the church rages. To some, the issue is theological in nature; to others, it is cultural. Attempts to derive answers from the Bible have resulted in a virtual proof-texting competition, leaving millions of adults confused, frustrated or angry.

Three out of four adults (76%) argue that "it is perfectly acceptable for a woman to be the pastor or head minister of a church." Interestingly, men are slightly more likely than are women themselves to promote this point of view (78% versus 74%). Boomers and busters are more likely than older adults to support women in the pastorate, although large majorities of all age groups accept this position. Even two-thirds of the born-again population (68%) and three-quarters of the Catholic mass (76%) endorse women as senior pastors. The segment most vehemently opposed to this concept is the evangelicals: 45% believe it is "perfectly acceptable" for a woman to lead a congregation; 54% oppose this notion.

Ministers' Behavior
Yet another insight into the perspectives of our culture deals with our

expectations regarding the behavior of ministers. An overwhelming majority (73%) acknowledge that they "expect ministers to live up to a higher moral and ethical standard" than they expect of other people. These expectations are most intense among adults 47 or older (63% feel strongly about this compared to 43% of their juniors), and among blacks (68% feel strongly, versus 47% of whites).

Interestingly, unchurched people do not have the lofty expectations of ministers that churched folk do: 63% of the unchurched agreed (either strongly or somewhat) that they have higher moral and ethical standards for ministers; 75% of the churched confessed to maintaining such a view.

A PERSONAL CHALLENGE

Read through this chapter and get a good glimpse at the theology of the typical American. From a biblical perspective, the profile that emerges is nothing less than frightening. The lack of accurate knowledge about God's Word, about His principles for life, and the apparent absence of influence the Church is having upon the thinking and behavior of this nation is a rude awakening for those who assume we are in the midst of a spiritual revival. Astoundingly, our research among pastors indicates that more than 4 out of 10 senior pastors believe we are in the midst of such a spiritual renaissance.[3]

The point of encouragement, however, is that we have nearly unrestricted opportunities to analyze the spiritual needs in our midst to minister to a confused culture in powerful ways. But time is of the essence.

In our efforts to influence a nation searching for meaning, one of the looming challenges is to make the unseen spiritual forces that people accept more tangible and real. It appears that today most people accept the existence of such forces, but the significance of those forces remains unexamined or underestimated. Past research has shown, for instance, that most people believe in evil but not in the existence of Satan.[4] How can you conceptualize and explicate the truth about the spiritual world in a way that commands people's attention, respect and active response?

In the same manner, we are challenged to help people understand Christianity in a way that differentiates it from all other religious systems. Currently, millions of Americans are less than impressed by Christianity because it is indistinguishable from other faiths to which they have exposure. The Christians they meet act no different from other people. The churches they pass on the way to work have little presence in the community and appear to do little apart from their Sunday morning rituals. The teachings of the faith seem like the same do-gooders code they hear from other religious entities.

Somehow, many Americans have heard about and accepted the notion that a fellow named Jesus Christ once lived and did some rather unusual things, but the connection between those events and their own lives is missing. Even their view of God has frequently remained untainted by the teachings of the Bible. Until we get our own house (of faith) in order, the chances of us leaving a lasting, life-changing impression on outsiders is negligible.

Ultimately, we must impress upon America that there is a crucial difference between Christianity and the pop religion of the day. God has clearly stated that regardless of how hard we try, and how many good deeds we do, entry into heaven is not available for purchase through the sweat of our brow. In a driven culture, this is hard to sell. Our job, as God's ambassadors to a confused and sinful world, is to continually use the resources He has provided—including our intelligence—to proclaim His way, and to pray for His blessing upon those efforts.

It is impossible to overemphasize the need for wholehearted, unrelenting, biblically sound evangelism. We need to be creative, articulate and practical as we reach out to skeptical and information-laden people with the Word of God. Somehow, whether through the energy of the evil one, the pigheadedness of those who are outside the community of faith, or through our own foibles and inabilities, non-Christians in this land simply are not getting it.

Often, it appears that non-Christians are so close that they are miles away. Sadly, because they believe they are on track, Christianity and religious faith is no longer an issue to them; they think they've got it, that they have arrived. What can we do to keep renewing our efforts to break through to them in ways that will introduce them to the real Jesus, and to be an agent of life transformation according to God's purposes?

Notes

1. See our findings on this, related on pages 210-212 in *What Americans Believe*, George Barna (Ventura, CA: Regal Books, 1991). In that study, we discovered that 64% said, "Christians, Jews, Buddhists, Muslims and all others pray to the same god, even though they use different names for that god."

2. We do not use the term "born again" in our surveys, as a means of having people classify themselves. Using the two questions alluded to here, we label adults in this manner after the fact, based on their answers. Please realize that is done in a good-faith effort to estimate people's spiritual nature, not to unfairly categorize them or to assume that we have a perfect means of knowing their hearts. Only God truly knows the nature of the human condition; our best efforts are riddled with error. Such survey results are simply an attempt to help us estimate what is happening regarding the spiritual condition of America.

3. See pages 204-206 of *What Americans Believe*, George Barna (Ventura, CA: Regal Books, 1991). Six out of 10 Americans, including 43% of born-again Christians, reject the existence of Satan, instead believing that the devil is merely a symbol of evil.

4. This is drawn from chapter 4 of *Today's Pastors*, George Barna (Ventura, CA: Regal Books, 1993). This study of senior pastors of Protestant churches indicated that large proportions of our pastors believe the Church is in a time of spiritual revival, and that a majority of Christians are undergoing significant spiritual renewal these days.

CHAPTER 5 GROWING SPIRITUALLY

CHAPTER HIGHLIGHTS

- Nine out of 10 people say they pray to God. Four out of 5 praying adults claim that prayer is a regular part of their lives, regardless of their daily circumstances. Among the adults who ever pray to God, almost 6 out of 10 (58%) claim they pray every day.
- Seven out of 10 people who pray say they are completely or usually satisfied with the quality of their prayer lives.
- Eight out of 10 adults who engage in prayer say they are "absolutely certain" that prayer makes a difference in their lives.
- Most adults who pray claim they do so more than once a day. Each prayer time averages less than five minutes.
- The most common reasons for prayer are to thank God for what He has done and to confess sins or ask for forgiveness. The least common prayer activity is to listen in silence for God to respond.
- One out of eight people who pray indicated that they sometimes pray in tongues or prayer languages.
- One-third of all adults claim they have been regularly mentored or discipled in their faith during the past year. One out of four adults claim they have served as a mentor or discipler.
- More than 9 out of 10 adults involved in the discipling process claim that it has been very or somewhat helpful to them.

WHAT WE DISCOVERED

Prayer and study. These two dimensions of people's religious faith are integral to mature in Christ. In a secularized culture, the pressures to devote time and energy to other, more materially productive or socially acceptable practices is considerable. Yet, most Americans pray. A substantial minority are involved in mentoring or discipleship processes.

FREQUENT GOD-TALK

"When I saw that blanket of rain comin' and was slapped in the face by that gustin' wind, all I could do was start prayin' to God that He would take care of us." The recollections of a woman whose house was ravaged by Hurricane Andrew reflect the nature of prayer in America. When in trouble, call heavenward for assistance. Prayer becomes the ultimate 911 call.

Of the various forms of spiritual activity people might engage in, prayer seems to be the most common to Americans. You may be surprised at people's claims about their experience with prayer.

Nine out of 10 adults (89%) say they sometimes pray to God. As might be expected, it is the people groups that are most sensitive to the power and value of religious conviction who are most likely to engage in prayer. Women, for example, are more likely to pray than are men; 95% of women pray, compared to 83% of men. Similarly, nonwhites are more likely to pray than are whites (95% versus 88%); churched folk are more likely than those who avoid churches (97% and 65%, respectively); and born-again Christians (99%) are more likely to pray than are other adults (83%).

Clearly, people find prayer is a source of comfort, strength, hope and perspective. However, because people pray does not mean they think they have perfected the art of communicating with God. Just one-fourth of all praying adults (26%) say they are completely satisfied with the quality of their prayer life. Another 43% say they are usually satisfied; most of the remaining praying adults (25%) admit to being sometimes satisfied, other times dissatisfied, with their prayer experiences.

Presumably, only 2% indicate they are usually or completely dissatisfied with their prayer times because most people would simply stop praying if they experienced such consistent disappointment.

Senior citizens and nonwhite adults were the two segments that stood out from the rest as being most likely to be completely satisfied with their prayer lives. It appears there is a link between the satisfaction received from prayer and characteristics such as the frequency of prayer, the time commitment to praying and having lower socioeconomic status. The elderly, blacks and Hispanics fit these criteria.

IF IT WORKS...

In an era of anxiety and opportunities in which time is one of the most carefully guarded personal resources, why would people commit time to pray to a God with whom relatively few of them have a personal, life-defining relationship? Quite simply, Americans believe that prayer works. Americans are practical in using their resources. Those endeavors that demonstrate or maintain the promise of a good return on the investment of resources will continue to reap a commitment of those resources. Prayer, to date, meets the standard.

Almost 6 out of 10 adults (56%) say they are "absolutely certain" that prayer really makes a difference in their lives. An additional 1 out of 4 adults (23%) are "somewhat certain." Overall, this is 8 out of 10 people who remain at least partially persuaded that prayer has the power to affect their lives in a real way (see Figure 5.1).

Interestingly, one out of five people who pray perceive prayer to be a gamble. They contend that they have no assurance or confidence in the power of prayer to make a difference, but they are hopeful it will work on their behalf.

"Look, it's a tough world out there. Does prayer really work? How would I know? How would anybody know? It's a chance you take, but I figure it doesn't cost me anything and it can't hurt. It's kinda like playin' the lottery. You lose, you haven't lost much. You win, you hit the jackpot, and it's all worth it."

There may be reason to doubt whether many who pray are doing so with total confidence, but a surprisingly low proportion (just 11%) say they generally rely upon prayer as a last resort in difficult times. Rather, four out of five praying adults (82%) said that prayer is a regular part of their lives, regardless of the circumstances in which they find themselves.

Among the adults who pray to God, the frequency of their prayers is surprising. Almost 6 out of 10 (58%) claim that they pray every day. Just 1% state that they pray less than once a week; the rest of the respondents were distributed fairly evenly in terms of how many days a week they pray. Again, the types of people most likely to pray daily included women, nonwhites, churched people and Christians. Add to that senior citizens, people of lesser means and Protestants, and you have the segments most committed to regular prayer sessions. The types of people who stand out as the least likely to pray during the course of a week are residents of the Northeast and suburbanites.

When people pray, they usually pray more than once during the day. Among the people who pray, half (52%) say they usually pray more than once during the days they speak with God; 8% say that it varies, sometimes more than once, sometimes once; and about 4 out of 10 claim they typically pray once during those days they pray at all.

For most people, prayer is not a prolonged activity. The average amount of time adults spend in prayer is about 5 minutes. Overall, the study discovered that 1 out of 14 people (7%) who pray claim their average prayer time lasts between 15 and 30 minutes; another 6% stated that they usually prayer for more than 30 minutes each time they pray (see Figure 5.2).

Worthy of note is the finding that although baby busters are among the least likely to pray at all, when they do pray they do so less often and once a day. They also emerged as being more aware of how much time they spend in prayer, and being somewhat more likely to pray for longer periods of time than do their elders.

Among evangelicals who pray—and that constitutes all of the evangelicals with whom we spoke—the average length of time spent in prayer is only a minute or two longer than is common among other segments. However, twice as many evangelicals as other adults (13%) said their typical prayer time lasts a half hour or more.

THE NATURE OF OUR PRAYERS

Why do we pray to God?

More than 9 out of 10 adults who pray (94%) do so to thank God for what He has done for them. This was equally true among Christians and non-Christians, the churched and the unchurched.

Does Prayer Really Make a Difference?

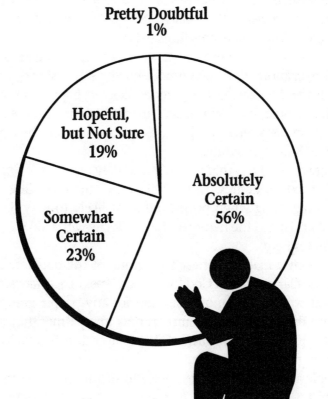

Pretty Doubtful
1%

Hopeful,
but Not Sure
19%

Absolutely
Certain
56%

Somewhat
Certain
23%

Figure 5.1

Source: Barna Research Group, Ltd. 1993

Although Protestants were slightly more likely than Catholics to list this as a reason for their prayers (97% versus 89%), the pattern remains intact.

Unexpectedly, we discovered that three-fourths of all adults who pray to God do so to ask Him to forgive specific sins they have committed. In a society in which prayer is relatively quick in nature, and sin is not a top-of-mind topic, for people to claim they ask for forgiveness is a source of encouragement. The types of people most likely to engage in such prayer were senior citizens (81%); those making less than $20,000 a year (89%); blacks (84%); Baptists (90%); born-again Christians (85%); and evangelicals (94%).

Two out of three praying Americans say they sometimes use their prayers to acknowledge God's unique qualities. Focusing on His special attributes and characteristics is more likely to happen among adults who live outside of the Northeast: Just 58% of those in the Northeast do so. A similarly small proportion of Hispanics use their prayers to recall God's unique nature.

Of great surprise is that just 61% said they pray to ask God to grant specific needs or desires. This conflicts with the prevailing notion of analysts regarding when people are most likely to pray (i.e., during times of crisis) and the nature of their dialogue with God (i.e., beseeching Him for help).

Although a majority of each subgroup of the population (except Hispanics) claimed to ask God for specific types of assistance, this form of prayer was not the most common for any people group studied. What we do not know, of course, is how many times they pray with special requests, or how much of their prayer time is actually devoted to focusing upon such needs.

People are considerably less likely to spend time listening silently for God's response to them. Just less than half of all praying adults (46%) claimed they take the time to await God's answer (see Figure 5.3). Such patience and solitude was least likely among men (41%); busters (34%); people from the suburbs (31%); Catholics (39%); and non-Christians (38%). Those who exhibit the greatest likelihood to wait for God's reply during their times of prayer are senior citizens (60%) and evangelicals (69%).

Prayer Time
The average number of minutes spent each time in prayer, by those who pray to God

Figure 5.2

Source: Barna Research Group, Ltd. 1993

PRAYING IN TONGUES

The growth of the charismatic movement in America and around the world has raised the profile of activities such as praying in tongues or spiritual languages. Although it is estimated that less than one out of every seven Christians in America employs a charismatic gift in his or her times of worship, prayer and personal ministry, awareness of such gifts has risen in recent years.

In total, we found 12% of the praying population claiming to usually speak in tongues or a spiritual language when they pray. This represents about 11% of the aggregate adult population praying in this manner.

GROWTH INDUSTRY: KNEE PADS?

The survey data on prayer provide a portrait that is nothing short of amazing. The figures suggest that 9 out of 10 adults pray, and surprisingly more than half of our nation's adults pray daily (52%). An overwhelming majority of all adults who pray, even on an irregular basis, do so out of a desire to communicate various messages to God, not out of a desperate desire to cajole the Mighty One to grant their heart's desire of the moment.

This unexpectedly high commitment to prayer corresponds with regional prayer movements that have begun to emerge in the past three years. These are most notable in the Pacific Northwest, in Southern California and in New England. Be encouraged that before revival explodes in a nation, it is always preceded by significant prayer.

THE BUDDY SYSTEM

Nearly 60 million adults (31%) say they are involved in some type of discipleship or mentoring process. Such activity takes many forms and apparently occurs with varying degrees of depth and sophistication.

Many more people are commited to help other believers mature in their faith than is typically assumed. One out of 4 adults, including 6 out of 10 evangelicals, claim to have mentored or discipled a less mature believer in their faith during the past year. The most common

The Content of Our Prayers
What we usually spend time praying about

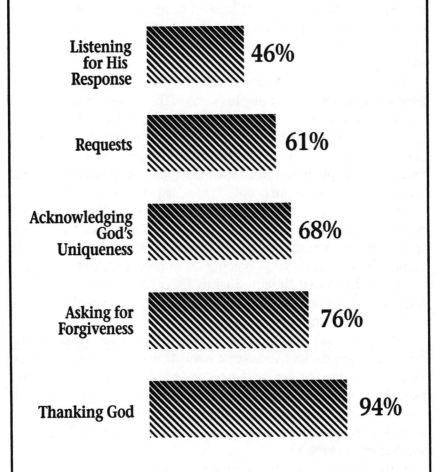

Listening for His Response — 46%

Requests — 61%

Acknowledging God's Uniqueness — 68%

Asking for Forgiveness — 76%

Thanking God — 94%

Figure 5.3

Source: Barna Research Group, Ltd. 1993

disciplers or mentors were women, parents, blacks and southerners, in addition to the born-again and evangelical segments.

The terms "discipling" and "mentoring" mean different things to different people, as the survey discovered. Among those who participated in the process in the past year, the average number of persons involved was nine. This is larger than many analysts of Christian development would consider to be part of the mentoring or discipling process. Many students of the Christian community define mentoring or discipling as one person taking one or a few less spiritually mature people under his or her wing for personalized tutoring in matters of the faith.

However, many Christians consider a Bible study group to be a "discipling" group, accounting for some of the confusion over the terminology used to define growth procedures. In other instances, churches sponsor "discipleship training" classes, which are deemed part of the discipleship arena. One-fifth of those who estimated the number of people involved in their discipling or mentoring process indicated that 20 or more people were usually involved.

In most of the groups that meet, prayer is used. Four out of five people involved in mentoring or discipling (79%) stated that they spend time in prayer. A similar proportion (75%) stated that they spend time discussing what is going on in their lives and how those conditions relate to their faith. Slightly fewer adults (68%) told us that their discipling or mentoring activity includes time devoted to reading or studying the Bible.

The typical meeting among the people involved in discipling efforts lasts just under two hours a week. One out of three spends an hour or less together, per meeting; one out of four spends up to two hours in their session; one out of seven spends five or more hours each week in these meetings. The people groups that spend the longest average amounts of time in their meetings include men, baby busters, southerners and blacks.

Is the discipling/mentoring process valued by its participants? For the most part it is. Six out of 10 adults involved said the experience is very helpful; most of the remaining participants (33%) said it was at least somewhat helpful. Only 5% said it was not too helpful or not at all helpful; 2% could not evaluate the process.

A PERSONAL CHALLENGE

If the information conveyed to us by respondents is accurate, Americans may be the most prayerful people on earth. What can we do to enhance our commitment to prayer?

How much time do you spend in meaningful conversations with friends when you are together? Probably more than the five minutes or less that we generally spend conversing with God. Perhaps we can begin to deepen our relationship with God through extended times of prayer in which we devote greater energy to listening to Him rather than ourselves. The data show that we are most comfortable speaking to God, and allocate little time to hear from Him. Undoubtedly, if we could increase our commitment to waiting for God's wisdom, we would be better off for the experience.

We might also consider how we know that prayer makes a difference in our lives. Given that most people spend time in prayer but barely half are convinced that the exercise makes a difference, a critical component to prayer is absent. When James wrote that we must pray without doubt, he taught a central element of the prayers of the faithful.[1]

Confidence in God's ability to hear our prayers, to respond in the most appropriate manner, and in the importance of our connectedness to Him through prayer are core realities of the Christian faith. If we permit people to define prayer as just another motion that we half-heartedly waltz through, we do them a great disservice. In this age, when an upwardly mobile people spread their risk by engaging in a variety of activities intended to enhance the quality of life, prayer must be embraced as more than a costless safety net that we dutifully cast one or two times a day, just in case there is a deity who can hear and deliver for us today.

If so many millions of adults are involved in a discipleship process, we must raise the question: What is really happening, in terms of spiritual challenge and growth, in those meetings? Year after year, our surveys demonstrate the paper-thin commitment of most Christians and the appalling lack of spiritual knowledge of those people.

If hundreds of thousands of hours are being spent by believers in a mentoring process each year, it is time that we evaluate what truly takes place in those meetings and critique the ways we are training, exhorting and encouraging believers to become more Christ-like. The entire blame for the lack of personal spiritual growth evident within the American Church cannot be placed on the shoulders of the mentoring process, but we have a responsibility to explore why more significant growth is not evident.

Note
1. See James 1:5-8.

CHAPTER 6
THE LIVES WE LEAD, AND HOW THEY ARE CHANGING

CHAPTER HIGHLIGHTS

- People's lives are in a constant state of flux. In the past 5 years, more than 1 out of 4 adults has changed churches; nearly 4 out of 10 have changed their address; most people in the labor pool have changed jobs; and half now live at a different financial level than they did in 1987.
- Despite the media attention given to 12-step groups, just 4% of all adults attend a meeting of a 12-step or recovery group in a typical week.
- Pleasure reading is becoming less and less common. Although 75% engaged in pleasure reading during a typical week in 1991, the proportion has fallen to 62% this year.
- During the past year, the typical adult spent the equivalent of two entire months watching television programming. We average about four hours a day of TV viewing.
- Most adults pray to God, attend church services, and read the Bible out of enjoyment. We consistently do a few activities out of habit or a sense of compulsion.
- Two-thirds of all adults donate money to charities or not-for-profit

groups in a typical month. The types of organizations deemed most in need of funding are those in the educational and health fields.
- Almost 9 out of 10 adults find telemarketing calls annoying. In contrast, just 8% describe singing hymns in a church as annoying.

WHAT WE DISCOVERED

Americans may struggle with the discomfort caused by change in their lives, but the facts make an indisputable case: The only thing constant in our lives is change. Whether we are examining our lifestyle patterns, our favorite leisure activities or our attitudes about how we live, little goes unchanged over the course of a decade.

FIVE YEARS AGO

Some aspects of our lives change more frequently than do others. We are constantly coping with changes—some we initiate; others are thrust upon us. And we regularly go through a metamorphosis that redefines how we live or what we do, as well as who we are.

Consider some of the changes that have taken place in just the last five years.

Religious Faith Transitions

Nine out of 10 adults claim they were affiliated with the same religious denomination or faith five years ago. We know from related research, however, that most adults perceive themselves to be Christian and therefore think that, although they may have transitioned from one Protestant denomination to another, they are still Protestant or Christian. In other words, because of the slipping influence or importance of denominational labels or ties for many adults, the core issue is the larger faith label with which they associate: Christian, Catholic, Protestant, Jewish, Buddhist and so on.

The interesting aberration are those adults who are unchurched. Just two out of three of the unchurched claimed they have maintained the same faith ties during the last five years. One out of every six unchurched adults (17%) said they do not have the same affiliation today; one out of every seven (14%) stated that the question was not pertinent for them as they have no faith connections.

Reclustering

One out of four adults is presently living with a different group of people than was the case five years earlier. This is to be expected from the baby busters, many of whom have gone through the process of leaving home for college, getting married, or making other lifestyle changes during their late teens and early 20s. Almost half of the busters (43%) indicated that they now live with a different group of people than they used to.

Busters were not the only group undergoing substantial reclustering, though. Among Hispanics, 44% are now in a different setting than they were five years ago. Other people groups experiencing above-average shifts in their housing situation include those with incomes less than $20,000 (39%); single adults (42%); and those who are not associated with any church (33%).

Political Party Changes
One-fifth of the electorate (20%) has shifted its political party allegiance since 1987, too. Again, the coming of voting age of millions of busters has an important influence on this figure. If the busters are removed from the statistics, we discover that the figure of party switchers drops to 15%. The groups that exhibit the greatest likelihood of having moved from one party to another include the baby boomers (20%); Hispanics (35%); adults in the western states (23%); Catholics (21%); the unchurched (26%); and non-Christians (23%). Relatively few evangelicals changed parties (11%).

Church Switching
Considerably less stability is evident in sticking with the same church or religious center. More than one-quarter of the population (27%) claim to have switched churches in the last five years. This church hopping has been most avid among baby busters (41%); baby boomers (31%); college graduates (34%); single adults (32%); Hispanics (36%); residents of the West (32%) (see Figure 6.1). Some of these segments would be expected to have a high rate of change, due to lifestyle transitions. Many busters, for instance, have changed churches because they have relocated in the last five years. Realize, though, that the rate of church changing is nearly three times that of having changed religious affiliations.

The unchurched are among those who are most likely to have moved from one church to another: 4 out of 10 have done so in the past 5 years. The data suggest a substantial amount of church shopping among the unchurched; only 30% of the current unchurched population claim that this question does not apply to them, primari-

We Change Churches Frequently

Percent who changed churches within the last five years

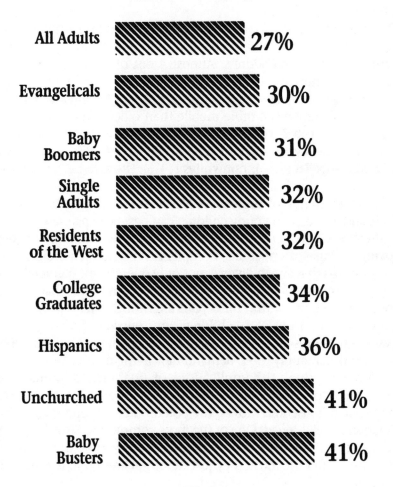

All Adults	27%
Evangelicals	30%
Baby Boomers	31%
Single Adults	32%
Residents of the West	32%
College Graduates	34%
Hispanics	36%
Unchurched	41%
Baby Busters	41%

Figure 6.1

Source: Barna Research Group, Ltd. 1993

ly because they have been outside the church world for more than 5 years.

Perhaps surprisingly, born-again Christians are no less likely than other adults to have gone through a church change. Evangelicals are slightly *more* likely than the typical adult to have changed their church home: 30% of evangelicals have transferred to a different congregation, compared to 26% of nonevangelicals.

Relocating

What might be most astounding about the incidence of church changing is that more people have changed their home address than have changed their church address. Almost 4 out of 10 adults (37%) say they lived at the same address 5 years ago. The most prolific movers have been the baby busters: two-thirds of them have relocated since 1987. Baby boomers are more mobile than older adults, too: 43% of them have relocated within the past 5 years. Other segments notable for their tendency to move include single adults (46%); adults with children under 18 (45%); nonwhites (44%); those living in the West (45%); and the unchurched (43%).

The coexistence of high rates of transition among both single adults and adults with young children can best be explained by several different realities. One of them, however, is the unusually frequent moving of single-parent adults. Complementary research projects have demonstrated that after a divorce, not only does the mother retain custody of the children in more than 7 out of 10 cases, but that she also moves several times within the 5 years after the divorce. Further, as we find more than 3 out of 10 children born outside of marriage these days, the pressures on the mother to make a living, a home and a life for her and her family often demand new living quarters.

Do not overlook the implications of unchurched adults being among the most prolific in relocating. Our research has shown that every time a household moves, the potential for dropping its church affiliation is heightened. One of the more common reasons for people becoming unchurched is that their church life was peripheral before their move; after the move they just never got around to looking for a new church.

Job Changes

Another important affiliation that experiences frequent change is where we work. Among people who were neither retired five years ago, nor have stayed outside the labor pool by choice during that entire time, more than half of all wage-earning adults have changed employers at least once. Aside from the expected people groups—busters and boomers—the most common job-changers were singles, nonwhites and city residents.

Financial Shifts

As much as our address is likely to change in a five-year period, our financial circumstances are even more likely to shift. Half of all adults (51%) stated that their financial level had changed in the past five years. Often, leaders overlook the fact that economic status shifts regularly. Poverty is fluid, as is affluence: People tend to slide from one economic level to another more frequently and silently than we know.

Who has shifted their economic standing in the past half-decade? Once again, the age factor arises as the pivotal characteristic. More than 6 out of 10 busters and boomers fit the mold. Hispanics are also more likely than the norm to have experienced an economic shift.

Taking these seven life conditions together, the survey found that relatively few adults—less than one out of four—have not had a change in at least two of those dimensions. Change is a regular part of the American way of life.

BEYOND THE JOB

Americans greatly value their time—especially their free time. Last year's study showed that when assigning value to different elements of life, such as family, health and friends, people's free time was rated as more important than most other aspects of life, including their religious lives, money and community. How do we spend our free time?

Variety is truly one of the spices that seasons our lives. The range of activities we participate in during a week is sometimes breathtaking—and stress-making! In some cases, how often we participate in an activity conflicts with the prevailing myths about who we are or how we live.

Earlier it was reported that in a given week, about 45% of adults attend a church service. That is more than claim to have rented a videocassette to play on their VCR (31%); more than volunteered any of their free time to help a nonprofit organization, other than a church (27%); and more than attended a 12-step or recovery group (4%). The fact that recovery groups reap such media attention again displays the incongruity between media coverage and popular involvement in the activity being focused upon.

Reading

Take reading, for instance. We know that watching television and listening to radio are more popular activities. We know that an alarmingly high proportion of Americans—perhaps as much as one-third of all adults—is deemed functionally illiterate. We know that "serious" reading—that is, books and journals related to historical, scientific, and nonfiction, analytical subject matter—has declined severely in the last 30 years. To hear the media tell the story, nobody in America reads these days, either out of the lack of skills to do so, the lack of time, or a general disinterest in the practice.

Yet, reading a book for pleasure remains one of the most common pastimes for adults in our country. Almost two out of three adults (62%) claim they read books for pleasure during the typical week. Although this practice is slightly less common among baby busters, a majority of that segment (56%) do so. Pleasure reading is most likely among those with a college degree, the affluent and evangelicals.

Compared to other activity levels measured in recent years, reading has experienced significant change in the past three years. The incidence of pleasure reading has dropped from 75% in 1991 to 67% in 1992 to the current level of 62% (see Figure 6.2). This is cause for concern, as the trend is clear, consistent, rapid—and unhealthy! Though pleasure reading is undertaken by a majority of adults, if this trend continues, this statement will be accurate for just a few more years.

Glued to the Tube

To be fair, realize that the Nielsen measures tell us the average television household has the set on for about 7 hours a day. Our study indicates that the typical adult spends about 4 hours each day consuming televised images. Three out of 10 adults stated that they usually watch 5 or more hours of television programming every day (see Figure 6.1)! More than 97% of all households have at least 1 working television set; 98% of the adults in those homes watch television regularly. Only

Pleasure Reading Is on the Decline

Percent who read part of a book
for pleasure in the past week

 75%

 67%

 62%

Figure 6.2

Source: Barna Research Group, Ltd. 1993

6% of all adult TV owners say that they usually watch less than an hour of television a day.

To put this addiction in context, realize that if we take the total number of hours the typical adult spends watching television during the course of the entire year, it adds up to the equivalent of viewing TV for 24 hours a day for 61 days. That means for 2 solid months of the year, every waking moment of our time is devoted to viewing the broadcast box.

The most prolific TV watchers are women, busters, the elderly and blacks. Evangelicals watch slightly less television than the average adult, but still average about 3 and one-half hours of TV programming every day. The typical evangelical, then, spends just less than 50 days a year glued to the tube—less than average, but significant nevertheless.

WE HAVE OUR REASONS

What motivates us to do those activities we typically do? In most cases, we are motivated either by necessity or enjoyment, but rarely, according to Americans, by habit.

Inviting Guests
One of our most enjoyable activities is inviting guests to visit us at home. When we do so, 87% of adults say the invitation is made out of a sense of enjoyment; just 5% say they offer the opportunity out of habit; 3% say they usually do so because they have to. Another 5% say they do not invite people to their home. Interestingly, nonwhites were three times more likely than whites to offer such invitations out of habit, and three times more likely to state that they do not invite people over. This is one of the more clear-cut instances of cultural differences emerging from the research.

Praying
Praying is usually done out of enjoyment. Two out of three adults enjoy praying; one out of seven do so out of habit; just 4% feel compelled to pray. Some of the demographic distinctions are worth noting. Three-quarters of all women pray out of enjoyment, but only half of all men do so. The older a respondent was, the more likely he or she

We Watch a Lot of TV – Even Though We Don't Like Much of Today's Television Programming

Hours watched, in an average day, per adult

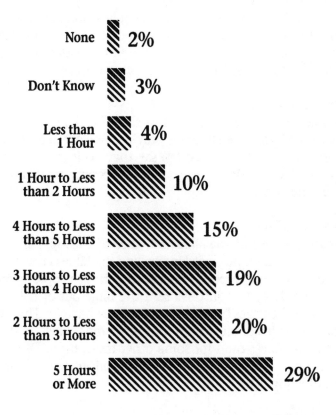

Figure 6.3

Source: Barna Research Group, Ltd. 1993

was to pray. Although two-thirds of whites are motivated by enjoyment to pray, three out of four blacks follow suit; but just half of Hispanics pray for this reason. Similarly, three-fourths of southern adults and two-thirds of midwesterners pray out of enjoyment, but only half of the praying adults in the Northeast and West are similarly motivated. Four out of five evangelicals say they pray out of enjoyment.

Attending Church Services

Two out of three adults also claim that they attend church services out of a sense of enjoyment. This motivation is four times more common than all other reasons combined. Note that among churchgoers, 11% attend on the basis of habit; 6% go because they feel they have to attend. Again, it is men and younger people who show the greatest reluctance to attend, doing so out of habit or other motives. Residents of the Northeast and the West also followed the pattern of being less excited about church, but attending for other reasons.

Yard or Garden Work

Most people who do yard or garden work (55%) claim they are motivated by the enjoyment such efforts provide. One out of four (26%) do such work out of necessity; just 5% say they do it out of habit. The folks least likely to gain pleasure from gardening or yard care are busters and nonwhites.

Reading the Bible

Just as many people read the Bible motivated by the joy it brings them (54%). The enjoyment produced by reading the Bible is just about the only motivation that appears capable of getting people to interact with Scripture. Note that just 8% read the Bible out of habit, and a mere 4% scan the pages because they feel they have to. Thus, people who read the Bible are more than four times more likely to do so for the joy this produces than for some other motivation. Of particular interest is the finding that 92% of all evangelicals say they read the Bible out of enjoyment.

Sharing Religious Beliefs

Another religious activity relatively few people participate in is telling others about their religious beliefs. Half of all Americans claim they do not evangelize other people. Among those who say they sometimes talk to others about their religious beliefs, 34% do so out of enjoyment; 8% out of habit; and just 2% out of a sense of necessity or compulsion. Although only 4% of the evangelicals feel compelled to share their faith views with others, that is double the proportion found among other adults.

Exercising

Some activities we do are less likely to be motivated by joy. Take exercising, for instance. Although the fitness craze that has enveloped America is well known, did you realize that people were nearly as likely to report exercising out of habit (11%) or necessity (28%) as out of enjoyment (45%)?

GIVING IT AWAY

Americans are a charitable people. Every year, people give away more than 100 billion dollars. We give away the largest proportion of our money to religious organizations, primarily churches.[1] Our past studies have indicated that we give our money to organizations and causes we believe in; only a handful of donors are motivated by the possibility of a tax write-off.

During the past year, two-thirds of all adults (67%) contributed money to not-for-profit organizations during a typical month (see Figure 6.4). This remains relatively consistent with past giving patterns.[2] Also consistent is the profile of who is most likely to have donated money. Those who support causes tend to be women; whites; churched adults; born-again Christians; and evangelicals. The data also show that the better educated and the more affluent a person is, the more likely he is to donate money to some not-for-profit entity.

On the age continuum, the youngest adults are the least likely to give money; but people from their mid-20s on up are equally likely to donate money to charity. This masks an important realization: Baby boomers are no less likely to give away their money than are other adults. Although boomers have a bad reputation for being stingy, the truth is that they are just as generous as other age groups. Compared to prior generations, boomers are no less likely to contribute money. What may be different is their choice of organizations they support. They tend to be more driven by the nature of the results achieved by the organizations they support, rather than by the purpose or intent of the organization.

Some significant omens are on the horizon for not-for-profit organizations. Because Americans are under no legal requirements to give away their money, confidence in not-for-profit organizations is a critical foundation that precedes giving. However, our study discovered that the recent scandals among nonprofit organizations is taking its toll on people's perceptions of the credibility of such organizations. Only 8% of all adults believe that the leaders of nonprofit organizations and charities are very trustworthy. Most people (58%) are cautiously skeptical of these leaders, citing them as somewhat trustworthy. An unfortunately large proportion of people (27%) describe these people as either not too or not at all trustworthy (see Figure 6.5).

Who tends to be most skeptical? Surprisingly, it is *not* the generations who have the least confidence in any type of organization or profession: baby busters and baby boomers. It is the builders and seniors who exhibit the greatest skepticism about nonprofit CEOs. Although just 20% of the two younger generations gave these leaders negative ratings, 36% of the builders (i.e., those 47-65 years of age) and 39% of the seniors (i.e., those 66 or older) said the leadership of such charitable entities was not trustworthy. This is particularly significant because people over 50 control the vast majority of the nation's wealth and represent the people most likely to transfer their wealth to such organizations within the coming decade.

The survey also revealed that if it were disclosed that the CEO of a particular charity the donor supported was earning $100,000 a year or more, most donors (59%) would cease giving to that entity. One out of three donors said such knowledge would not influence their giving. Six percent said this would actually make them more likely to support that organization. Why? In some cases, the donor was impressed that the organization would admit to such a salary structure. More often, however, this tendency was because they assumed the organization had hired a person who was a top-notch leader and was worth that amount of money. Having such a leader made them feel their investment was being better protected.

The Status Quo
Despite occasional signs that the economy is recovering, our survey revealed that people will likely continue to give away their money at

Most People Part with
Their Money – Willingly

Percent who gave a contribution to
a nonprofit or charitable organization
within the past month

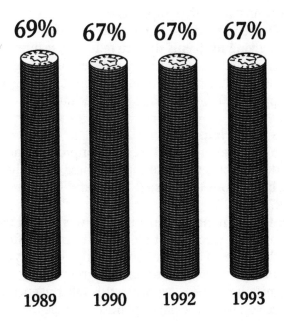

69% 67% 67% 67%

1989 1990 1992 1993

Figure 6.4

Source: Barna Research Group, Ltd. 1993

the same rate they have been doing in the past. Seven out of 10 adults said they will give the same amount of money to nonprofits and charities as they gave in the past 6 months. The remaining adults were evenly divided between intending to give more money (13%) and those who expect to give away less money (11%). The people most likely to increase their aggregate giving were the younger, less skeptical adults. Nonwhites and evangelicals also intimated that they will likely give more money in the coming months.

In the same way, more than three out of four adults (77%) expect to give money to the same number of nonprofit organizations as they did in the preceding six months. If there is any change, it might be that people slowly begin to constrict the number of entities they support, perhaps out of a lack of confidence in the integrity of nonprofit organizations. Overall, just 5% of all adults plan to support an expanded number of charities; meanwhile, 12% plan to cut back on the number of organizations they support.

Bucking the trend are black adults, who were slightly more likely to increase their giving recipients than to reduce that number. The people group most likely to substantially reduce the number of charities supported is senior citizens. Less than 1% plan to increase the number of groups supported; 14% plan to reduce that number.

Who Needs Your Help?

According to most adults, two types of nonprofit organizations are most in need of people's financial support these days. Those types are educational institutions (34% listed these) and health-related groups (named by 27%).

No other type of nonprofit organization was named by even 10% of all adults as being among that type most in need of financial assistance. The other types of organizations included religious entities (chosen as most needy by 9%); environmental groups (8%); civic or community organizations (7%); overseas crisis-relief agencies (4%); and organizations working for social or political change (3%).

As for those who cited religious organizations as the most needy, the people most likely to do so were senior citizens (16% listed this category of organizations); married adults (13%, twice the proportion of single adults who listed these groups); rural residents (14%); Protestants (14%, more than double the proportion of Catholics); churched adults (12%); born-again Christians (19%, versus just 4% among oth-

Many People Are Suspicious of the Leaders of Nonprofit Organizations

Percent saying how trustworthy nonprofit leaders are

Not At All Trustworthy

Don't Know

Very Trustworthy

8%

6%

8%

Not Too Trustworthy 19%

Somewhat Trustworthy 58%

Figure 6.5

Source: Barna Research Group, Ltd. 1993

ers); and evangelicals (28%). Evangelicals stood out as the only people group that made religious organizations their top choice.

YOU ARE BUGGING ME

Americans have clear notions of what they consider annoying. As we determine our daily schedules, the people we choose to befriend and the types of activities we participate in, our choices are influenced by our expectations. And when we anticipate annoyance, we alter our schedules accordingly.

Telemarketing Calls
Of the six conditions we tested, the one that was deemed annoying by the largest proportion of adults was receiving a telephone call from someone trying to sell a product or service. Although telemarketing has blossomed into a multibillion-dollar industry in less than a decade, 85% of all adults say they find such intrusions annoying (see Figure 6.6). People from high-income households are particularly likely to note their distaste for such calls—perhaps because they are among the most targeted of households and may receive more calls than other people receive.

People Talking at the Movies
Have you been to a movie theater recently and had trouble hearing the movie because other people in the audience were talking? If so, you are not alone. Eight out of 10 adults find this circumstance to be annoying.

Profanity on Radio
Another incident that perturbs most adults (60%) is hearing profanity on the radio. Despite the rise to prominence of "shock jocks" such as Howard Stern, most adults find crude language coming over the airwaves to be offensive. In this regard, however, substantial differences of opinion were noticed between people groups. For instance, three-fourths of all women find radio profanity unacceptable, but less than half of all men concur. And, although more than two-thirds of adults 28 or older find such programming offensive, just one-third of the baby busters feel the same way. Although Christians lead the way in

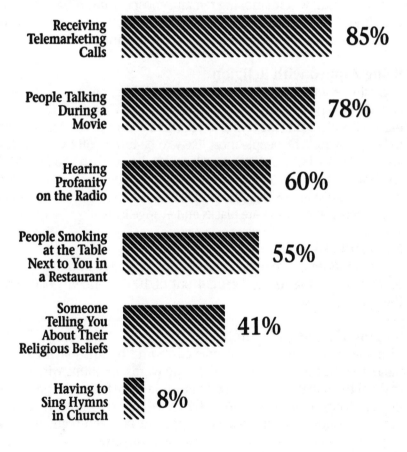

Want to Annoy Your Friends?
Try These Activities...
Percent who find the activity annoying

Receiving Telemarketing Calls — 85%

People Talking During a Movie — 78%

Hearing Profanity on the Radio — 60%

People Smoking at the Table Next to You in a Restaurant — 55%

Someone Telling You About Their Religious Beliefs — 41%

Having to Sing Hymns in Church — 8%

Figure 6.6

Source: Barna Research Group, Ltd. 1993

feeling that such language is annoying (75% of all born-again Christians and 89% of evangelicals), realize that a majority of non-Christians (51%) also find such content inappropriate.

Smoking in Restaurants
A majority of Americans also construe smoking in a restaurant to be unacceptable behavior. Fifty-five percent of the adults we spoke to described people smoking at the next table to be annoying. This was partially predicated upon people's region. Those living in the Northeast and South, where smoking remains most common, were less likely to find this offensive. In the Midwest and West, however, a considerable majority found smoking to be an annoyance.

Being Zapped with Religion
Regarding evangelism, a large minority of adults expressed their dismay at having to endure such communications. More than 4 out of 10 adults (42%) consider someone trying to tell them about their religious beliefs to be annoying. The people most likely to be turned off by such efforts are men (47%); busters (50%); people making more than $60,000 (56%); residents of the West (54%); Catholics (52%); the unchurched (56%); and non-Christians (52%). The people who are least likely to be offended by such conversation are blacks and evangelicals.

Magazine Ads
Just as unappealing to most adults is finding a large number of advertisements in a magazine. Again, 4 out of 10 respondents (41%) said this is annoying.

Singing Hymns in Church
Although you would be hard pressed to find hymns playing on the radio, to find people who can recite the words, or adults who consider them to be their favorite type of music, a mere 8% of the adult population deems hymns sung in a church service to be annoying. Once again, substantial differences were apparent between segments. Men were three times more likely than women to consider hymns sung in church as annoying. Baby busters were four times more likely to think that way as are older adults. Unchurched people were more than twice as likely as churched people to hold such a view of hymns. However,

no single people group we studied revealed that more than 20% viewed singing hymns in church as an annoyance.

This raises an interesting question. Why do so many people view hymns as outdated and irrelevant if they do not consider them an annoyance? Perhaps the views of one baby buster, who did not describe hymns as annoying, sums up the feelings of many people.

"It's not that I like hymns. I don't. But if you're gonna go to a church, you kinda expect them to sing hymns. It's part of what they do at churches. So I don't think of them as annoying. They don't mean anything to me, they sound ridiculous and I don't sing them."

But if you dislike them and the singing of such hymns colors your impressions of the experience, wouldn't you describe them as annoying?

"Well, the thing is, if you go to a church, expect hymns. If you find them annoying, just don't go to church. Or, like me, I find them irrelevant, so I don't attend."

A PERSONAL CHALLENGE

Think about how you and your church respond to visitors. Americans being as transient as they are, and knowing that one out of three people have changed their church home in just the past five years, even churches that may not be actively seeking newcomers are likely to have some of them drop in on any given Sunday. How well prepared are you to address their needs and expectations?

Regarding Bible reading, many people choose not to do so. About one out of every five adults who reads the Bible does so for purposes other than the enjoyment or pleasure it gives. The challenge to us is to help all people recognize that those who consistently read the Scriptures generally find the exercise to be a fulfilling, satisfying experience.

What can you do to help those who you know ignore the Bible to view Bible reading as an enjoyable activity? Whether it be exposing people to reader-friendly versions, engaging them in conversation about what they read, pointing out passages that address acute personal needs, providing ancillary materials that provide a helpful context for understanding Bible content—what can you do to help people accept the Bible as a fun and viable resource for life in the '90s?

Notes

1. These figures are based on the annual research conducted by the American Association of Fund Raising Counsel (AAFRC). Each year the AAFRC releases information pertaining to Americans' giving patterns during the prior year. Their most recent reports show that more than 80% of all funds given to charity come from individuals; a small proportion comes from foundations and corporations.
2. These figures are based on research conducted for the *Non-Profit Times* by the Barna Research Group. The data are part of a semiannual tracking study conducted for that publication.

CHAPTER 7 THE MEDIA IN AMERICA

CHAPTER HIGHLIGHTS

- Only one out of every six adults describes today's television programming as very enjoyable.
- Most adults believe that television programs show too much violence, air too much foul language and show too much explicit sexual content. Large proportions also believe that TV is increasing the amounts of each of the objectionable forms of content in comparison to what was aired five years ago.
- MTV is comparatively less enjoyable, according to TV viewers, than other channels. Yet its influence is enormous. Christians are just as likely to watch and to enjoy MTV as are non-Christians.
- Most adults believe that the mass media favor liberal views on politics and public issues.
- A significant minority of adults believe that the mass media are biased against Christian beliefs.
- Only one-third of all adults contend that the media are objective in the ways they report events and information.

WHAT WE DISCOVERED

Americans have a tremendous amount of exposure to the mass media. As noted in the previous chapter, the typical adult watched the equivalent of two full months of television programming last year. We also listen to tremendous amounts of radio programming, most people read a newspaper each day and most people read magazines every week.

What do we know about people's reactions to the media to which they are exposed?

TV AIN'T WHAT IT USED TO BE

Talk to older adults about television and you hear stories about the good ol' days of television. Recollections of some of the early or classic programs still bring a smile to the faces of those who used to set aside an hour here or there to watch Milton Berle, Carol Burnett, Walt Disney and other favorites.

Attitudes and opinions about television are different today. Parents are just as likely to struggle with whether to own a television set as they are to allow their children to watch unrestricted television. Increasingly, adults are chagrined by what they view being broadcast into their living rooms.

Our study found that just 16% of adults consider television programming to be very enjoyable overall. Most adults (60%), aware that there is some outstanding programming mixed in with the less appealing material, describe today's TV content as somewhat enjoyable. A rising proportion of adults—currently 21%—call TV programming either not too or not at all enjoyable (see Figure 7.1).

Baby busters are the most accepting of today's TV programming. Twenty-five percent of them say it is very enjoyable; 92% consider it to be either very or somewhat enjoyable. In contrast, the people groups most apprehensive about today's programming are those in the 47-65 age bracket; Republicans; the wealthy; residents of the western states; and evangelicals. About 3 out of 10 people from each of those segments (4 out of 10 among evangelicals) call television not too or not at all enjoyable these days.

A related study we conducted for the American Family Association

The Majority of People Do Not Think TV Programs Are Very Enjoyable

Descriptions of TV programming, among television set owners

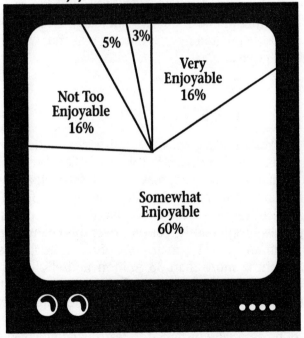

Not at All Enjoyable

Don't Know

5%

3%

Very Enjoyable 16%

Not Too Enjoyable 16%

Somewhat Enjoyable 60%

Figure 7.1

Source: Barna Research Group, Ltd. 1993

in 1992 also uncovered the fatigue of Americans with the insensitivity of television programming to the moral sensibilities of Americans.[1] A national random sample of 1,215 adults found that 72% said they believe today's television programming contains too much violence; 57% said TV uses too much profane language; 65% believe that TV shows too much explicit sexual content. Almost half of the public contends that TV programs provide too much coverage of nontraditional or liberal values and lifestyles.

Are things getting better? Not according to most TV viewers. Although the majority of adults are dissatisfied with TV content, as depicted above, even more substantial majorities contend that things have gotten worse compared to five years ago. Three out of four (76%) say the amount of violence broadcast has increased; 85% state that the sexual content has increased; and 84% maintain that profane language is more common today. A majority (57%) indicate that the depiction of nontraditional or liberal values has increased. Clearly, the direction television programming is moving is at odds with the desires of the viewing population.

THE MTV CONTROVERSY

To many Christian leaders, MTV, the fast-paced, cutting-edge music television channel, is the channel of the devil. Sermons are preached about it; the channel is used as an example of the evils and immorality of the age; and some ministries intentionally pray for MTV's programming executives out of the belief that those executives are confused, lost souls. In spite of the concern over this channel within the Christian community, MTV remains one of the more successful cable channels, reaching more than 35 million households in America alone. In fact, a majority of Christian households in this nation have access to this channel. The born-again population represents a significant viewing group of MTV.

You may be especially intrigued to learn what emerged when we asked a national sample of adults who can receive MTV (as a cable channel, it is not available to every household) and have watched that channel, what they felt about MTV's programming. Comparing the opinions of viewers of five different cable channels, we discovered that MTV had by far the lowest positive rating of those channels.

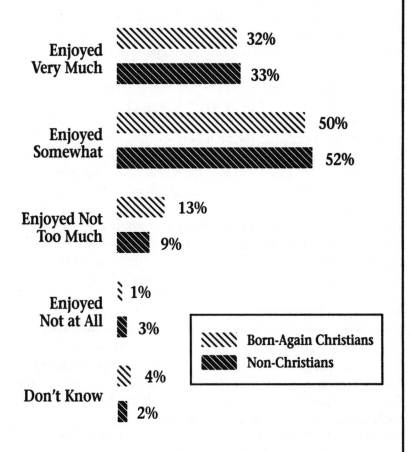

MTV: Marginal Television

How people who have watched MTV
in the last month rate its programming

Enjoyed Very Much
32%
33%

Enjoyed Somewhat
50%
52%

Enjoyed Not Too Much
13%
9%

Enjoyed Not at All
1%
3%

Don't Know
4%
2%

Born-Again Christians
Non-Christians

Figure 7.2

Source: Barna Research Group, Ltd. 1993

Whereas two-thirds of the viewers of CNN and ESPN said they enjoyed the programming on those channels very much, just half as many of MTV's viewers (33%) said they enjoyed the programming of that channel very much.

The channel clearly appeals to a younger audience. Almost half of the baby busters (47%) said they found MTV to be very enjoyable, compared to just 18% of the baby boomers sharing that perspective. Perhaps the most amazing statistic, though, was that among the born-again Christians who viewed the channel, their levels of enjoyment of MTV were almost identical to those of non-Christians (see Figure 7.2). In the same manner, the opinions of churched adults about MTV were indistinguishable from those of unchurched people.

OBJECTIVE MEDIA?

Others have conducted research and written persuasively about the myth of the objective media in America.[2] When you explore the ideological leanings, information sources and perceived purposes of the media among its executives, you quickly discover that the mass media make little effort and have no intention of acting objectively. The media are intentionally used by those in authority as a means of promoting particular ideas and perspectives to the public.

The views of Americans are at odds with those who control the media, however. Consider the following viewpoints.

Insensitive Reporting
Although the media's coverage of the 1992 presidential campaign seemed to be built upon sexual innuendo, moral inconsistencies and spiritual dispersions cast by the media at the major candidates, many voters were disappointed by the lack of substance in such reporting. Our study showed that Americans are less than wholeheartedly behind such investigative reporting. Overall, 39% strongly agree that the mass media should report information on the moral behavior of political candidates and leaders; an additional 26% agree somewhat.

Biased Reporting
Most adults believe that they can discern a particular bias in the nature of the media's reporting of current affairs. Two out of 3 adults agree

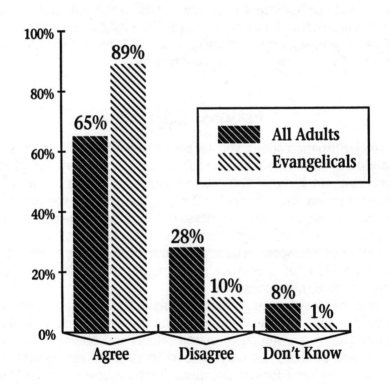

The Mass Media Are Not Objective in Their Reporting

Responses to the statement:
Overall, the mass media seem to favor liberal views on politics and issues

Figure 7.3

Source: Barna Research Group, Ltd. 1993

that "the mass media seem to favor liberal views on politics and issues." A majority of Democrats, Republicans and independent voters concur on this matter. Not surprisingly, 9 out of 10 evangelicals hold this opinion (see Figure 7.3).

A considerable minority—but a minority nevertheless—believe that the mass media seem to be biased against Christian beliefs (see Figure 7.4). Nearly 4 out of 10 adults (38%) either agree strongly or somewhat with this contention. Recognize that only one-third of busters and boomers, combined, buy this view; half of the adults 47 or older accept it. Nine out of 10 evangelicals believe this is true; 71% agree strongly with this sentiment.

When people are asked outright if they believe that the media are objective—"that is, they do not interpret events and information, they just report them without any type of bias"—only one out of three adults defends the objectivity of the media. A majority of people, from all of the people groups examined, believe that the mass media interject bias in reporting events and information.

A PERSONAL CHALLENGE

If you are like most adults, you live with a paradox. That is, at the same time that you harbor a distaste for the content of much of what is broadcast on television, you devote a significant amount of your free time to viewing what TV has to offer. The challenge for you may be to reconcile those competing realities so that your values are paralleled by your behavior. What leisure alternatives are available to you that could replace your time spent in front of the television set? Or, if you choose to watch TV, what alternative programming is available that meets your standards more consistently?

Is there a way you, and others who share concerns about the influence of a subjective media, might bring those concerns to the forefront? The media, similar to manufacturers and other producers of goods and services, can only exist when their market supports the product they offer for consumption. Consider how you spend your time, money and other resources in relation to media, and what could be done to inform and influence the media executives to be more sensitive to the values and desires of you and others who possess similar views.

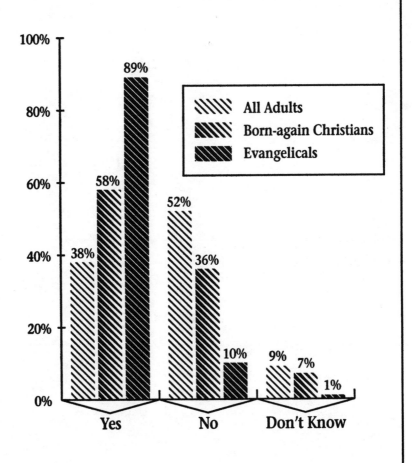

Are the Media Biased Against Christianity? Most Christians Think So

100%

89%

80%

58%

60%

52%

38%

40%

36%

20%

10%

9% 7%

1%

0%

Yes   No   Don't Know

All Adults
Born-again Christians
Evangelicals

Figure 7.4

Source: Barna Research Group, Ltd. 1993

Notes

1. This study was conducted in March 1992 by a telephone survey of 1,205 randomly selected adults from across the continental United States. The results have been used with the permission of the American Family Association, Tupelo, Mississippi.
2. Examples of such research include *Watching America,* R. Robert Lichter, Linda Lichter, Stanley Rothman (New York: Prentice Hall Press, 1991) and *The Media Elite,* R. Robert Lichter, Linda Lichter, Stanley Rothman (New York: Hastings House, 1990).

Closing Thoughts

At no period in American history has the Church had an easy time trying to make Christianity a significant and cherished part of people's lives. Although the temptation is great to argue that things are worse now than they have ever been, such a grandiose statement might be nothing more than supreme arrogance.

The heart of the matter is not whether things are more challenging than ever before but how faithfully we attempt to serve our God by reaching out to the millions of hurting, needy, searching, discouraged people, in His name, for His glory. Toward that end, we must identify the condition of people and endeavor to lovingly and efficiently facilitate both personal and cultural transformation.

Having read the preceding chapters, would you please take a few minutes to write down some of your thoughts regarding what you can do to be an agent of change for God's purposes? Without such a commitment to play a pivotal role in shaping human history, you are squandering important resources entrusted to you by God. God allows time, energy, experiences, information and many opportunities for your ministry. As an act of good stewardship, please think through what difference the information contained in this book is going to make in how you minister, to whom you will minister, and what criteria for evaluating your ministry you will use in the coming weeks and months.

Allow me to offer nine closing challenges to you, sparked by some of the insights gained through this year's studies. If these thoughts resonate within you, create the detailed plans that will make them operational in your ministry. If you do not like these exhortations, cast them aside and develop your own list of strategies that you will pursue. The key is not whose plans or ideas you implement, but that you respond to human need and God's calling with sincerity, wisdom and urgency. That passion for immediate and intelligent outreach is well stated in the letter from James, especially in 1:22: "Obey God's message! Don't fool yourselves by just listening to it" *(CEV)*.

WHERE ARE THE LEADERS?

At such a critical time for the Church, *the need for strong, visionary leadership is acute.* Every successful movement in recorded history has been headed by a strong leader. Conditions are no different today. For our churches to make their mark on a skeptical, unbelieving, spiritually complacent world, we must ensure that our churches are pastored by strong leaders.[1] Most people are followers, and one of the purposes of the local church is to provide followers with a leader. Therefore, we must ensure that congregations are led by people who lead out of a passion and calling to serve God; who will envision the better future that God wills for His people; who will motivate people to action; who will create intelligent plans for positive change; and who will spearhead the implementation of those plans, for the enduring glory of God.

Take a hard look at the church and other organizations through which you minister. Is the person in charge truly a leader, or simply a highly trained person holding a position of leadership? What are the strategies and plans promoted by the person in charge? Are your limited ministry resources being allocated for maximum influence?

Ministry is different from business. Unlike many business entities, we cannot justify the existence of the local church if the goal is simply to survive, to get by yet another week in the desperate hope that Christ will return immediately. Our aim is to serve God by acting as pliable but capable conduits for His love, grace and transformation of people's lives. To revolutionize a secularized culture such as ours, we need the cream of the crop at the helm of each church, to motivate, encourage and direct our ministry energies.

How strong is the leadership at your church?

BACK TO THE BASICS

Spiritually speaking, many Christians try to run before they have learned how to walk. Lacking the fundamentals, they eventually get snarled up in their faith, hindered by the absence of a strong foundation on which to build their faith. The American church must pause to return and bolster that foundation within the body of believers today.

Do you realize that most Christians do not live with a holistic, biblical worldview? Their decisions are made off-the-cuff, based on whatever seems right at the moment—without prayer, without a biblical checkpoint, without a true concern for how Jesus might have dealt with the same circumstances.

Have you reflected on the aggregate belief system of Americans? Based on the information revealed in the three annual reports we have produced, let's piece together the belief system of the typical American. That system would contain the following components:

- Four out of 10 people believe Jesus made mistakes;
- Two out of three people reject the notion of absolute truth;
- One out of three adults believe that God is something or someone other than the perfect, all-powerful, omniscient Creator of the universe who lives and rules that world today;
- Three out of five adults do not believe in Satan;
- About half of all Americans believe that all religious faiths are basically the same;
- Three out of five people say that all people pray to the same god, regardless of what name or character we ascribe to the god to whom we pray;
- People's Bible knowledge is abysmally thin: They cannot name half of the Ten Commandments, or who preached the Sermon on the Mount.

Before we can hope to create a Church that is a spiritual force to be reckoned with, the people who are the Church must have a solid comprehension of what they believe and why. To reach that point, reassess the spiritual depth and commitment of the people who comprise your faith community. What will it take to make them intelligent and articulate to understand and proclaim their faith in Christ? Why shouldn't you make a carefully tailored process of growing those people according to their spiritual need a top priority in your ministry?

FOCUS ON THE UNCHURCHED

One out of four adults is currently unchurched, and at least that many are nominally churched. In other words, probably more than half of all adults in this country are not really living in a true community of faith. We can do better than that.

How long has the American Church ministered on automatic pilot? Evangelistically, we have a terrible track record. Concerning discipleship, our record is no better. Granted, we are engaged in a sophisticated spiritual war in which we do not control the outcome. The Holy Spirit is responsible for the conversion of people to God's side and their maturation in that faith. We are simply the means through which the Holy Spirit works.

But how often and how intensely do we invoke the power and presence of God's spirit? This is not a question designed to rekindle a debate between charismatics and fundamentalists. Rather, it is an honest and important query regarding how we approach our task as God's ambassadors to a world of doubters and sinners.

Indeed, how much of our effort is devoted to fulfilling the Great Commission? An objective analysis would conclude, "not much." The ways we use our resources and the manner we approach in sharing our faith suggests that we do not take this seriously enough to give it our absolute best efforts. Frankly, God deserves better than what we give Him in our too-infrequent attempts to reach those who live outside of His Kingdom.

Ponder what you do to reach the lost, and how you could intentionally become a better agent of God's love and grace. Identify specific ways you and your colleagues in ministry might enhance your efforts, through God's empowerment, to bring greater glory and honor to His name.[2]

LIVE LOVE

As our society becomes more fractured and anxiety-ridden, one of the ways Christians could stand out and make a difference is by modeling an entirely disparate lifestyle. One profound way of doing so would be to aggressively pursue interracial harmony.

What a clear and powerful message we would send to a me-first, materialistic, distrusting world by truly serving other people, sacrificing to meet their needs, consistently striving for unity with others—especially when those others are of a different color, upbringing or locale. And this cannot be a forced, image-driven show of piety. Instead, it must be an authentic demonstration of color-blind love and compassion.

We can virtually count on race riots ripping America apart in the next 10 years unless radical steps are taken by key people in our nation to defuse the impending explosion. Who are those key people? That status is up for grabs. It could be political leaders and policy makers. It could be educators. It could be social activists. Or it could be you and other followers of Jesus Christ who truly believe that all people are equal in God's eyes, and that as His disciples we must exude similar unconditional acceptance of all people regardless of their background.

What is your church doing to foster racial harmony? Even if you live in a single-race community, or worship in a congregation that lacks variation in skin tone, take the responsibility to build bridges to different types of people seriously. Jesus did.

ACT OUT YOUR FAITH

Why is it that in survey after survey born-again believers are nearly indistinguishable from non-Christians? Thankfully, when we winnow down the body of believers to those whom we label "evangelicals," many differences are evident. But this segment of the believer population is small. Doesn't the Bible teach us that once we have accepted Christ we ought to be open to the inner working of His Spirit such that we become continually transformed beings?

Perhaps our churches and ministry leaders must consciously create ways believers are held accountable for their gradual transformation. Maybe ministries should be more specific in outlining ways believers are to grow, or to be different from the rest of the pack, or to envision their life's goals. The most appropriate response to such a challenge likely differs from church to church, from ministry to ministry, from believer to believer. But there must be a definite response to address this spiritual calamity.

If we were dissecting the behavior of any other group of people—students, athletes, professionals, parents—we would demand evidence of growth over the course of time. Why should we accept anything less regarding the character and commitment of Christians?

How disturbing it is to consistently analyze data that show there is no difference between the faithful and the faithless. Imagine how God must perceive this condition.

FISCAL FITNESS

We know that the Christian Church in America has plenty of money, cumulatively, to get the job done. Each year, more than 50 billion dollars is donated to local churches. That is more than the annual budget of many nations of the world. Given the work of the early church, which was impoverished at best, this stockpile of funds is certainly sufficient to influence the nation.

The issue we must focus on is not a lack of funds but how we use the resources at our disposal. If a distinguished financial analyst were to examine Christianity in America, many probing questions would be raised.

Why do we have more than 300,000 religious outlets? Couldn't we produce the same (or better) results with fewer outposts?

Why do some pastors work part-time jobs to finance their ministry efforts while others have salary packages in excess of $100,000 a year? Are these higher-paid pastors more spiritual? Are they more important in God's economy than the less heavily endowed laborers?

Why do we spend five dollars on buildings and maintenance of church-related properties for every one dollar we spend on evangelistic activity? Is this the ultimate statement of our ministry priorities?

How can we explain the fact that less than one-quarter of all believers tithe? Or the fact that the average person who regularly attends church gives less than 2% of his or her income to the church?

The questions could continue. Do we have reasonable, viable answers?

STRENGTHEN THE FAMILY

What an incredible state of affairs. The family is deteriorating before our very eyes and little is being done to save it. Millions of Americans cannot even describe the meaning of "family values." How amazing it is to live in a day when most young people expect marriages to dissolve; when a large and growing percentage of babies are born to single mothers; when cohabitation and sexual intercourse before marriage are assumed to be normal, moral and rational behaviors; and when one out of four adults accepts homosexual couples as viable parents.[3]

What is your church doing to protect and restore traditional family systems and the values that underlie a strong family? This means doing more than just talking about the importance of a healthy family and how significant families used to be in our culture. Most of the churched people we interviewed said they hear more than enough vague lectures about family, but not nearly enough practical helps regarding what to do in a culture that rejects traditional family living and thinking. How will you provide tangible, practical assistance to those who are relying upon you for help?

Americans define relationships as critically important, but we believe we have too few—and the ones we have suffer for lack of time spent developing trust and intimacy. So what will you do? Traditionally, the Church has played a central role in developing close, personal relationships, both within and outside of the family. Today, the Church more often avoids a core role in facilitating relationship building. What will you do, now that you know there is an unmet need that the Church could feasibly help to meet?

Even the public policy arena suffers from the Church's waning influence in matters of family policy. Perhaps you can justify the absence of the Church from political activity on scriptural grounds. But you cannot justify the emasculation of the family, through the persistent efforts of political leaders, on those same grounds. How will you enter the political or policy arena in the coming days, knowing that God's design for people is to be related in traditional family units; and that contemporary immorality, in the name of freedom, tolerance or diversity, is a weak excuse for watching God's plan for His people being dismantled?

WISE UP REGARDING THE WORLD

Over and over, the writer of Proverbs admonishes us to "get wisdom; just get wisdom!" Sage advice, indeed, but easier said than done.

One step we could take is to act with greater discernment regarding the use of the mass media. Many avenues are open to us; all of those avenues require us to scrutinize the content being offered and to make a wise decision about what sources of information and entertainment are worthy of our attention and acceptance. We must be increasingly sensitive to the biases and values promoted by these external influences, and we must also be ready to offer alternatives to people who desire a different basis of information and entertainment.

ON YOUR KNEES

The final exhortation is that you pray to God for the health of His Church, for the health of your family, for your own spiritual growth and depth, and for the health of this nation.

Too often Christians end their conversations with a perfunctory, "I'll pray for you." If only such commitment were maintained and people truly communicated with God as intercessors for all of the situations we encounter!

In the past three years, I have studied many churches that have become models of healthy ministry, and others that have been turned around from severe decline to become stable and healthy once again. I have been struck by the realization that two particular conditions have been present in almost every case: (1) the presence of a visionary leader; and (2) a deep, lasting commitment to prayer. Clever promotional campaigns, truckloads of money, world-renowned preachers, or ostentatious buildings were not significant dimensions of those ministries. It was leaders, ordained by God, who truly sought His plan and His dreams, who (along with their congregations) were connected to His will through heartfelt, constant prayer that were the key.

In the spiritual battle we are a part of, we must seek the mind and the power of God through dedicated prayer. We cannot overestimate the power of prayer; nor can we overutilize the privilege we have of interacting directly with God. Pray for wisdom, guidance, power and influence in these trying times. As Paul wrote, we are to "pray continually" (1 Thess. 5:17, *NIV)* for God hears and answers the prayer of the righteous. You can do nothing greater today than to beg God for mercy, insight and a chance to play a role in His redemptive plan for this deteriorating nation.

Notes

1. For a deeper discussion of why I believe this is such a crucial need today, please refer to a recent study we conducted of senior pastors of Protestant churches, described in *Today's Pastors,* George Barna (Ventura, CA: Regal Books, 1993). The most important conclusion discussed in this book is that our churches are failing to have much influence because we have good-hearted, well-intentioned pastors in our churches who, by their own admission, do not possess the ability to lead people.

2. For some ideas on how to creatively evangelize, you might consider reading some related works. Try *Inside the Mind of Unchurched Harry,* Lee Strobel (Grand Rapids, MI: Zondervan Publishing, 1993); *Never on a Sunday,* a report by the Barna Research Group, P.O. Box 4152, Glendale, CA, 91222-0152; *Reinventing Evangelism,* Don Posterski (Downers Grove, IL: InterVarsity Press, 1989); and *Evangelism Through the Local Church,* Michael Green (Nashville, TN: Thomas Nelson Publishers, 1992).

3. These and other startling realities about changes in the American family are drawn from the research we conducted for the book *The Future of the American Family,* George Barna (Chicago, IL: Moody Press, 1993). Other excellent sources of insight into the changing nature of the family are *Free to Be Family,* produced by the Family Research Council, Washington, D.C.; 1992; *Faithful Attraction,* Andrew Greeley (New York: Tor Books, 1991); and *New Families, No Families,* Frances Goldschneider and Linda Waite (Berkeley, CA: University of California Press, 1991).

APPENDICES

APPENDIX I DEFINITIONS AND SURVEY METHODOLOGY

DEFINITIONS

The following represent the definitions for each of the population sub-groups referred to in the data tables throughout this book.

Total Population: The adults who were interviewed as part of the study.

Age: These categories reflect the age of the adult who was interviewed. Only people 18 or older were included in the surveys. Note that people in the 18 to 27 age-group are sometimes referred to as "baby busters" (people born between 1965-1983); those in the 28 to 46 age bracket are sometimes called "baby boomers" (born between 1946-1964); those in the 47-65 age bracket are sometimes called "builders" (born between 1928-1945).

Education: People who have formal education through a high school diploma are included in the "high school or less" group. Those who attended college but did not graduate are in the "some college" category. Those termed "college graduate" have received a college degree; this includes bachelors, masters, doctorates and other professional degrees.

Household Income: These categories refer to the total annual household income earned by all household members before taxes are removed.

Marital Status: Refers to the person's current status, listed as either married or not married. Those in the "not married" category include people who have never been married, are currently separated, are divorced and not currently remarried, and widowed adults. Those who have been divorced but are now remarried are included in the "married" category.

Have Kids: Those respondents who have children under the age of 18 are listed in the "yes" category; adults without children under 18 appear in the "no" group.

Community Type: The categories used here were read to respondents who then made a choice of one of the three options.

Region: The following states were included in these four regional groupings:
Northeast: ME, VT, NH, MA, RI, CT, NY, NJ, PA, DE, MD
South: VA, WV, KY, TN, NC, SC, GA, FL, AL, LA, MS, AR, OK, TX
Midwest: OH, MI, IN, IL, IA, WI, ND, SD, MO, KS, NE, MN
West: AZ, NM, UT, CO, ID, WY, MT, NV, CA, OR, WA

Born Again: To qualify for the "yes" category, people had to say that they have made a personal commitment to Jesus Christ that is still important in their lives today, and to believe that when they die they will go to heaven because they have confessed their sins and have accepted Jesus Christ as their Savior. Anyone who did not meet both of those conditions appears in the "no" category.

Denominational Affiliation: People were asked to describe themselves as either Protestant, Catholic, Jewish or of some other faith. Due to the low incidence of people in non-Christian faiths, only Protestants and Catholics, as major umbrella groupings, are shown. In addition, Protestants were asked to describe the type of church they usually attend. The data provide two columns, one for those attending a Baptist church and one for those who attend "mainline Protestant" churches. The mainline churches include Methodist, Lutheran, Episcopal, Presbyterian and United Church of Christ congregations.

Churched: Those in the "yes" category were adults who said that in a typical month they attend church one or more times. Those in the "no" category said they attend church less often than once a month, if at all.

Voter Registration: Each respondent indicated whether or not they were registered to vote at the time of the survey interview. Those who were not are listed under the "not registered" label. Among registered voters, they were asked if they had registered in affiliation with a political party. The three categories shown are for those who are registered as Democrats, those registered as Republicans and those who are registered but are independent of any political party. People registered in affiliation with minor parties are not shown.

Evangelical: These are people who meet several criteria. In addition to meeting the born-again definition (see above) they also believe that the Bible is totally accurate in all it teaches; believe that they personally have a responsibility to tell others about their religious beliefs; say that religion is very or somewhat important in their lives; and define God as the all-powerful, all-knowing, perfect Creator of the universe who rules the world today.

Survey Methodology

Data Collection
The data referred to in this book were collected through two nationwide telephone surveys conducted by the Barna Research Group, Ltd. The first of those surveys was conducted in July 1992 and included 1,004 adults. The second was conducted in January 1993 among 1,205 adults. The survey respondents, all 18 or older, were chosen through the use of a national random-digit dial (RDD) sample provided by Maritz, Inc. The response rate for the surveys were 61% and 63%, respectively.

Interviews
The average interview length was 20 minutes in the July survey, 22 minutes in the January study. The January survey also employed a split-sample technique; the sample was randomly divided into two equivalent portions, and certain questions were asked of one split but not the other. All of the interviews were conducted from the centralized telephone facility of Barna Research, located in Glendale, California. Calls were placed between 5:00 P.M. and 9:00 P.M. in a given time

zone on weeknights, from 10:00 A.M. to 4:00 P.M. on Saturdays and from noon to 8:00 P.M. on Sundays.

Quotas

Quotas were established to ensure that the number of completed interviews in a given geographic area corresponded with the population proportion in that area.

Weighting

To balance the sample according to true population proportions, statistical weighting was employed, based upon respondent gender and ethnicity. The population and survey sample distributions, by demographic categories, are shown below.

Demographic		Adult Population	July Sample	January Sample
Gender:	Male	49%	49%	48%
	Female	51	51	52
Age:	18-27	15	19	19
	28-46	41	43	41
	47-65	23	24	22
	66+	21	14	18
Ethnicity:	White	76	74	75
	Black	13	12	12
	Asian	3	4	4
	Hispanic	9	8	8

Source: Statistical Abstract of the United States, 1992; U.S. Department of Commerce, Washington, D.C.

PARAMETERS FOR ANALYZING SURVEY DATA

Every survey of people's attitudes and experiences that is based upon a sample of the population is a representation of the attitudes and experiences of the people who comprise the aggregate population.

Error

If the sample is selected properly—that is, survey respondents are chosen in accordance with the principles of probability sampling—then it is possible to estimate the potential amount of error attributable to sampling inaccuracies in the survey data. The only way to fully eliminate that potential error is to conduct a census rather than a sample.

Statisticians have developed means of identifying how much error could be in survey measurements due to sampling inaccuracies, assuming that random sampling procedures are conscientiously applied. The Sampling Accuracy Table at the end of Appendix 1 outlines such estimates of how much error might be found in surveys, based upon the sample size and the response levels to survey questions. All of the figures shown assume that we are working at the 95% confidence interval, meaning that we would expect these statistics to be accurate in 95 out of 100 cases. This is the standard confidence level used in most survey research.

In general, the following conditions are true:

- The larger the sample size, the more reliable are the survey data. However, there is not a simple one-to-one relationship between sample size and sampling error reduction.
- The larger the difference in opinion evident through the response distribution related to the question, the less likely it is that the survey statistics are erroneous due to sampling.

Response Levels and Accuracy

The data in the Sampling Accuracy Table shown below indicate how accurate the data are at specific response levels and at different sample sizes. For instance, in a survey of 1,000 people, if the answers were about evenly divided (i.e., 50% said "yes," 50% said "no"), those responses are probably accurate to within plus or minus three percentage points of what the survey actually found. Thus, you could say that the most likely response to the question was 50% saying "yes," with a 3-point margin of error at the 95% confidence interval. And that means that in this situation, the true population response would be somewhere between 47% and 53% in 95 out of 100 cases.

Here is another example. Let's say you ask the question regarding whether or not people have attended a church worship service in the past year. You find that 71% say they have, and 29% say they have not. Assume that the question was asked of 380 adults.

To determine the approximate level of sampling error associated with this finding you would look under the 30%/70% column (since the 71%-29% outcome is closest to the 30%-70% distribution). You would use the figures on the row representing the sample size of 400 people. The intersection point of that row with the 30%/70% column indicates a maximum sampling error of four percentage points.

You might say that 71% of all adults have attended a church worship service in the past year; this information is accurate to within plus or minus four percentage points at the 95% confidence level.

In some cases, the sample size or response distributions you use might vary markedly from the parameters shown in this table. You can either extrapolate from the figures shown to arrive at a closer interpretation of the error statistic or consult a good statistics book that might have a more detailed table. If you really want to test your patience and mental acuity, you might use the statistical formula for determining the error figures and calculate the number from scratch. That formula is provided in most decent statistics textbooks.

Sampling Accuracy Table

.05 Confidence Interval
Response Distribution

Sample Size	50/50	40/60	30/70	20/80	10/90
2,000	2	2	2	2	2
1,500	3	3	2	2	2
1,200	3	3	3	2	2
1,000	3	3	3	2	2
800	3	3	3	3	2
600	4	4	4	3	2
400	5	5	4	4	3
200	7	7	6	5	4
100	10	10	9	8	6
50	14	14	13	12	8

READING THE DATA TABLES

Many people look at a page filled with data—percentages, raw scores, indexes, frequencies or whatever—and break out in a cold sweat. Let me emphasize that you can get a multitude of insights out of this book without having to look at the data tables in the appendix. The statistics on which the survey commentary is based are provided for those hearty souls who can make sense out of the data, and who may wish to do some of their own data interpretation.

If you want to examine the data tables, here are a few clues to help you through the process. The sample data table below is coded to help you understand what each of the elements on the page represents.

A

Do you you agree strongly, agree somewhat, disagree somewhat, or disagree strongly with the statement: "One person cannot make a difference in the world"?

B

D   **C**

	N	Agree Strongly	Agree Somewhat	Disagree Somewhat	Disagree Strongly	Don't Know
Total Responding	1060	11%	11%	25%	51%	1%
Gender: Male	510	14	8	25	52	1
Female	549	9	13	26	51	1
Age: 18 to 26	226	13	9	33	45	1
27-45	476	10	11	26	53	1
46-64	234	10	10	23	56	0
65 Plus	115	18	12	16	50	4
Education: High School or Less	480	16	13	25	44	2
Some College	289	7	8	28	57	0
College Graduate	286	8	9	25	58	0
Ethnicity: White	778	9	9	26	55	1
Black	131	25	15	14	46	0
Hispanic	90	18	9	34	36	3
Marital: Married	575	10	10	26	54	0
Single	311	13	10	27	50	0
Divorced/Separated	100	8	14	26	48	4
Widowed	70	19	15	19	43	3
Kids Under 18: Yes	453	10	11	28	52	0
No	607	13	11	24	51	2

E

A This is similar wording of the questions asked in the survey.

B Each of these columns represents one of the answers that respondents might have given. Also remember that each of the figures in any of the columns is a percentage, not the total number of respondents who gave that particular answer.

C This is the total number (not a percentage) of survey respondents who are described by the label in the far left column of the row, and who answered this question. For the question on the sample page, 1,060 adults were asked the question. The second row, which is the results among males, shows the responses of the 510 people in that age group who were interviewed for the survey.

D The "total responding" row presents the aggregate survey data. Among all of the people involved in the survey who answered the question, their answers are always shown in the top row.

E The rest of the population segments listed on the page represent the other people groups who were interviewed, and how they responded. In this table, for instance, six independent variables were measured: gender, age, education, ethnicity, marital status, and having kids under 18. The statistics across from the male respondents tell us that 14% agreed strongly with the statement "one person cannot make a difference in the world," 8% agreed somewhat, 25% disagreed somewhat, 52% disagreed strongly, and 1% volunteered that they did not know (which is what DK stands for). The data in the row labeled "total responding" and beneath the column label "male" tells us that 510 men answered this question. The next row of data shows the responses of the female respondents. Among them, 9% agreed strongly with the statement, 13% agreed somewhat, 26% disagreed somewhat, 51% disagreed strongly, and 1% did not know. The subgroup size was 549 women. Notice that for any row of data shown in the table, the answers will add up to 100%. If the numbers are off by one or two percentage points, it is due to the rounding off of the figures.

DATA TABLES DIRECTORY

JULY 1992 SURVEY TABLES

I. How Much Do Certain Situations Annoy Us?

1. People talking during a movie
2. People smoking at a nearby table in a restaurant
3. A large number of ads in a magazine
4. Someone sharing their religious beliefs with us
5. Receiving telemarketing calls
6. Having to sing hymns in a church service
7. Hearing profanity on radio programs

II. Our Activities Rated for Enjoyment, Pressure or Habit

8. Praying to God
9. Exercising
10. Having guests over to visit at our homes
11. Attending church or religious service
12. Telling others about our religious beliefs
13. Working in the yard or garden
14. Reading the Bible

III. Our Views About Life in General

15. Trusting anyone other than family and close friends
16. Our system of government is not perfect, but it works well
17. Satisfaction of life
18. State of moral and ethical standards of Americans
19. Anger and hostility between ethnic groups in America
20. The stability of American society dependent on the strength of the traditional family unit
21. The abortion issue in the spotlight
22. Freedom based on doing anything you want to do
23. Life is too complex these days

IV. Where We Were in 1988

24. Living at the same address
25. Attending the same church or religious center
26. Registered to vote with the same political party
27. Affiliated with the same religious denomination or faith
28. Working with the same company
29. Living with the same people
30. Living at the same financial level

V. Since 1988, Have Influences on Society Changed?

31. Churches
32. Political parties
33. U.S. Supreme Court
34. Marriage
35. Journalists and media personalities

VI. Nonprofit Organizations

36. Views on most needy organizations
37. Views on organizations with high-salaried chief executives

VII. People's Beliefs About Religious Issues

38. God hears and answers our prayers
39. Higher moral and ethical standards expected of ministers
40. Did Jesus sometimes made mistakes?

41. Will Jesus come back?
42. Believing in similarity of religious faiths
43. Was Jesus as human as the rest of the people on earth?

VIII. Our Religious Activity in Past Year: Mentoring, Discipling, Small Groups

44. Percentage of people being mentored
45. Percentage who mentor others
46. Shared religious faith with others and were accepted
47. People who have attended small groups regularly
48. Praying in discipling process
49. Reading the Bible in discipling activity
50. Discussing life issues related to religious faith when being mentored
51. Number of people involved in mentoring process
52. Number of hours devoted each week to mentoring
53. How helpful is the mentoring and discipling process?

IX. Our Views on Government Issues and the 1992 Presidential Candidates

54. Finances and the economy
55. Domestic and social policies
56. International and foreign policies
57. July 1992 voter poll of presidential candidates: Clinton, Bush and Perot

JANUARY 1993 SURVEY TABLES

X. Our TV Viewing Habits

58. Number of hours watched Monday through Friday
59. Cable TV subscribers
60. Premium cable channels (pay extra)
61. MTV—Music Television
62. ESPN—Sports Channel
63. USA Network
64. The Family Channel
65. CNN—Cable News Network
66. How enjoyable, overall, is today's TV programming?

XI. Our Activities in an Average Week
67. Read a book
68. Attend a recovery group or 12-step program
69. Read the Book of Mormon
70. Rent a videocassette
71. Attend a church worship service
72. Read from the Bible
73. Use a computer
74. Volunteer time to a nonprofit organization other than a church
75. Volunteer time in a church

XII. Influences and Decisions in our Lives
76. Moral and ethical matters
77. Views and beliefs about various aspects in life
78. Will things be better or worse for us five years from now?

XIII. Importance of What We Represent
79. The United States
80. Church or Synagogue
81. Ethnic Heritage
82. Parents
83. Jesus Christ

XIV. How We View the Mass Media
84. Biased against Christian beliefs?
85. Liberal views on politics and issues?
86. Report information on moral behavior of political candidates and leaders?
87. Unbiased reporting, are objective?

XV. Nonprofit Organizations
88. Contributions given in 30-day period
89. Trustworthiness of nonprofit leaders
90. Volume of giving increase or decrease
91. Change number or type of organizations for contributions in future

July 1992
Survey Tables

TABLE 1   165

Is "people talking during a movie" usually annoying to you or not?

		N	Yes	No	Don't Know
Total Responding		1004	78%	20%	2%
Gender:	Male	492	77	22	2
	Female	512	78	19	3
Age:	18 to 27	188	77	22	1
	28-46	404	81	18	1
	47-65	223	77	20	3
	66-98	130	65	26	9
Income:	Under $20,000	213	67	30	3
	$20,000 to $40,000	349	78	19	2
	$40,000 to $60,000	163	83	16	1
	$60,000 or more	149	82	16	3
Education:	High School or Less	441	70	26	3
	Some College	237	81	17	2
	College Graduate	317	85	14	2
Marital Status:	Married	538	78	19	3
	Not Married	461	76	21	2
Have Kids Under 18:	Yes	364	79	20	1
	No	633	76	20	3
Ethnicity:	White	743	80	18	3
	Black	124	65	33	2
	Hispanic	85	80	20	0
Region:	Northeast	222	80	18	2
	South	210	77	21	2
	Central	402	75	22	3
	West	170	79	19	2
Community Type:	Urban	411	77	20	3
	Suburban	212	79	20	2
	Rural	372	77	20	2
Voter Registration:	Not Registered	243	73	26	1
	Reg. Democrat	315	74	24	2
	Reg. Republican	244	81	16	4
	Reg. Independent	143	86	12	2
Denominational	Protestant	541	77	20	3
Affiliation:	Catholic	280	78	21	1
	Baptist	168	75	22	3
	Mainline Protestant	162	83	15	3
Churched:	Yes	774	79	18	2
	No	205	72	26	2
Born Again:	Yes	373	78	19	3
	No	630	77	20	2
	Evangelical	118	80	15	5

TABLE 2

Is "people smoking at a table next to you in a restaurant" usually annoying to you or not?

		N	Yes	No	Don't Know
Total Responding		1004	55%	44%	1%
Gender:	Male	492	54	45	1
	Female	512	56	43	1
Age:	18 to 27	188	57	43	0
	28-46	404	56	43	1
	47-65	223	46	51	3
	66-98	130	58	42	0
Income:	Under $20,000	213	55	45	0
	$20,000 to $40,000	349	50	49	1
	$40,000 to $60,000	163	62	37	2
	$60,000 or more	149	60	40	1
Education:	High School or Less	441	51	48	1
	Some College	237	53	46	1
	College Graduate	317	62	37	1
Marital Status:	Married	538	56	43	2
	Not Married	461	54	46	0
Have Kids Under 18:	Yes	364	56	43	1
	No	633	54	45	1
Ethnicity:	White	743	53	45	2
	Black	124	55	45	0
	Hispanic	85	67	33	0
Region:	Northeast	222	49	51	0
	South	210	48	50	1
	Central	402	58	41	1
	West	170	64	34	2
Community Type:	Urban	411	56	43	1
	Suburban	212	59	41	1
	Rural	372	52	47	2
Voter Registration:	Not Registered	243	53	45	2
	Reg. Democrat	315	54	45	1
	Reg. Republican	244	59	40	1
	Reg. Independent	143	52	46	2
Denominational Affiliation:	Protestant	541	58	41	1
	Catholic	280	51	48	1
	Baptist	168	54	45	0
	Mainline Protestant	162	60	40	0
Churched:	Yes	774	58	41	1
	No	205	44	55	1
Born Again:	Yes	373	61	38	1
	No	630	51	48	1
	Evangelical	118	71	28	1

TABLE 3   167

Is "a large number of advertisements in a magazine" usually annoying to you or not?

		N	Yes	No	Don't Know
Total Responding		1004	41%	57%	2%
Gender:	Male	492	39	59	2
	Female	512	43	56	1
Age:	18 to 27	188	33	67	1
	28-46	404	45	54	0
	47-65	223	39	58	3
	66-98	130	42	53	5
Income:	Under $20,000	213	38	60	2
	$20,000 to $40,000	349	39	59	1
	$40,000 to $60,000	163	52	48	0
	$60,000 or more	149	37	62	1
Education:	High School or Less	441	36	62	2
	Some College	237	41	56	2
	College Graduate	317	48	52	0
Marital Status:	Married	538	42	56	2
	Not Married	461	41	58	1
Have Kids Under 18:	Yes	364	40	58	1
	No	633	42	57	2
Ethnicity:	White	743	43	55	1
	Black	124	19	77	4
	Hispanic	85	52	48	0
Region:	Northeast	222	43	56	2
	South	210	34	65	1
	Central	402	43	55	2
	West	170	44	55	1
Community Type:	Urban	411	40	59	1
	Suburban	212	46	53	1
	Rural	372	40	58	2
Voter Registration:	Not Registered	243	40	59	2
	Reg. Democrat	315	36	62	2
	Reg. Republican	244	45	54	2
	Reg. Independent	143	45	54	1
Denominational Affiliation:	Protestant	541	41	57	1
	Catholic	280	43	55	2
	Baptist	168	34	63	3
	Mainline Protestant	162	51	49	0
Churched:	Yes	774	38	60	2
	No	205	51	47	1
Born Again:	Yes	373	40	58	2
	No	630	42	57	1
	Evangelical	118	40	57	4

TABLE 4

Is "someone trying to tell you about their religious beliefs" usually annoying to you or not?

		N	Yes	No	Don't Know
Total Responding		1004	42%	55%	3%
Gender:	Male	492	47	52	1
	Female	512	38	58	4
Age:	18 to 27	188	50	50	0
	28-46	404	42	55	4
	47-65	223	43	55	2
	66-98	130	34	62	4
Income:	Under $20,000	213	38	58	4
	$20,000 to $40,000	349	43	55	3
	$40,000 to $60,000	163	47	50	3
	$60,000 or more	149	56	44	0
Education:	High School or Less	441	39	56	5
	Some College	237	45	54	1
	College Graduate	317	45	54	2
Marital Status:	Married	538	40	58	2
	Not Married	461	45	51	3
Have Kids Under 18:	Yes	364	40	57	3
	No	633	44	54	2
Ethnicity:	White	743	45	53	2
	Black	124	21	73	6
	Hispanic	85	47	47	6
Region:	Northeast	222	45	52	3
	South	210	31	63	5
	Central	402	42	57	2
	West	170	54	45	1
Community Type:	Urban	411	44	54	2
	Suburban	212	43	54	3
	Rural	372	40	56	4
Voter Registration:	Not Registered	243	37	60	4
	Reg. Democrat	315	43	54	3
	Reg. Republican	244	42	55	3
	Reg. Independent	143	54	46	0
Denominational Affiliation:	Protestant	541	36	62	3
	Catholic	280	52	45	2
	Baptist	168	28	68	4
	Mainline Protestant	162	46	52	2
Churched:	Yes	774	39	59	2
	No	205	56	40	4
Born Again:	Yes	373	26	70	4
	No	630	52	46	2
	Evangelical	118	12	84	4

TABLE 5 169

Is "receiving a telephone call from someone trying to sell you a product or service" usually annoying to you or not?

		N	Yes	No	Don't Know
Total Responding		1004	85%	14%	1%
Gender:	Male	492	82	17	1
	Female	512	88	12	1
Age:	18 to 27	188	81	18	1
	28-46	404	88	10	1
	47-65	223	84	15	1
	66-98	130	80	20	0
Income:	Under $20,000	213	79	21	0
	$20,000 to $40,000	349	84	15	1
	$40,000 to $60,000	163	86	13	1
	$60,000 or more	149	94	4	2
Education:	High School or Less	441	84	16	0
	Some College	237	86	12	2
	College Graduate	317	86	13	1
Marital Status:	Married	538	87	12	1
	Not Married	461	83	16	1
Have Kids Under 18:	Yes	364	85	14	1
	No	633	85	14	1
Ethnicity:	White	743	87	12	1
	Black	124	69	30	1
	Hispanic	85	90	10	0
Region:	Northeast	222	82	16	2
	South	210	84	15	1
	Central	402	85	15	0
	West	170	89	10	2
Community Type:	Urban	411	82	17	1
	Suburban	212	89	10	1
	Rural	372	86	14	1
Voter Registration:	Not Registered	243	83	15	2
	Reg. Democrat	315	83	16	0
	Reg. Republican	244	86	12	2
	Reg. Independent	143	91	9	0
Denominational Affiliation:	Protestant	541	87	12	1
	Catholic	280	83	16	0
	Baptist	168	79	20	1
	Mainline Protestant	162	91	9	0
Churched:	Yes	774	85	14	1
	No	205	85	13	2
Born Again:	Yes	373	86	14	1
	No	630	84	14	1
	Evangelical	118	90	9	1

TABLE 6

Is "having to sing hymns in a church service" usually annoying to you or not?

		N	Yes	No	Don't Know
Total Responding		1004	8%	88%	4%
Gender:	Male	492	12	83	4
	Female	512	4	92	4
Age:	18 to 27	188	19	78	3
	28-46	404	5	90	5
	47-65	223	5	90	4
	66-98	130	4	91	5
Income:	Under $20,000	213	14	82	5
	$20,000 to $40,000	349	7	90	2
	$40,000 to $60,000	163	8	88	4
	$60,000 or more	149	6	89	5
Education:	High School or Less	441	9	88	3
	Some College	237	8	88	4
	College Graduate	317	7	87	6
Marital Status:	Married	538	5	91	3
	Not Married	461	12	83	5
Have Kids Under 18:	Yes	364	7	91	2
	No	633	9	86	5
Ethnicity:	White	743	6	89	5
	Black	124	12	88	0
	Hispanic	85	11	86	4
Region:	Northeast	222	10	86	5
	South	210	5	90	5
	Central	402	7	90	3
	West	170	13	82	5
Community Type:	Urban	411	9	86	5
	Suburban	212	8	87	5
	Rural	372	7	90	3
Voter Registration:	Not Registered	243	12	85	3
	Reg. Democrat	315	9	87	4
	Reg. Republican	244	4	94	2
	Reg. Independent	143	7	88	5
Denominational Affiliation:	Protestant	541	5	93	2
	Catholic	280	10	89	1
	Baptist	168	5	95	1
	Mainline Protestant	162	2	96	2
Churched:	Yes	774	6	92	2
	No	205	14	73	13
Born Again:	Yes	373	4	95	1
	No	630	11	83	6
	Evangelical	118	2	97	1

TABLE 7   171

Is "hearing profanity on radio programs" usually annoying to you or not?

		N	Yes	No	Don't Know
Total Responding		1004	60%	38%	2%
Gender:	Male	492	47	51	2
	Female	512	72	27	1
Age:	18 to 27	188	31	68	1
	28-46	404	62	36	2
	47-65	223	67	30	2
	66-98	130	77	20	2
Income:	Under $20,000	213	59	41	1
	$20,000 to $40,000	349	61	38	1
	$40,000 to $60,000	163	66	32	3
	$60,000 or more	149	50	49	2
Education:	High School or Less	441	61	37	2
	Some College	237	58	41	1
	College Graduate	317	60	38	2
Marital Status:	Married	538	68	30	2
	Not Married	461	50	48	2
Have Kids Under 18:	Yes	364	62	37	1
	No	633	59	39	2
Ethnicity:	White	743	62	37	1
	Black	124	53	45	2
	Hispanic	85	50	48	2
Region:	Northeast	222	60	39	1
	South	210	61	38	1
	Central	402	62	36	2
	West	170	53	44	3
Community Type:	Urban	411	55	43	2
	Suburban	212	62	36	2
	Rural	372	63	35	1
Voter Registration:	Not Registered	243	53	46	1
	Reg. Democrat	315	61	37	2
	Reg. Republican	244	67	31	1
	Reg. Independent	143	52	44	4
Denominational	Protestant	541	69	30	1
Affiliation:	Catholic	280	53	45	1
	Baptist	168	69	31	0
	Mainline Protestant	162	67	31	2
Churched:	Yes	774	64	35	1
	No	205	45	52	3
Born Again:	Yes	373	75	24	1
	No	630	51	47	2
	Evangelical	118	89	11	0

Do you "pray to God" out of enjoyment, because you have to, out of habit, or do you never pray?

		N	Enjoyment	Have To	Habit	Don't Do It	Don't Know
Total Responding		1004	63%	4%	17%	12%	5%
Gender:	Male	492	53	4	19	17	7
	Female	512	72	3	15	7	3
Age:	18 to 27	188	53	5	21	15	6
	28-46	404	62	4	16	13	5
	47-65	223	65	4	14	13	4
	66-98	130	72	2	20	4	3
Income:	Under $20,000	213	63	5	16	10	6
	$20,000 to $40,000	349	66	3	17	11	3
	$40,000 to $60,000	163	58	8	17	12	5
	$60,000 or more	149	57	0	20	18	5
Education:	High School or Less	441	65	3	19	9	4
	Some College	237	63	3	15	14	4
	College Graduate	317	59	4	16	15	6
Marital Status:	Married	538	67	3	17	10	3
	Not Married	461	58	4	17	15	6
Have Kids Under 18:	Yes	364	69	2	16	8	5
	No	633	59	4	18	15	5
Ethnicity:	White	743	63	3	16	13	4
	Black	124	77	3	17	3	0
	Hispanic	85	50	4	24	11	11
Region:	Northeast	222	57	4	21	12	6
	South	210	73	3	14	8	3
	Central	402	64	3	16	12	5
	West	170	53	4	18	20	5
Community Type:	Urban	411	64	4	16	12	4
	Suburban	212	59	3	16	17	5
	Rural	372	63	3	18	10	4
Voter Registration:	Not Registered	243	61	5	14	14	6
	Reg. Democrat	315	64	2	18	12	4
	Reg. Republican	244	66	4	17	8	5
	Reg. Independent	143	58	3	20	15	3
Denominational Affiliation:	Protestant	541	72	4	15	7	2
	Catholic	280	60	4	23	7	7
	Baptist	168	82	4	12	2	0
	Mainline Protestant	162	70	1	20	7	2
Churched:	Yes	774	69	4	17	6	3
	No	205	35	2	17	37	9
Born Again:	Yes	373	83	3	12	2	1
	No	630	51	4	20	19	7
	Evangelical	118	88	3	9	0	0

TABLE 9 173

Do you "exercise" out of enjoyment, because you have to, out of habit, or do you never exercise?

		N	Enjoyment	Have To	Habit	Don't Do It	Don't Know
Total Responding		1004	45%	28%	11%	15%	1%
Gender:	Male	492	50	22	15	13	1
	Female	512	41	33	7	18	1
Age:	18 to 27	188	51	22	19	7	1
	28-46	404	43	32	10	15	1
	47-65	223	42	30	6	20	1
	66-98	130	46	23	9	22	0
Income:	Under $20,000	213	48	22	12	18	1
	$20,000 to $40,000	349	42	27	12	18	1
	$40,000 to $60,000	163	48	31	12	8	1
	$60,000 or more	149	48	32	10	9	1
Education:	High School or Less	441	44	25	11	19	1
	Some College	237	45	30	9	15	1
	College Graduate	317	46	30	12	11	1
Marital Status:	Married	538	44	31	7	17	1
	Not Married	461	47	24	15	14	1
Have Kids Under 18:	Yes	364	45	29	11	14	1
	No	633	46	27	10	16	1
Ethnicity:	White	743	48	28	10	14	1
	Black	124	39	29	9	23	0
	Hispanic	85	33	28	23	16	0
Region:	Northeast	222	42	32	9	15	1
	South	210	43	29	10	17	1
	Central	402	46	24	14	16	1
	West	170	52	30	7	11	1
Community Type:	Urban	411	48	26	11	14	1
	Suburban	212	42	31	10	17	0
	Rural	372	45	28	10	16	1
Voter Registration:	Not Registered	243	49	27	9	14	1
	Reg. Democrat	315	43	27	12	18	0
	Reg. Republican	244	46	29	10	14	0
	Reg. Independent	143	45	28	9	17	1
Denominational Affiliation:	Protestant	541	44	28	9	18	1
	Catholic	280	48	27	13	12	0
	Baptist	168	48	26	11	15	0
	Mainline Protestant	162	45	32	8	14	0
Churched:	Yes	774	46	29	11	14	1
	No	205	42	23	11	22	1
Born Again:	Yes	373	47	28	10	15	0
	No	630	45	27	11	16	1
	Evangelical	118	49	28	12	11	0

Do you "have guests over to your house" out of enjoyment, because you have to, out of habit, or do you never invite guests to your house?

		N	Enjoyment	Have To	Habit	Don't Do It	Don't Know
Total Responding		1004	87%	3%	5%	5%	0%
Gender:	Male	492	85	2	6	6	1
	Female	512	89	3	3	4	0
Age:	18 to 27	188	90	1	6	3	0
	28-46	404	87	3	4	5	1
	47-65	223	86	3	4	6	1
	66-98	130	83	4	6	8	0
Income:	Under $20,000	213	83	2	7	8	0
	$20,000 to $40,000	349	88	3	5	4	0
	$40,000 to $60,000	163	87	2	6	5	0
	$60,000 or more	149	95	1	2	1	0
Education:	High School or Less	441	85	3	6	5	1
	Some College	237	90	1	5	4	0
	College Graduate	317	88	3	3	6	0
Marital Status:	Married	538	90	2	4	3	0
	Not Married	461	84	3	6	7	1
Have Kids Under 18:	Yes	364	90	3	4	3	0
	No	633	86	3	5	6	1
Ethnicity:	White	743	91	2	3	3	0
	Black	124	72	3	13	12	1
	Hispanic	85	81	2	9	9	0
Region:	Northeast	222	90	3	3	3	1
	South	210	84	3	5	7	1
	Central	402	84	2	6	7	0
	West	170	93	2	4	1	0
Community Type:	Urban	411	85	3	5	6	0
	Suburban	212	90	3	2	5	0
	Rural	372	88	2	5	4	1
Voter Registration:	Not Registered	243	87	1	6	6	0
	Reg. Democrat	315	83	2	8	7	0
	Reg. Republican	244	88	4	3	4	1
	Reg. Independent	143	95	2	2	1	1
Denominational Affiliation:	Protestant	541	87	3	5	5	1
	Catholic	280	89	2	5	4	0
	Baptist	168	82	3	8	5	1
	Mainline Protestant	162	89	3	5	4	0
Churched:	Yes	774	88	3	5	4	0
	No	205	85	2	3	10	0
Born Again:	Yes	373	90	3	4	2	0
	No	630	85	2	5	7	0
	Evangelical	118	93	2	1	4	0

TABLE 11   175

Do you "attend church or a religious service" out of enjoyment, because you have to, out of habit, or do you never attend a church or religious service?

		N	Enjoyment	Have To	Habit	Don't Do It	Don't Know
Total Responding		1004	62%	6%	11%	19%	2%
Gender:	Male	492	53	5	14	25	3
	Female	512	71	6	8	14	1
Age:	18 to 27	188	45	12	18	22	3
	28-46	404	63	4	9	20	2
	47-65	223	65	4	8	22	1
	66-98	130	77	5	8	8	1
Income:	Under $20,000	213	61	7	8	21	3
	$20,000 to $40,000	349	62	5	12	19	2
	$40,000 to $60,000	163	64	5	12	17	3
	$60,000 or more	149	54	8	16	21	1
Education:	High School or Less	441	61	5	12	20	2
	Some College	237	61	7	10	20	2
	College Graduate	317	62	5	11	19	3
Marital Status:	Married	538	70	4	10	16	0
	Not Married	461	52	8	12	24	4
Have Kids Under 18:	Yes	364	71	4	11	12	2
	No	633	56	6	11	24	2
Ethnicity:	White	743	64	5	11	19	1
	Black	124	69	7	12	12	0
	Hispanic	85	46	9	15	24	6
Region:	Northeast	222	52	8	18	19	3
	South	210	72	4	9	14	1
	Central	402	67	4	10	16	2
	West	170	49	7	8	34	2
Community Type:	Urban	411	61	4	12	20	2
	Suburban	212	55	8	12	24	1
	Rural	372	65	6	10	16	3
Voter Registration:	Not Registered	243	53	9	10	26	2
	Reg. Democrat	315	67	6	8	18	1
	Reg. Republican	244	62	5	14	15	3
	Reg. Independent	143	62	2	14.	19	2
Denominational Affiliation:	Protestant	541	73	4	8	14	1
	Catholic	280	58	10	19	10	3
	Baptist	168	79	4	9	8	0
	Mainline Protestant	162	70	3	12	15	1
Churched:	Yes	774	73	6	13	7	2
	No	205	19	6	5	67	3
Born Again:	Yes	373	85	2	8	4	1
	No	630	48	8	13	28	3
	Evangelical	118	93	2	3	1	1

Table 12

Do you "tell other people about your religious beliefs" out of enjoyment, because you have to, out of habit, or do you never tell other people about your religious beliefs?

		N	Enjoyment	Have To	Habit	Don't Do It	Don't Know
Total Responding		1004	34%	2%	8%	52%	4%
Gender:	Male	492	29	2	9	57	4
	Female	512	39	3	7	48	4
Age:	18 to 27	188	30	2	14	53	0
	28-46	404	33	3	8	52	5
	47-65	223	37	3	4	52	4
	66-98	130	39	0	7	49	5
Income:	Under $20,000	213	43	2	9	42	5
	$20,000 to $40,000	349	33	3	9	52	3
	$40,000 to $60,000	163	31	2	9	54	4
	$60,000 or more	149	27	1	7	63	2
Education:	High School or Less	441	39	2	9	47	3
	Some College	237	32	3	6	55	4
	College Graduate	317	28	3	8	57	5
Marital Status:	Married	538	38	2	7	49	3
	Not Married	461	29	3	9	56	4
Have Kids Under 18:	Yes	364	37	3	10	47	3
	No	633	32	2	7	55	4
Ethnicity:	White	743	33	3	7	54	3
	Black	124	56	2	14	25	3
	Hispanic	85	13	0	10	69	9
Region:	Northeast	222	24	4	6	63	3
	South	210	46	2	6	42	4
	Central	402	35	2	10	47	5
	West	170	28	1	7	62	2
Community Type:	Urban	411	35	3	11	48	4
	Suburban	212	28	1	4	62	5
	Rural	372	36	3	7	51	3
Voter Registration:	Not Registered	243	36	3	10	46	4
	Reg. Democrat	315	35	2	8	49	6
	Reg. Republican	244	36	3	8	52	1
	Reg. Independent	143	26	1	6	65	3
Denominational Affiliation:	Protestant	541	46	3	8	40	3
	Catholic	280	16	2	8	70	3
	Baptist	168	55	1	10	31	2
	Mainline Protestant	162	34	3	6	52	5
Churched:	Yes	774	39	2	9	46	4
	No	205	13	3	2	78	4
Born Again:	Yes	373	59	3	10	25	3
	No	630	19	2	7	68	4
	Evangelical	118	84	4	7	3	3

TABLE 13   177

Do you "work in the yard or garden" out of enjoyment, because you have to, out of habit, or do you never work in the yard or garden?

		N	Enjoyment	Have To	Habit	Don't Do It	Don't Know
Total Responding		1004	55%	26%	5%	14%	1%
Gender:	Male	492	50	31	7	12	1
	Female	512	59	21	4	15	1
Age:	18 to 27	188	36	33	10	19	1
	28-46	404	53	32	4	11	0
	47-65	223	60	22	5	12	0
	66-98	130	67	9	4	18	1
Income:	Under $20,000	213	56	22	3	17	1
	$20,000 to $40,000	349	55	23	6	16	1
	$40,000 to $60,000	163	55	31	5	9	0
	$60,000 or more	149	49	35	6	8	0
Education:	High School or Less	441	55	23	7	14	1
	Some College	237	52	27	4	16	1
	College Graduate	317	55	31	3	11	0
Marital Status:	Married	538	63	25	3	8	0
	Not Married	461	45	28	7	20	1
Have Kids Under 18:	Yes	364	54	31	4	10	1
	No	633	55	23	6	16	0
Ethnicity:	White	743	60	23	4	12	0
	Black	124	37	28	9	26	0
	Hispanic	85	35	35	9	20	2
Region:	Northeast	222	53	24	4	19	0
	South	210	55	27	2	15	1
	Central	402	55	27	7	11	0
	West	170	57	28	5	10	0
Community Type:	Urban	411	53	25	7	15	0
	Suburban	212	56	25	3	15	1
	Rural	372	56	28	4	11	1
Voter Registration:	Not Registered	243	44	34	4	16	1
	Reg. Democrat	315	59	18	8	15	0
	Reg. Republican	244	62	25	3	11	0
	Reg. Independent	143	51	29	5	13	2
Denominational	Protestant	541	57	27	4	12	0
Affiliation:	Catholic	280	52	27	7	13	0
	Baptist	168	51	31	5	13	0
	Mainline Protestant	162	65	25	2	8	0
Churched:	Yes	774	55	27	5	12	0
	No	205	53	24	4	19	1
Born Again:	Yes	373	60	26	4	10	0
	No	630	51	26	6	16	1
	Evangelical	118	60	31	2	7	0

Do you "read the Bible" out of enjoyment, because you have to, out of habit, or do you never read the Bible?

		N	Enjoyment	Have To	Habit	Don't Do It	Don't Know
Total Responding		1004	54%	4%	8%	32%	2%
Gender:	Male	492	45	4	9	39	3
	Female	512	63	3	7	25	1
Age:	18 to 27	188	45	3	12	38	2
	28-46	404	53	5	8	31	3
	47-65	223	53	3	6	36	2
	66-98	130	70	1	9	20	0
Income:	Under $20,000	213	57	5	10	24	3
	$20,000 to $40,000	349	58	2	8	29	3
	$40,000 to $60,000	163	51	5	7	36	1
	$60,000 or more	149	43	3	8	43	2
Education:	High School or Less	441	56	3	10	29	2
	Some College	237	50	4	6	38	1
	College Graduate	317	54	5	7	31	3
Marital Status:	Married	538	59	4	8	28	1
	Not Married	461	49	3	8	37	3
Have Kids Under 18:	Yes	364	59	5	8	25	3
	No	633	51	3	8	36	2
Ethnicity:	White	743	56	3	7	32	2
	Black	124	65	4	17	15	0
	Hispanic	85	34	8	5	45	9
Region:	Northeast	222	46	3	11	37	3
	South	210	67	1	9	22	1
	Central	402	55	5	8	30	2
	West	170	46	4	4	43	3
Community Type:	Urban	411	53	4	9	32	2
	Suburban	212	47	4	6	39	4
	Rural	372	59	3	9	28	2
Voter Registration:	Not Registered	243	50	5	7	35	3
	Reg. Democrat	315	57	2	10	29	2
	Reg. Republican	244	56	4	9	29	2
	Reg. Independent	143	51	4	6	37	3
Denominational Affiliation:	Protestant	541	68	3	9	19	1
	Catholic	280	39	5	8	45	3
	Baptist	168	72	3	14	11	0
	Mainline Protestant	162	61	4	9	24	3
Churched:	Yes	774	62	3	9	24	2
	No	205	25	3	5	64	2
Born Again:	Yes	373	81	2	7	9	1
	No	630	38	4	9	46	3
	Evangelical	118	92	1	4	2	1

TABLE 15   179

Do you agree strongly, agree somewhat, disagree somewhat, or disagree strongly with the following statement: "You cannot trust anyone other than your family and close friends these days"?

		N	Agree Strongly	Agree Somewhat	Disagree Somewhat	Disagree Strongly	Don't Know
Total Responding		1004	17%	15%	32%	35%	1%
Gender:	Male	492	16	15	32	36	1
	Female	512	18	15	32	33	1
Age:	18 to 27	188	24	19	27	28	2
	28-46	404	13	15	37	34	1
	47-65	223	14	15	30	40	0
	66-98	130	26	10	26	35	2
Income:	Under $20,000	213	20	16	26	36	2
	$20,000 to $40,000	349	19	17	29	35	1
	$40,000 to $60,000	163	14	14	41	30	1
	$60,000 or more	149	10	10	34	45	1
Education:	High School or Less	441	24	18	29	28	1
	Some College	237	15	15	32	37	0
	College Graduate	317	8	11	36	43	1
Marital Status:	Married	538	15	13	34	37	1
	Not Married	461	20	18	29	32	1
Have Kids Under 18:	Yes	364	17	16	33	33	1
	No	633	17	15	31	36	1
Ethnicity:	White	743	16	14	31	37	1
	Black	124	26	19	27	28	1
	Hispanic	85	13	19	34	34	0
Region:	Northeast	222	18	16	32	32	1
	South	210	20	16	30	32	2
	Central	402	14	16	33	36	1
	West	170	19	10	32	39	1
Community Type:	Urban	411	21	17	28	34	1
	Suburban	212	10	12	36	41	1
	Rural	372	16	16	34	32	1
Voter Registration:	Not Registered	243	21	20	27	30	3
	Reg. Democrat	315	17	13	34	36	0
	Reg. Republican	244	15	14	31	39	1
	Reg. Independent	143	16	12	38	32	2
Denominational Affiliation:	Protestant	541	15	16	33	35	1
	Catholic	280	20	17	31	32	1
	Baptist	168	19	19	31	30	1
	Mainline Protestant	162	13	13	36	38	0
Churched:	Yes	774	17	15	32	35	1
	No	205	17	14	32	37	0
Born Again:	Yes	373	17	16	28	37	1
	No	630	17	14	34	34	1
	Evangelical	118	12	17	31	40	0

TABLE 16

Do you agree strongly, agree somewhat, disagree somewhat, or disagree strongly with the following statement: "Our system of government is not perfect, but it works well"?

		N	Agree Strongly	Agree Somewhat	Disagree Somewhat	Disagree Strongly	Don't Know
Total Responding		1004	26%	40%	14%	18%	2%
Gender:	Male	492	31	40	10	17	2
	Female	512	20	40	18	19	3
Age:	18 to 27	188	22	41	14	20	3
	28-46	404	21	46	12	19	2
	47-65	223	32	37	14	15	2
	66-98	130	30	29	16	19	6
Income:	Under $20,000	213	21	38	13	25	3
	$20,000 to $40,000	349	27	38	12	22	1
	$40,000 to $60,000	163	27	44	14	14	2
	$60,000 or more	149	32	47	11	9	1
Education:	High School or Less	441	24	35	15	23	3
	Some College	237	21	48	15	15	1
	College Graduate	317	32	41	11	14	3
Marital Status:	Married	538	29	39	14	16	2
	Not Married	461	22	41	14	20	3
Have Kids Under 18:	Yes	364	22	45	14	17	3
	No	633	28	37	14	19	2
Ethnicity:	White	743	27	39	13	19	2
	Black	124	14	38	19	25	3
	Hispanic	85	28	43	9	11	10
Region:	Northeast	222	23	40	15	20	2
	South	210	25	39	12	20	3
	Central	402	26	40	14	17	3
	West	170	28	42	13	16	1
Community Type:	Urban	411	24	40	14	19	3
	Suburban	212	25	42	16	15	2
	Rural	372	28	39	11	19	2
Voter Registration:	Not Registered	243	17	41	15	22	4
	Reg. Democrat	315	26	40	13	19	2
	Reg. Republican	244	35	38	11	15	1
	Reg. Independent	143	22	46	17	13	2
Denominational Affiliation:	Protestant	541	25	40	15	18	2
	Catholic	280	28	44	9	16	3
	Baptist	168	24	39	18	18	2
	Mainline Protestant	162	28	40	15	14	3
Churched:	Yes	774	27	40	14	17	2
	No	205	21	40	13	23	4
Born Again:	Yes	373	25	40	15	18	2
	No	630	26	40	13	18	3
	Evangelical	118	30	37	16	16	1

TABLE 17   181

Do you agree strongly, agree somewhat, disagree somewhat, or disagree strongly with the following statement: "Life is very satisfying for you"?

		N	Agree Strongly	Agree Somewhat	Disagree Somewhat	Disagree Strongly	Don't Know
Total Responding		1004	61%	25%	8%	4%	1%
Gender:	Male	492	59	28	9	3	1
	Female	512	63	23	8	5	1
Age:	18 to 27	188	55	30	7	7	0
	28-46	404	58	28	10	4	0
	47-65	223	65	22	10	3	0
	66-98	130	73	13	5	6	4
Income:	Under $20,000	213	57	22	10	9	2
	$20,000 to $40,000	349	56	29	10	5	0
	$40,000 to $60,000	163	65	27	7	1	0
	$60,000 or more	149	72	21	5	1	1
Education:	High School or Less	441	58	24	10	7	1
	Some College	237	65	27	5	3	0
	College Graduate	317	63	25	9	1	1
Marital Status:	Married	538	70	21	7	2	0
	Not Married	461	51	31	10	7	1
Have Kids Under 18:	Yes	364	59	26	10	4	0
	No	633	62	25	8	4	1
Ethnicity:	White	743	65	25	6	3	0
	Black	124	54	20	15	8	4
	Hispanic	85	51	26	15	8	0
Region:	Northeast	222	60	27	7	6	0
	South	210	65	24	8	2	1
	Central	402	61	25	9	4	1
	West	170	60	26	9	5	1
Community Type:	Urban	411	59	28	9	4	1
	Suburban	212	57	28	9	5	1
	Rural	372	66	21	8	4	1
Voter Registration:	Not Registered	243	50	29	13	8	1
	Reg. Democrat	315	65	21	9	4	1
	Reg. Republican	244	71	23	5	2	0
	Reg. Independent	143	55	36	6	3	1
Denominational Affiliation:	Protestant	541	63	26	7	4	1
	Catholic	280	60	26	10	4	1
	Baptist	168	64	24	8	4	1
	Mainline Protestant	162	62	30	4	2	2
Churched:	Yes	774	63	25	8	4	1
	No	205	54	28	12	5	0
Born Again:	Yes	373	66	25	5	3	1
	No	630	58	26	10	5	1
	Evangelical	118	75	20	3	1	1

TABLE 18

Do you agree strongly, agree somewhat, disagree somewhat, or disagree strongly with the following statement: "The moral and ethical standards of Americans these days are just as high as ever"?

		N	Agree Strongly	Agree Somewhat	Disagree Somewhat	Disagree Strongly	Don't Know
Total Responding		1004	10%	12%	25%	50%	3%
Gender:	Male	492	11	13	28	45	3
	Female	512	10	11	21	55	3
Age:	18 to 27	188	12	19	27	41	1
	28-46	404	10	13	28	46	4
	47-65	223	11	8	22	57	2
	66-98	130	11	8	14	61	7
Income:	Under $20,000	213	16	12	18	51	3
	$20,000 to $40,000	349	9	16	23	50	2
	$40,000 to $60,000	163	6	9	28	53	4
	$60,000 or more	149	10	11	33	43	4
Education:	High School or Less	441	13	15	19	49	3
	Some College	237	9	11	27	52	1
	College Graduate	317	7	9	31	48	4
Marital Status:	Married	538	9	10	25	54	3
	Not Married	461	12	15	25	45	3
Have Kids Under 18:	Yes	364	9	15	26	48	1
	No	633	11	10	24	51	4
Ethnicity:	White	743	8	12	25	53	3
	Black	124	23	15	14	43	5
	Hispanic	85	17	11	27	43	2
Region:	Northeast	222	10	10	26	50	4
	South	210	13	12	17	56	2
	Central	402	9	12	27	49	3
	West	170	11	13	29	44	3
Community Type:	Urban	411	13	14	24	48	1
	Suburban	212	8	10	31	47	4
	Rural	372	8	12	22	53	4
Voter Registration:	Not Registered	243	13	12	25	45	4
	Reg. Democrat	315	12	13	23	49	2
	Reg. Republican	244	7	12	22	56	3
	Reg. Independent	143	5	11	30	51	2
Denominational Affiliation:	Protestant	541	9	10	23	55	2
	Catholic	280	10	15	25	48	3
	Baptist	168	12	12	16	58	3
	Mainline Protestant	162	7	13	30	48	1
Churched:	Yes	774	9	12	25	52	2
	No	205	12	14	26	44	4
Born Again:	Yes	373	7	10	19	63	1
	No	630	12	13	28	42	4
	Evangelical	118	3	4	15	78	1

TABLE 19   183

Do you agree strongly, agree somewhat, disagree somewhat, or disagree strongly with the following statement: "There is a lot of anger and hostility between the different ethnic and racial groups in America today"?

		N	Agree Strongly	Agree Somewhat	Disagree Somewhat	Disagree Strongly	Don't Know
Total Responding		1004	58%	30%	7%	3%	2%
Gender:	Male	492	57	31	6	4	1
	Female	512	59	28	7	3	3
Age:	18 to 27	188	71	23	3	1	2
	28-46	404	57	33	6	3	1
	47-65	223	54	31	9	5	1
	66-98	130	57	24	9	4	7
Income:	Under $20,000	213	63	25	5	5	3
	$20,000 to $40,000	349	67	24	5	3	1
	$40,000 to $60,000	163	52	36	9	2	1
	$60,000 or more	149	48	39	6	4	4
Education:	High School or Less	441	65	24	5	4	2
	Some College	237	59	28	9	3	2
	College Graduate	317	49	40	8	2	2
Marital Status:	Married	538	53	32	9	4	3
	Not Married	461	65	27	4	2	2
Have Kids Under 18:	Yes	364	58	30	7	4	1
	No	633	59	29	7	3	2
Ethnicity:	White	743	56	31	7	3	2
	Black	124	69	15	6	8	2
	Hispanic	85	64	25	10	0	2
Region:	Northeast	222	65	26	5	2	2
	South	210	57	30	6	4	3
	Central	402	54	31	8	5	2
	West	170	60	30	7	1	2
Community Type:	Urban	411	67	23	6	3	1
	Suburban	212	50	34	9	2	4
	Rural	372	53	35	6	4	2
Voter Registration:	Not Registered	243	64	29	5	2	1
	Reg. Democrat	315	60	27	7	4	3
	Reg. Republican	244	54	32	7	4	2
	Reg. Independent	143	55	33	8	2	2
Denominational Affiliation:	Protestant	541	55	32	7	4	3
	Catholic	280	61	26	8	3	2
	Baptist	168	58	29	4	7	2
	Mainline Protestant	162	47	39	7	3	3
Churched:	Yes	774	57	30	7	4	3
	No	205	60	30	6	2	1
Born Again:	Yes	373	58	29	6	4	3
	No	630	58	30	7	3	2
	Evangelical	118	55	34	6	3	3

TABLE 20

Do you agree strongly, agree somewhat, disagree somewhat, or disagree strongly with the following statement: "If the traditional family unit falls apart, the stability of American society will collapse"?

		N	Agree Strongly	Agree Somewhat	Disagree Somewhat	Disagree Strongly	Don't Know
Total Responding		1004	48%	22%	16%	10%	3%
Gender:	Male	492	44	25	16	12	3
	Female	512	52	18	17	9	3
Age:	18 to 27	188	34	24	27	13	2
	28-46	404	45	26	16	11	3
	47-65	223	60	16	11	9	4
	66-98	130	59	14	13	8	5
Income:	Under $20,000	213	49	15	18	13	5
	$20,000 to $40,000	349	49	23	16	9	3
	$40,000 to $60,000	163	49	25	14	10	1
	$60,000 or more	149	41	26	23	10	1
Education:	High School or Less	441	49	19	16	10	5
	Some College	237	54	19	16	10	1
	College Graduate	317	43	26	18	11	2
Marital Status:	Married	538	55	20	14	6	4
	Not Married	461	40	24	19	15	3
Have Kids Under 18:	Yes	364	50	21	18	7	4
	No	633	47	22	15	12	3
Ethnicity:	White	743	51	21	16	9	3
	Black	124	44	18	16	15	7
	Hispanic	85	39	30	17	12	2
Region:	Northeast	222	42	25	15	14	5
	South	210	53	19	12	12	3
	Central	402	50	19	19	7	4
	West	170	44	27	17	11	1
Community Type:	Urban	411	44	21	18	13	4
	Suburban	212	48	25	16	9	3
	Rural	372	52	21	15	9	3
Voter Registration:	Not Registered	243	44	23	14	11	7
	Reg. Democrat	315	48	20	18	10	4
	Reg. Republican	244	54	22	15	8	0
	Reg. Independent	143	44	23	20	11	1
Denominational Affiliation:	Protestant	541	55	19	15	8	4
	Catholic	280	44	26	19	9	2
	Baptist	168	55	17	15	10	4
	Mainline Protestant	162	50	21	19	8	2
Churched:	Yes	774	52	21	16	9	2
	No	205	33	24	20	16	7
Born Again:	Yes	373	62	18	11	7	2
	No	630	40	24	20	13	4
	Evangelical	118	81	10	3	6	1

TABLE 21   185

Do you agree strongly, agree somewhat, disagree somewhat, or disagree strongly with the following statement: "The abortion issue gets more attention than it deserves"?

		N	Agree Strongly	Agree Somewhat	Disagree Somewhat	Disagree Strongly	Don't Know
Total Responding		1004	40%	18%	14%	23%	5%
Gender:	Male	492	41	20	16	19	3
	Female	512	39	16	11	27	7
Age:	18 to 27	188	37	17	17	28	1
	28-46	404	39	20	15	22	4
	47-65	223	43	18	13	20	6
	66-98	130	45	11	7	27	11
Income:	Under $20,000	213	44	11	15	24	7
	$20,000 to $40,000	349	41	21	10	24	3
	$40,000 to $60,000	163	42	18	16	19	6
	$60,000 or more	149	37	20	19	21	4
Education:	High School or Less	441	42	17	11	24	6
	Some College	237	40	18	15	22	5
	College Graduate	317	38	19	17	22	4
Marital Status:	Married	538	39	18	14	24	5
	Not Married	461	42	18	13	22	5
Have Kids Under 18:	Yes	364	41	17	15	23	4
	No	633	40	18	13	23	6
Ethnicity:	White	743	38	18	14	24	5
	Black	124	50	13	9	23	6
	Hispanic	85	52	23	13	12	0
Region:	Northeast	222	37	17	16	26	4
	South	210	44	15	11	26	4
	Central	402	41	17	13	22	7
	West	170	39	24	15	18	4
Community Type:	Urban	411	44	14	13	25	4
	Suburban	212	39	20	16	21	4
	Rural	372	37	21	13	22	7
Voter Registration:	Not Registered	243	39	21	13	21	6
	Reg. Democrat	315	42	17	11	23	7
	Reg. Republican	244	43	15	13	24	5
	Reg. Independent	143	38	18	22	21	1
Denominational Affiliation:	Protestant	541	40	18	13	22	6
	Catholic	280	45	15	16	19	5
	Baptist	168	40	17	14	22	6
	Mainline Protestant	162	43	19	16	17	5
Churched:	Yes	774	39	18	15	24	5
	No	205	46	18	12	18	5
Born Again:	Yes	373	37	17	14	25	6
	No	630	42	18	14	22	5
	Evangelical	118	27	13	16	37	6

Do you agree strongly, agree somewhat, disagree somewhat, or disagree strongly with the following statement: "Freedom means being able to do anything you want to do"?

		N	Agree Strongly	Agree Somewhat	Disagree Somewhat	Disagree Strongly	Don't Know
Total Responding		1004	23%	16%	25%	35%	2%
Gender:	Male	492	25	15	25	33	2
	Female	512	22	16	24	36	1
Age:	18 to 27	188	28	21	29	21	1
	28-46	404	22	17	28	33	0
	47-65	223	21	12	24	41	3
	66-98	130	29	12	14	40	5
Income:	Under $20,000	213	37	14	25	23	2
	$20,000 to $40,000	349	21	19	24	36	0
	$40,000 to $60,000	163	18	12	28	41	1
	$60,000 or more	149	18	15	25	40	2
Education:	High School or Less	441	34	16	23	25	2
	Some College	237	16	20	26	36	2
	College Graduate	317	14	13	25	47	1
Marital Status:	Married	538	21	15	23	40	2
	Not Married	461	26	16	27	29	1
Have Kids Under 18:	Yes	364	23	18	24	33	1
	No	633	23	14	25	36	2
Ethnicity:	White	743	22	15	25	37	1
	Black	124	37	20	13	25	5
	Hispanic	85	21	13	39	28	0
Region:	Northeast	222	24	18	27	28	2
	South	210	26	15	24	33	1
	Central	402	25	12	23	38	2
	West	170	16	22	25	36	2
Community Type:	Urban	411	26	17	23	32	2
	Suburban	212	15	14	29	41	2
	Rural	372	25	15	24	35	2
Voter Registration:	Not Registered	243	25	19	25	28	3
	Reg. Democrat	315	27	16	21	35	1
	Reg. Republican	244	17	14	24	43	1
	Reg. Independent	143	20	14	33	34	0
Denominational Affiliation:	Protestant	541	23	14	23	39	1
	Catholic	280	24	18	27	29	2
	Baptist	168	26	17	21	35	0
	Mainline Protestant	162	20	13	23	43	1
Churched:	Yes	774	22	16	25	36	2
	No	205	27	16	24	32	2
Born Again:	Yes	373	19	16	21	43	1
	No	630	26	16	27	30	2
	Evangelical	118	13	12	24	51	0

TABLE 23　　　　　　　　　187

Do you agree strongly, agree somewhat, disagree somewhat, or disagree strongly with the following statement: "Life is too complex these days"?

		N	Agree Strongly	Agree Somewhat	Disagree Somewhat	Disagree Strongly	Don't Know
Total Responding		1004	30%	32%	23%	13%	3%
Gender:	Male	492	26	32	25	15	2
	Female	512	35	31	21	10	3
Age:	18 to 27	188	28	33	26	11	2
	28-46	404	31	33	21	13	1
	47-65	223	28	28	28	13	3
	66-98	130	38	28	15	13	6
Income:	Under $20,000	213	41	31	15	7	6
	$20,000 to $40,000	349	32	29	25	14	1
	$40,000 to $60,000	163	26	33	26	15	0
	$60,000 or more	149	18	37	25	16	3
Education:	High School or Less	441	37	30	18	9	5
	Some College	237	28	29	25	17	1
	College Graduate	317	23	35	27	14	1
Marital Status:	Married	538	30	31	23	14	2
	Not Married	461	31	32	23	11	3
Have Kids Under 18:	Yes	364	33	35	18	12	2
	No	633	29	29	25	13	3
Ethnicity:	White	743	31	31	23	13	2
	Black	124	30	28	21	12	9
	Hispanic	85	32	28	28	11	2
Region:	Northeast	222	33	29	21	14	2
	South	210	34	29	20	14	4
	Central	402	29	32	24	12	3
	West	170	26	37	24	12	2
Community Type:	Urban	411	30	31	23	13	3
	Suburban	212	27	32	24	14	2
	Rural	372	32	31	22	12	3
Voter Registration:	Not Registered	243	37	29	25	7	2
	Reg. Democrat	315	27	34	21	14	4
	Reg. Republican	244	26	29	25	20	0
	Reg. Independent	143	30	38	21	8	2
Denominational Affiliation:	Protestant	541	32	33	21	11	3
	Catholic	280	30	30	23	15	2
	Baptist	168	34	33	19	10	4
	Mainline Protestant	162	31	36	21	9	3
Churched:	Yes	774	31	32	22	13	2
	No	205	28	32	24	13	3
Born Again:	Yes	373	29	37	21	11	2
	No	630	31	28	24	14	3
	Evangelical	118	33	37	16	14	0

TABLE 24

Think about your life five years ago: In 1987, were you "living at the same address"?

		N	Yes	No	Don't Know
Total Responding		1004	63%	37%	0%
Gender:	Male	492	61	39	0
	Female	512	64	36	0
Age:	18 to 27	188	34	66	0
	28-46	404	57	43	0
	47-65	223	80	20	0
	66-98	130	91	9	0
Income:	Under $20,000	213	61	39	0
	$20,000 to $40,000	349	58	42	0
	$40,000 to $60,000	163	68	32	0
	$60,000 or more	149	62	38	0
Education:	High School or Less	441	65	35	0
	Some College	237	62	38	0
	College Graduate	317	59	41	0
Marital Status:	Married	538	70	30	0
	Not Married	461	54	46	0
Have Kids Under 18:	Yes	364	55	45	0
	No	633	67	33	0
Ethnicity:	White	743	66	34	0
	Black	124	58	42	0
	Hispanic	85	51	49	0
Region:	Northeast	222	65	35	0
	South	210	60	40	0
	Central	402	66	34	0
	West	170	55	45	0
Community Type:	Urban	411	60	40	0
	Suburban	212	64	36	0
	Rural	372	65	35	0
Voter Registration:	Not Registered	243	41	59	0
	Reg. Democrat	315	68	32	0
	Reg. Republican	244	73	27	0
	Reg. Independent	143	65	35	0
Denominational Affiliation:	Protestant	541	65	35	0
	Catholic	280	63	37	0
	Baptist	168	61	39	0
	Mainline Protestant	162	74	26	0
Churched:	Yes	774	65	35	0
	No	205	57	43	0
Born Again:	Yes	373	65	35	0
	No	630	61	39	0
	Evangelical	118	72	28	0

TABLE 25   189

Think about your life five years ago: In 1987, were you "attending the same local church or religious center"?

		N	Yes	No	Does Not Apply	Don't Know
Total Responding		1004	65%	27%	7%	0%
Gender:	Male	492	62	28	9	0
	Female	512	68	26	6	0
Age:	18 to 27	188	53	41	5	0
	28-46	404	61	31	7	0
	47-65	223	73	17	11	0
	66-98	130	82	15	3	0
Income:	Under $20,000	213	64	29	7	0
	$20,000 to $40,000	349	65	28	7	0
	$40,000 to $60,000	163	67	25	7	0
	$60,000 or more	149	60	30	10	0
Education:	High School or Less	441	70	24	6	0
	Some College	237	67	24	8	0
	College Graduate	317	58	34	8	0
Marital Status:	Married	538	72	22	6	0
	Not Married	461	58	32	9	0
Have Kids Under 18:	Yes	364	67	29	4	0
	No	633	65	26	9	0
Ethnicity:	White	743	66	25	9	0
	Black	124	72	26	3	0
	Hispanic	85	64	36	0	0
Region:	Northeast	222	70	24	6	0
	South	210	65	30	5	0
	Central	402	67	25	8	0
	West	170	58	32	10	0
Community Type:	Urban	411	65	28	7	0
	Suburban	212	63	30	7	0
	Rural	372	67	24	9	0
Voter Registration:	Not Registered	243	56	35	8	0
	Reg. Democrat	315	72	22	6	0
	Reg. Republican	244	71	24	5	0
	Reg. Independent	143	61	31	7	0
Denominational	Protestant	541	68	26	5	0
Affiliation:	Catholic	280	76	21	3	0
	Baptist	168	71	27	2	0
	Mainline Protestant	162	74	20	5	0
Churched:	Yes	774	75	23	2	0
	No	205	29	41	30	0
Born Again:	Yes	373	72	27	1	0
	No	630	62	27	11	0
	Evangelical	118	69	30	1	0

TABLE 26

Think about your life five years ago: In 1987, were you "registered to vote with the same political party"?

		N	Yes	No	Does Not Apply	Don't Know
Total Responding		1004	72%	20%	7%	1%
Gender:	Male	492	70	22	8	0
	Female	512	75	17	7	1
Age:	18 to 27	188	38	48	13	0
	28-46	404	74	20	6	0
	47-65	223	89	6	5	1
	66-98	130	88	6	5	1
Income:	Under $20,000	213	70	23	6	0
	$20,000 to $40,000	349	70	22	7	1
	$40,000 to $60,000	163	80	15	4	0
	$60,000 or more	149	73	14	13	0
Education:	High School or Less	441	68	23	8	1
	Some College	237	72	22	6	0
	College Graduate	317	78	14	8	0
Marital Status:	Married	538	82	11	6	0
	Not Married	461	61	30	9	1
Have Kids Under 18:	Yes	364	73	20	7	1
	No	633	72	19	8	0
Ethnicity:	White	743	75	17	7	1
	Black	124	72	19	8	1
	Hispanic	85	52	35	14	0
Region:	Northeast	222	71	21	7	1
	South	210	72	19	9	1
	Central	402	74	18	7	1
	West	170	71	23	6	0
Community Type:	Urban	411	76	17	7	0
	Suburban	212	72	18	10	0
	Rural	372	69	23	7	1
Voter Registration:	Not Registered	243	42	41	16	1
	Reg. Democrat	315	89	9	2	0
	Reg. Republican	244	87	12	1	0
	Reg. Independent	143	65	23	12	1
Denominational Affiliation:	Protestant	541	77	15	7	1
	Catholic	280	73	21	6	0
	Baptist	168	80	13	7	0
	Mainline Protestant	162	77	13	9	2
Churched:	Yes	774	76	17	6	1
	No	205	60	26	14	1
Born Again:	Yes	373	82	13	4	1
	No	630	67	23	9	1
	Evangelical	118	84	11	4	0

TABLE 27   191

Think about your life five years ago: In 1987, were you "affiliated with the same religious denomination or faith"?

		N	Yes	No	Does Not Apply	Don't Know
Total Responding		1004	87%	10%	3%	1%
Gender:	Male	492	85	10	4	1
	Female	512	88	9	2	0
Age:	18 to 27	188	84	13	2	1
	28-46	404	84	13	3	0
	47-65	223	89	6	5	0
	66-98	130	93	5	1	1
Income:	Under $20,000	213	85	11	3	1
	$20,000 to $40,000	349	88	10	2	0
	$40,000 to $60,000	163	88	7	5	0
	$60,000 or more	149	86	10	4	0
Education:	High School or Less	441	90	8	1	1
	Some College	237	86	8	5	0
	College Graduate	317	82	13	5	0
Marital Status:	Married	538	90	7	3	0
	Not Married	461	83	12	4	1
Have Kids Under 18:	Yes	364	87	11	2	0
	No	633	86	9	4	1
Ethnicity:	White	743	87	9	4	1
	Black	124	90	7	3	0
	Hispanic	85	85	15	0	0
Region:	Northeast	222	85	13	2	0
	South	210	88	8	3	1
	Central	402	89	9	2	0
	West	170	82	9	8	1
Community Type:	Urban	411	85	11	4	1
	Suburban	212	82	14	4	0
	Rural	372	91	6	2	1
Voter Registration:	Not Registered	243	83	14	3	1
	Reg. Democrat	315	89	8	3	0
	Reg. Republican	244	90	7	3	0
	Reg. Independent	143	85	10	4	1
Denominational Affiliation:	Protestant	541	90	8	1	0
	Catholic	280	94	5	1	0
	Baptist	168	92	8	0	0
	Mainline Protestant	162	91	7	2	1
Churched:	Yes	774	92	8	0	0
	No	205	68	17	14	1
Born Again:	Yes	373	93	7	0	0
	No	630	83	11	5	1
	Evangelical	118	91	9	0	0

Table 28

Think about your life five years ago: In 1987, were you "working with the same company"?

		N	Yes	No	Does Not Apply	Don't Know
Total Responding		1004	42%	44%	14%	0%
Gender:	Male	492	48	43	8	0
	Female	512	36	44	19	0
Age:	18 to 27	188	14	78	7	0
	28-46	404	53	44	3	0
	47-65	223	57	30	12	0
	66-98	130	23	23	55	0
Income:	Under $20,000	213	24	51	25	0
	$20,000 to $40,000	349	42	48	10	0
	$40,000 to $60,000	163	63	29	7	0
	$60,000 or more	149	44	47	9	0
Education:	High School or Less	441	36	44	20	0
	Some College	237	43	47	10	0
	College Graduate	317	50	42	9	0
Marital Status:	Married	538	49	35	15	0
	Not Married	461	34	54	12	0
Have Kids Under 18:	Yes	364	49	44	7	1
	No	633	38	44	18	0
Ethnicity:	White	743	43	41	15	0
	Black	124	36	51	13	0
	Hispanic	85	43	49	8	0
Region:	Northeast	222	43	39	17	0
	South	210	39	47	14	0
	Central	402	43	43	14	0
	West	170	43	47	10	0
Community Type:	Urban	411	38	49	12	1
	Suburban	212	47	41	12	0
	Rural	372	44	40	16	0
Voter Registration:	Not Registered	243	30	57	12	1
	Reg. Democrat	315	46	40	14	0
	Reg. Republican	244	47	33	20	0
	Reg. Independent	143	44	49	7	0
Denominational Affiliation:	Protestant	541	42	41	16	0
	Catholic	280	45	41	13	0
	Baptist	168	38	46	15	0
	Mainline Protestant	162	45	34	21	0
Churched:	Yes	774	43	41	15	0
	No	205	39	52	9	0
Born Again:	Yes	373	44	38	18	0
	No	630	41	47	12	0
	Evangelical	118	53	32	15	0

TABLE 29   193

Think about your life five years ago: In 1987, were you "living with the same people"?

		N	Yes	No	Does Not Apply	Don't Know
Total Responding		1004	73%	26%	1%	0%
Gender:	Male	492	70	29	1	0
	Female	512	76	23	1	0
Age:	18 to 27	188	57	43	0	0
	28-46	404	72	28	0	0
	47-65	223	82	16	1	0
	66-98	130	80	15	5	0
Income:	Under $20,000	213	57	39	3	0
	$20,000 to $40,000	349	71	28	1	0
	$40,000 to $60,000	163	85	15	0	0
	$60,000 or more	149	81	19	0	0
Education:	High School or Less	441	77	21	1	0
	Some College	237	69	30	2	0
	College Graduate	317	71	29	0	0
Marital Status:	Married	538	88	12	0	0
	Not Married	461	55	42	3	0
Have Kids Under 18:	Yes	364	80	20	0	0
	No	633	69	29	2	0
Ethnicity:	White	743	75	23	1	0
	Black	124	70	28	1	0
	Hispanic	85	56	44	0	0
Region:	Northeast	222	72	27	1	0
	South	210	73	24	2	1
	Central	402	74	25	1	0
	West	170	73	25	2	0
Community Type:	Urban	411	70	28	1	0
	Suburban	212	75	25	0	0
	Rural	372	75	23	2	0
Voter Registration:	Not Registered	243	59	39	1	0
	Reg. Democrat	315	75	24	1	0
	Reg. Republican	244	80	19	1	0
	Reg. Independent	143	79	21	0	0
Denominational	Protestant	541	76	23	1	0
Affiliation:	Catholic	280	72	26	2	0
	Baptist	168	75	25	0	0
	Mainline Protestant	162	80	18	1	0
Churched:	Yes	774	76	24	1	0
	No	205	65	33	2	1
Born Again:	Yes	373	77	22	1	0
	No	630	71	28	1	0
	Evangelical	118	79	20	1	0

TABLE 30

Think about your life five years ago: In 1987, were you "living at the same financial level"?

		N	Yes	No	Does Not Apply	Don't Know
Total Responding		1004	47%	51%	0%	1%
Gender:	Male	492	46	52	0	1
	Female	512	48	51	0	1
Age:	18 to 27	188	35	64	1	1
	28-46	404	40	60	0	0
	47-65	223	55	44	0	1
	66-98	130	75	23	0	2
Income:	Under $20,000	213	50	49	0	1
	$20,000 to $40,000	349	43	56	0	0
	$40,000 to $60,000	163	47	53	0	0
	$60,000 or more	149	50	50	0	0
Education:	High School or Less	441	51	47	0	2
	Some College	237	44	55	0	1
	College Graduate	317	46	54	0	0
Marital Status:	Married	538	51	48	0	0
	Not Married	461	43	55	0	1
Have Kids Under 18:	Yes	364	42	57	0	1
	No	633	51	48	0	1
Ethnicity:	White	743	49	50	0	1
	Black	124	44	55	0	1
	Hispanic	85	37	63	0	0
Region:	Northeast	222	45	54	1	1
	South	210	50	49	0	1
	Central	402	49	51	0	1
	West	170	46	54	0	0
Community Type:	Urban	411	44	55	0	1
	Suburban	212	47	52	0	1
	Rural	372	51	47	0	1
Voter Registration:	Not Registered	243	35	63	0	2
	Reg. Democrat	315	51	49	0	0
	Reg. Republican	244	55	44	0	1
	Reg. Independent	143	50	50	1	0
Denominational Affiliation:	Protestant	541	52	47	0	1
	Catholic	280	42	55	1	1
	Baptist	168	45	55	0	0
	Mainline Protestant	162	57	42	0	1
Churched:	Yes	774	48	51	0	1
	No	205	45	54	0	1
Born Again:	Yes	373	53	46	0	1
	No	630	44	54	0	1
	Evangelical	118	53	47	0	0

TABLE 31   195

Do you think that "churches" have more influence, less influence, or the same level of influence in our society compared to five years ago?

		N	More Influence	Same Level of Influence	Less Influence	Don't Know
Total Responding		1004	21%	40%	33%	5%
Gender:	Male	492	20	42	33	5
	Female	512	22	39	33	5
Age:	18 to 27	188	23	43	32	2
	28-46	404	21	46	29	3
	47-65	223	17	33	43	7
	66-98	130	25	33	33	9
Income:	Under $20,000	213	28	34	34	5
	$20,000 to $40,000	349	23	45	29	3
	$40,000 to $60,000	163	14	41	41	4
	$60,000 or more	149	15	44	36	4
Education:	High School or Less	441	25	38	32	5
	Some College	237	21	47	27	5
	College Graduate	317	17	40	40	4
Marital Status:	Married	538	22	37	36	5
	Not Married	461	21	45	30	4
Have Kids Under 18:	Yes	364	26	39	31	5
	No	633	19	41	35	5
Ethnicity:	White	743	19	42	35	5
	Black	124	32	25	38	5
	Hispanic	85	33	41	23	3
Region:	Northeast	222	25	35	35	6
	South	210	21	44	32	3
	Central	402	22	40	33	5
	West	170	16	45	34	5
Community Type:	Urban	411	25	41	31	4
	Suburban	212	18	40	35	7
	Rural	372	20	40	35	5
Voter Registration:	Not Registered	243	24	40	32	4
	Reg. Democrat	315	25	36	33	5
	Reg. Republican	244	19	41	36	4
	Reg. Independent	143	13	49	34	4
Denominational Affiliation:	Protestant	541	23	39	33	5
	Catholic	280	19	44	35	3
	Baptist	168	25	36	36	3
	Mainline Protestant	162	19	45	34	3
Churched:	Yes	774	21	41	34	3
	No	205	21	41	29	9
Born Again:	Yes	373	25	39	32	4
	No	630	19	41	34	5
	Evangelical	118	25	33	41	1

TABLE 32

Do you think that "political parties" have more influence, less influence, or the same level of influence in our society compared to five years ago?

		N	More Influence	Same Level of Influence	Less Influence	Don't Know
Total Responding		1004	21%	35%	38%	6%
Gender:	Male	492	21	36	39	4
	Female	512	21	34	37	8
Age:	18 to 27	188	29	36	32	3
	28-46	404	21	38	38	4
	47-65	223	16	34	45	6
	66-98	130	23	27	36	14
Income:	Under $20,000	213	29	29	34	8
	$20,000 to $40,000	349	25	38	32	4
	$40,000 to $60,000	163	16	40	40	3
	$60,000 or more	149	12	38	48	2
Education:	High School or Less	441	28	34	29	9
	Some College	237	19	37	40	4
	College Graduate	317	13	35	50	3
Marital Status:	Married	538	20	34	40	6
	Not Married	461	23	35	36	5
Have Kids Under 18:	Yes	364	25	33	37	4
	No	633	19	36	39	6
Ethnicity:	White	743	19	36	40	6
	Black	124	35	24	34	7
	Hispanic	85	34	37	27	2
Region:	Northeast	222	21	32	40	6
	South	210	21	40	33	5
	Central	402	22	32	40	7
	West	170	21	39	37	3
Community Type:	Urban	411	25	33	37	5
	Suburban	212	16	32	48	4
	Rural	372	20	38	34	7
Voter Registration:	Not Registered	243	24	33	36	7
	Reg. Democrat	315	25	34	36	5
	Reg. Republican	244	18	36	42	3
	Reg. Independent	143	16	35	44	6
Denominational Affiliation:	Protestant	541	21	35	37	7
	Catholic	280	21	39	36	4
	Baptist	168	24	34	35	7
	Mainline Protestant	162	15	39	39	7
Churched:	Yes	774	21	35	40	5
	No	205	24	35	34	7
Born Again:	Yes	373	22	35	38	5
	No	630	21	35	38	6
	Evangelical	118	22	37	35	6

TABLE 33 197

Do you think that the "Supreme Court" has more influence, less influence, or the same level of influence in our society compared to five years ago?

		N	More Influence	Same Level of Influence	Less Influence	Don't Know
Total Responding		1004	30%	44%	17%	10%
Gender:	Male	492	33	44	17	7
	Female	512	28	43	17	12
Age:	18 to 27	188	35	42	16	7
	28-46	404	28	48	17	7
	47-65	223	33	44	15	8
	66-98	130	30	33	18	19
Income:	Under $20,000	213	34	36	16	14
	$20,000 to $40,000	349	31	44	18	7
	$40,000 to $60,000	163	29	47	18	7
	$60,000 or more	149	28	55	12	5
Education:	High School or Less	441	33	36	18	13
	Some College	237	26	48	18	8
	College Graduate	317	30	52	13	6
Marital Status:	Married	538	30	45	17	9
	Not Married	461	31	42	17	11
Have Kids Under 18:	Yes	364	31	45	16	8
	No	633	30	42	17	10
Ethnicity:	White	743	30	45	16	9
	Black	124	34	35	21	10
	Hispanic	85	32	39	17	12
Region:	Northeast	222	31	43	16	10
	South	210	27	49	15	10
	Central	402	32	40	17	11
	West	170	30	47	17	5
Community Type:	Urban	411	34	41	18	7
	Suburban	212	25	50	13	12
	Rural	372	30	42	17	11
Voter Registration:	Not Registered	243	27	42	18	13
	Reg. Democrat	315	36	40	15	9
	Reg. Republican	244	30	45	17	8
	Reg. Independent	143	28	52	15	5
Denominational Affiliation:	Protestant	541	32	41	16	11
	Catholic	280	29	45	20	6
	Baptist	168	34	40	16	10
	Mainline Protestant	162	29	45	16	11
Churched:	Yes	774	31	43	17	9
	No	205	28	46	17	9
Born Again:	Yes	373	30	44	17	9
	No	630	31	43	16	10
	Evangelical	118	28	48	18	6

Do you think that "marriage, in general" has more influence, less influence, or the same level of influence in our society compared to five years ago?

		N	More Influence	Same Level of Influence	Less Influence	Don't Know
Total Responding		1004	18%	35%	41%	6%
Gender:	Male	492	18	39	37	6
	Female	512	18	30	45	6
Age:	18 to 27	188	20	30	45	5
	28-46	404	21	38	35	6
	47-65	223	16	37	40	6
	66-98	130	12	20	60	8
Income:	Under $20,000	213	13	23	55	9
	$20,000 to $40,000	349	17	35	43	5
	$40,000 to $60,000	163	20	42	33	5
	$60,000 or more	149	23	47	25	4
Education:	High School or Less	441	17	29	45	8
	Some College	237	17	39	39	5
	College Graduate	317	20	39	37	4
Marital Status:	Married	538	21	38	37	4
	Not Married	461	15	31	46	8
Have Kids Under 18:	Yes	364	23	33	38	6
	No	633	15	36	43	6
Ethnicity:	White	743	17	36	41	6
	Black	124	23	24	47	5
	Hispanic	85	22	37	34	7
Region:	Northeast	222	17	32	46	5
	South	210	18	31	46	5
	Central	402	17	36	40	7
	West	170	20	41	32	7
Community Type:	Urban	411	20	35	40	5
	Suburban	212	23	34	36	7
	Rural	372	13	34	45	7
Voter Registration:	Not Registered	243	18	30	43	9
	Reg. Democrat	315	19	34	42	4
	Reg. Republican	244	20	37	41	2
	Reg. Independent	143	15	42	35	8
Denominational Affiliation:	Protestant	541	19	33	42	6
	Catholic	280	15	39	40	5
	Baptist	168	21	28	45	5
	Mainline Protestant	162	13	41	42	4
Churched:	Yes	774	17	34	44	5
	No	205	20	38	33	10
Born Again:	Yes	373	17	31	47	5
	No	630	18	37	38	7
	Evangelical	118	15	30	54	2

TABLE 35   199

Do you think that "journalists and media personalities" have more influence, less influence, or the same level of influence in our society compared to five years ago?

		N	More Influence	Same Level of Influence	Less Influence	Don't Know
Total Responding		1004	58%	26%	12%	4%
Gender:	Male	492	55	27	16	3
	Female	512	60	26	8	6
Age:	18 to 27	188	67	25	8	1
	28-46	404	62	28	9	2
	47-65	223	51	27	17	5
	66-98	130	49	21	16	13
Income:	Under $20,000	213	54	21	18	7
	$20,000 to $40,000	349	62	26	10	1
	$40,000 to $60,000	163	59	29	10	3
	$60,000 or more	149	54	35	10	1
Education:	High School or Less	441	55	24	14	7
	Some College	237	65	22	11	2
	College Graduate	317	55	34	10	1
Marital Status:	Married	538	57	26	13	4
	Not Married	461	58	27	11	4
Have Kids Under 18:	Yes	364	63	26	8	3
	No	633	54	27	14	5
Ethnicity:	White	743	57	27	11	4
	Black	124	53	27	15	5
	Hispanic	85	72	14	11	4
Region:	Northeast	222	57	26	12	5
	South	210	56	29	10	5
	Central	402	59	25	11	4
	West	170	56	27	15	2
Community Type:	Urban	411	60	25	12	3
	Suburban	212	60	27	10	4
	Rural	372	55	27	13	5
Voter Registration:	Not Registered	243	59	24	13	5
	Reg. Democrat	315	55	25	16	4
	Reg. Republican	244	61	27	8	4
	Reg. Independent	143	56	29	12	3
Denominational Affiliation:	Protestant	541	57	26	12	5
	Catholic	280	59	28	11	1
	Baptist	168	55	25	13	7
	Mainline Protestant	162	57	27	11	5
Churched:	Yes	774	58	26	12	4
	No	205	57	28	11	4
Born Again:	Yes	373	58	25	13	5
	No	630	57	27	11	4
	Evangelical	118	58	29	12	1

I'm going to mention some types of nonprofit organizations. Please tell me which of these organizations you think are most in need of financial help right now.

		N	Religious Organizations	Educational Organizations	Health And Health Care Groups	Overseas Crisis Relief Groups	Environmental Groups
Total Responding		1004	9%	34%	27%	4%	8%
Gender:	Male	492	8	34	26	4	9
	Female	512	11	33	28	4	6
Age:	18 to 27	188	5	49	23	3	9
	28 to 46	404	7	34	28	5	8
	47 to 65	223	12	28	30	4	7
	66 to 98	130	16	21	26	5	5
Income:	Under $20,000	213	11	28	34	1	6
	$20,000 to $40,000	349	11	34	29	3	7
	$40,000 to $60,000	163	9	37	25	7	6
	$60,000 or more	149	5	36	20	6	11
Education:	High School or Less	441	9	32	33	3	6
	Some College	237	9	34	27	2	9
	College Graduate	317	10	36	20	7	9
Marital Status:	Married	538	13	34	25	5	7
	Not Married	461	6	34	30	3	8
Have Kids Under 18:	Yes	364	9	37	25	5	7
	No	633	10	32	29	4	8
Ethnicity:	White	743	10	31	27	4	9
	Black	124	10	38	26	4	2
	Hispanic	85	4	44	28	2	6
Region:	Northeast	222	7	31	29	6	10
	South	210	10	33	32	5	7
	Central	402	12	32	24	4	7
	West	170	6	42	29	2	6
Community Type:	Urban	411	8	37	27	2	7
	Suburban	212	5	40	24	6	8
	Rural	372	14	26	30	5	8
Voter Registration:	Not Registered	243	6	35	32	6	6
	Democrat	315	10	36	28	4	6
	Republican	244	13	31	21	3	7
	Independent	143	8	36	29	5	10
Denominational Affiliation:	Protestant	541	14	31	26	4	6
	Catholic	280	6	36	27	5	8
	Baptist	168	18	33	29	3	3
	Mainline Protestant	162	11	30	24	7	7
Churched:	Yes	774	12	33	27	4	6
	No	205	1	34	31	4	13
Born Again	Yes	373	19	28	28	4	5
	No	630	4	37	27	4	9
	Evangelical	118	28	18	26	8	3

TABLE 36 (continued)   201

I'm going to mention some types of nonprofit organizations. Please tell me which of these organizations you think are most in need of financial help right now.

		Civic or Community Organizations	Organ. Work For Polit. / Soc. Change	Other: (Write Answer)	None / All / Can't Select Just One	Don't Know
Total Responding		7	3	1	4	3
Gender:	Male	7	3	1	5	2
	Female	6	2	0	4	5
Age:	18 to 27	6	2	1	1	1
	28 to 46	8	3	1	3	3
	47 to 65	6	1	0	8	4
	66 to 98	6	4	0	8	9
Income:	Under $20,000	5	3	2	6	3
	$20,000 to $40,000	6	2	0	3	2
	$40,000 to $60,000	7	1	0	5	2
	$60,000 or more	14	3	0	4	1
Education:	High School or Less	4	3	1	4	4
	Some College	9	0	0	4	5
	College Graduate	9	3	0	4	1
Marital Status:	Married	7	1	0	5	3
	Not Married	6	4	1	3	4
Have Kids Under 18:	Yes	8	3	1	2	2
	No	6	2	0	6	4
Ethnicity:	White	7	3	0	4	4
	Black	7	1	0	9	2
	Hispanic	3	6	3	0	5
Region:	Northeast	7	4	0	2	5
	South	5	1	0	3	3
	Central	8	4	1	6	3
	West	7	1	1	5	2
Community Type:	Urban	8	3	1	5	3
	Suburban	8	3	0	2	3
	Rural	5	3	1	5	4
Voter Registration:	Not Registered	4	3	0	4	4
	Democrat	5	4	1	3	3
	Republican	12	3	0	6	4
	Independent	7	0	0	2	2
Denominational Affiliation:	Protestant	8	2	0	4	4
	Catholic	7	4	1	3	2
	Baptist	8	1	1	2	2
	Mainline Protestant	10	3	0	4	5
Churched:	Yes	7	2	1	4	4
	No	6	3	1	7	1
Born Again	Yes	6	1	0	3	5
	No	7	4	1	5	3
	Evangelical	6	1	0	1	8

TABLE 37

Let's say that you learned the chief executive or director of your favorite charity earned more than $100,000 a year at that job. Would that make you more likely to donate money to that charity, less likely, or not make a difference to you?

		N	More Likely	No Difference	Less Likely	Don't Know
Total Responding		1004	6%	32%	59%	3%
Gender:	Male	492	7	35	55	3
	Female	512	5	28	63	4
Age:	18 to 27	188	11	38	50	0
	28-46	404	7	33	56	4
	47-65	223	4	24	67	5
	66-98	130	4	26	67	3
Income:	Under $20,000	213	9	31	58	2
	$20,000 to $40,000	349	6	30	61	3
	$40,000 to $60,000	163	5	28	64	2
	$60,000 or more	149	3	45	49	3
Education:	High School or Less	441	8	32	55	4
	Some College	237	6	27	65	1
	College Graduate	317	3	34	59	4
Marital Status:	Married	538	5	30	62	3
	Not Married	461	8	34	55	3
Have Kids Under 18:	Yes	364	7	31	58	4
	No	633	6	33	59	2
Ethnicity:	White	743	6	26	65	4
	Black	124	10	52	35	3
	Hispanic	85	9	39	50	2
Region:	Northeast	222	5	38	52	5
	South	210	9	33	54	4
	Central	402	7	27	64	2
	West	170	3	34	61	2
Community Type:	Urban	411	8	36	53	3
	Suburban	212	4	35	57	4
	Rural	372	5	26	66	3
Voter Registration:	Not Registered	243	9	31	56	4
	Reg. Democrat	315	6	32	58	4
	Reg. Republican	244	3	32	63	2
	Reg. Independent	143	5	35	55	4
Denominational Affiliation:	Protestant	541	7	28	62	3
	Catholic	280	7	36	54	4
	Baptist	168	9	34	54	3
	Mainline Protestant	162	5	23	70	2
Churched:	Yes	774	6	32	59	3
	No	205	5	31	61	4
Born Again:	Yes	373	7	30	62	2
	No	630	6	33	57	4
	Evangelical	118	7	23	69	2

TABLE 38   203

Do you agree strongly, agree somewhat, disagree somewhat, or disagree strongly with the following statement: "There is a God who hears people's prayers and has the power to answer those prayers"?

		N	Agree Strongly	Agree Somewhat	Disagree Somewhat	Disagree Strongly	Don't Know
Total Responding		1004	71%	15%	4%	5%	4%
Gender:	Male	492	62	20	7	7	4
	Female	512	80	11	2	3	4
Age:	18 to 27	188	61	27	5	5	2
	28-46	404	71	15	5	5	4
	47-65	223	73	12	3	7	5
	66-98	130	81	8	3	4	4
Income:	Under $20,000	213	73	14	3	4	5
	$20,000 to $40,000	349	74	15	4	5	2
	$40,000 to $60,000	163	71	16	3	8	2
	$60,000 or more	149	61	22	8	4	4
Education:	High School or Less	441	76	14	3	4	3
	Some College	237	67	17	8	4	4
	College Graduate	317	69	15	4	7	5
Marital Status:	Married	538	77	12	4	4	3
	Not Married	461	65	20	5	5	5
Have Kids Under 18:	Yes	364	78	14	4	3	1
	No	633	68	16	5	6	5
Ethnicity:	White	743	71	15	5	5	4
	Black	124	90	6	0	1	2
	Hispanic	85	61	26	6	6	2
Region:	Northeast	222	68	20	3	4	5
	South	210	83	7	4	2	4
	Central	402	75	15	4	3	4
	West	170	53	22	7	14	4
Community Type:	Urban	411	72	16	4	5	4
	Suburban	212	68	15	6	6	5
	Rural	372	73	15	3	4	4
Voter Registration:	Not Registered	243	70	16	4	6	4
	Reg. Democrat	315	73	13	3	6	4
	Reg. Republican	244	78	12	5	4	2
	Reg. Independent	143	61	23	8	3	5
Denominational Affiliation:	Protestant	541	82	11	3	2	3
	Catholic	280	71	21	3	3	2
	Baptist	168	91	7	0	0	1
	Mainline Protestant	162	77	14	3	1	5
Churched:	Yes	774	79	14	2	3	2
	No	205	45	21	12	12	10
Born Again:	Yes	373	95	4	0	0	0
	No	630	57	22	7	8	6
	Evangelical	118	100	0	0	0	0

TABLE 39

Do you agree strongly, agree somewhat, disagree somewhat, or disagree strongly with the following statement: "Overall, you expect ministers to live up to a higher moral and ethical standard than you expect of other people"?

		N	Agree Strongly	Agree Somewhat	Disagree Somewhat	Disagree Strongly	Don't Know
Total Responding		1004	51%	22%	14%	11%	2%
Gender:	Male	492	50	23	14	11	2
	Female	512	51	22	14	12	2
Age:	18 to 27	188	43	26	17	13	1
	28-46	404	43	27	17	13	1
	47-65	223	61	19	10	7	3
	66-98	130	66	11	10	11	2
Income:	Under $20,000	213	62	18	7	12	1
	$20,000 to $40,000	349	51	20	15	13	1
	$40,000 to $60,000	163	43	30	16	9	1
	$60,000 or more	149	43	30	17	10	1
Education:	High School or Less	441	57	17	12	12	2
	Some College	237	49	27	11	11	1
	College Graduate	317	43	26	18	11	2
Marital Status:	Married	538	49	22	14	12	2
	Not Married	461	52	22	14	11	1
Have Kids Under 18:	Yes	364	44	24	17	13	2
	No	633	54	21	12	11	2
Ethnicity:	White	743	47	24	14	13	2
	Black	124	68	16	6	8	3
	Hispanic	85	53	14	28	6	0
Region:	Northeast	222	53	22	14	10	1
	South	210	54	20	12	11	3
	Central	402	48	24	14	13	2
	West	170	49	21	17	12	0
Community Type:	Urban	411	53	21	12	11	2
	Suburban	212	46	24	18	10	2
	Rural	372	50	23	14	13	1
Voter Registration:	Not Registered	243	51	22	10	16	1
	Reg. Democrat	315	55	22	15	7	1
	Reg. Republican	244	50	20	15	14	1
	Reg. Independent	143	43	25	19	11	2
Denominational Affiliation:	Protestant	541	50	23	13	12	1
	Catholic	280	58	19	14	7	1
	Baptist	168	57	25	8	9	1
	Mainline Protestant	162	44	29	16	10	1
Churched:	Yes	774	51	24	14	10	1
	No	205	49	17	13	17	4
Born Again:	Yes	373	54	21	12	12	2
	No	630	48	23	15	11	2
	Evangelical	118	54	24	7	14	0

TABLE 40   205

Do you agree strongly, agree somewhat, disagree somewhat, or disagree strongly with the following statement: "Jesus sometimes made mistakes"?

		N	Agree Strongly	Agree Somewhat	Disagree Somewhat	Disagree Strongly	Don't Know
Total Responding		1004	18%	26%	7%	40%	9%
Gender:	Male	492	19	30	8	35	8
	Female	512	17	22	7	44	10
Age:	18 to 27	188	22	34	6	32	5
	28-46	404	19	27	10	38	7
	47-65	223	15	22	6	44	13
	66-98	130	14	19	6	51	10
Income:	Under $20,000	213	18	23	5	46	7
	$20,000 to $40,000	349	15	25	10	44	7
	$40,000 to $60,000	163	18	31	6	40	6
	$60,000 or more	149	27	29	8	25	10
Education:	High School or Less	441	18	25	7	44	7
	Some College	237	15	27	8	42	9
	College Graduate	317	21	28	8	32	12
Marital Status:	Married	538	17	23	8	45	8
	Not Married	461	19	30	7	34	10
Have Kids Under 18:	Yes	364	16	24	6	48	5
	No	633	19	27	8	35	11
Ethnicity:	White	743	19	27	8	36	9
	Black	124	12	10	5	68	6
	Hispanic	85	17	32	8	39	5
Region:	Northeast	222	20	32	8	31	10
	South	210	14	14	8	52	11
	Central	402	16	26	8	42	7
	West	170	25	33	4	29	9
Community Type:	Urban	411	19	25	7	40	8
	Suburban	212	19	28	10	32	12
	Rural	372	17	25	6	44	7
Voter Registration:	Not Registered	243	18	23	9	40	10
	Reg. Democrat	315	16	27	7	42	7
	Reg. Republican	244	16	24	8	44	7
	Reg. Independent	143	23	31	8	30	8
Denominational Affiliation:	Protestant	541	15	21	6	52	6
	Catholic	280	20	33	11	30	5
	Baptist	168	13	13	6	64	3
	Mainline Protestant	162	19	30	8	34	9
Churched:	Yes	774	17	24	7	46	6
	No	205	24	33	7	16	20
Born Again:	Yes	373	10	14	7	67	2
	No	630	23	33	8	24	13
	Evangelical	118	6	5	2	87	0

TABLE 41

Do you agree strongly, agree somewhat, disagree somewhat, or disagree strongly with the following statement: "Jesus will come back"?

		N	Agree Strongly	Agree Somewhat	Disagree Somewhat	Disagree Strongly	Don't Know
Total Responding		1004	58%	13%	9%	11%	10%
Gender:	Male	492	51	15	11	13	9
	Female	512	64	10	6	9	11
Age:	18 to 27	188	50	16	14	10	10
	28-46	404	56	17	7	10	9
	47-65	223	59	7	7	13	14
	66-98	130	69	6	4	14	5
Income:	Under $20,000	213	62	11	8	10	9
	$20,000 to $40,000	349	61	12	8	10	9
	$40,000 to $60,000	163	60	15	6	12	7
	$60,000 or more	149	44	15	13	13	15
Education:	High School or Less	441	64	11	9	9	7
	Some College	237	59	13	9	9	11
	College Graduate	317	48	14	8	15	15
Marital Status:	Married	538	62	10	7	12	9
	Not Married	461	52	15	11	10	12
Have Kids Under 18:	Yes	364	63	14	9	9	6
	No	633	55	11	9	12	13
Ethnicity:	White	743	56	13	8	11	12
	Black	124	84	5	0	8	2
	Hispanic	85	45	21	20	8	6
Region:	Northeast	222	45	15	9	16	15
	South	210	70	8	4	8	10
	Central	402	65	12	9	7	7
	West	170	41	16	13	18	11
Community Type:	Urban	411	57	13	7	12	12
	Suburban	212	44	18	9	15	14
	Rural	372	66	9	10	8	7
Voter Registration:	Not Registered	243	57	14	9	12	9
	Reg. Democrat	315	58	13	7	13	8
	Reg. Republican	244	63	10	9	6	11
	Reg. Independent	143	52	15	12	9	13
Denominational Affiliation:	Protestant	541	74	9	5	5	7
	Catholic	280	49	20	13	8	10
	Baptist	168	87	6	1	3	3
	Mainline Protestant	162	60	11	10	5	14
Churched:	Yes	774	66	12	7	8	7
	No	205	28	14	15	21	22
Born Again:	Yes	373	93	4	1	1	1
	No	630	37	18	13	17	16
	Evangelical	118	99	0	0	1	0

TABLE 42   207

Do you agree strongly, agree somewhat, disagree somewhat, or disagree strongly with the following statement: "It does not matter what religious faith you follow because all faiths teach similar lessons about life"?

		N	Agree Strongly	Agree Somewhat	Disagree Somewhat	Disagree Strongly	Don't Know
Total Responding		1004	38%	24%	10%	24%	4%
Gender:	Male	492	36	27	8	25	4
	Female	512	40	20	12	24	4
Age:	18 to 27	188	39	27	10	23	2
	28-46	404	35	26	11	26	3
	47-65	223	46	17	8	25	4
	66-98	130	37	19	9	29	6
Income:	Under $20,000	213	40	20	9	27	4
	$20,000 to $40,000	349	42	24	7	25	2
	$40,000 to $60,000	163	31	25	16	27	2
	$60,000 or more	149	38	29	8	21	4
Education:	High School or Less	441	39	22	11	24	5
	Some College	237	42	23	6	25	4
	College Graduate	317	35	27	12	25	1
Marital Status:	Married	538	36	23	10	27	4
	Not Married	461	41	24	10	22	4
Have Kids Under 18:	Yes	364	35	25	10	28	2
	No	633	40	23	10	23	4
Ethnicity:	White	743	37	24	11	23	5
	Black	124	40	18	9	31	2
	Hispanic	85	54	27	0	19	0
Region:	Northeast	222	42	32	7	17	2
	South	210	36	15	13	33	5
	Central	402	39	20	11	25	4
	West	170	35	31	9	22	3
Community Type:	Urban	411	39	22	9	27	3
	Suburban	212	39	27	9	21	5
	Rural	372	37	24	11	24	4
Voter Registration:	Not Registered	243	37	22	11	27	3
	Reg. Democrat	315	42	21	9	25	3
	Reg. Republican	244	34	24	11	29	2
	Reg. Independent	143	40	30	10	16	3
Denominational Affiliation:	Protestant	541	33	19	13	31	4
	Catholic	280	48	28	7	14	3
	Baptist	168	30	15	14	40	2
	Mainline Protestant	162	41	25	12	16	6
Churched:	Yes	774	36	23	10	28	3
	No	205	49	27	8	11	4
Born Again:	Yes	373	25	18	14	40	3
	No	630	46	27	8	15	4
	Evangelical	118	7	4	10	75	4

TABLE 43

Do you agree strongly, agree somewhat, disagree somewhat, or disagree strongly with the following statement: "When Jesus was on earth, He was as much a human being as you are"?

		N	Agree Strongly	Agree Somewhat	Disagree Somewhat	Disagree Strongly	Don't Know
Total Responding		1004	66%	16%	5%	8%	5%
Gender:	Male	492	61	19	6	8	6
	Female	512	71	12	4	8	5
Age:	18 to 27	188	56	25	7	8	3
	28-46	404	67	15	6	8	3
	47-65	223	66	14	4	6	10
	66-98	130	75	9	1	10	4
Income:	Under $20,000	213	71	10	4	9	5
	$20,000 to $40,000	349	66	19	6	6	4
	$40,000 to $60,000	163	63	14	7	11	4
	$60,000 or more	149	64	19	3	6	9
Education:	High School or Less	441	71	14	6	6	4
	Some College	237	63	22	3	8	4
	College Graduate	317	62	14	6	9	8
Marital Status:	Married	538	73	13	4	6	4
	Not Married	461	58	19	7	9	7
Have Kids Under 18:	Yes	364	70	14	6	8	2
	No	633	64	17	5	7	8
Ethnicity:	White	743	69	15	4	6	6
	Black	124	72	6	8	10	4
	Hispanic	85	46	34	5	13	3
Region:	Northeast	222	62	16	5	9	8
	South	210	72	9	6	9	4
	Central	402	69	14	5	8	5
	West	170	57	26	6	4	6
Community Type:	Urban	411	68	14	4	8	6
	Suburban	212	59	17	9	9	6
	Rural	372	68	17	4	7	4
Voter Registration:	Not Registered	243	57	19	7	12	5
	Reg. Democrat	315	69	12	6	7	5
	Reg. Republican	244	73	15	5	5	3
	Reg. Independent	143	63	21	3	6	7
Denominational Affiliation:	Protestant	541	74	10	5	7	4
	Catholic	280	61	21	5	9	4
	Baptist	168	77	7	5	8	3
	Mainline Protestant	162	73	11	6	7	3
Churched:	Yes	774	69	14	5	8	4
	No	205	54	24	4	7	11
Born Again:	Yes	373	78	8	5	6	2
	No	630	59	20	5	8	7
	Evangelical	118	85	5	3	5	1

TABLE 44   209

During the past year have you "been regularly mentored or discipled in your religious faith by someone who is more mature or experienced in that faith"?

		N	Yes	No	Don't Know
Total Responding		1004	31%	66%	3%
Gender:	Male	492	28	69	2
	Female	512	33	63	4
Age:	18 to 27	188	40	60	0
	28-46	404	29	68	3
	47-65	223	29	67	4
	66-98	130	27	66	7
Income:	Under $20,000	213	31	65	3
	$20,000 to $40,000	349	34	63	3
	$40,000 to $60,000	163	28	70	2
	$60,000 or more	149	28	71	1
Education:	High School or Less	441	32	64	4
	Some College	237	30	67	3
	College Graduate	317	30	68	2
Marital Status:	Married	538	31	66	4
	Not Married	461	31	66	3
Have Kids Under 18:	Yes	364	38	60	2
	No	633	27	70	4
Ethnicity:	White	743	28	69	3
	Black	124	49	48	4
	Hispanic	85	24	72	4
Region:	Northeast	222	23	71	5
	South	210	36	59	5
	Central	402	32	65	3
	West	170	29	70	0
Community Type:	Urban	411	30	67	3
	Suburban	212	28	67	4
	Rural	372	33	65	3
Voter Registration:	Not Registered	243	29	67	3
	Reg. Democrat	315	34	63	3
	Reg. Republican	244	31	65	4
	Reg. Independent	143	27	71	2
Denominational	Protestant	541	36	60	3
Affiliation:	Catholic	280	27	69	4
	Baptist	168	47	52	1
	Mainline Protestant	162	29	66	5
Churched:	Yes	774	37	60	4
	No	205	9	89	2
Born Again:	Yes	373	50	47	3
	No	630	19	77	4
	Evangelical	118	62	36	2

TABLE 45

During the past year have you "been a committed mentor or discipler of someone else to help them mature in their religious faith"?

		N	Yes	No	Don't Know
Total Responding		1004	24%	74%	2%
Gender:	Male	492	19	80	1
	Female	512	30	68	3
Age:	18 to 27	188	17	83	0
	28-46	404	24	74	2
	47-65	223	27	71	1
	66-98	130	29	68	3
Income:	Under $20,000	213	26	72	2
	$20,000 to $40,000	349	26	73	1
	$40,000 to $60,000	153	22	77	1
	$60,000 or more	149	22	77	1
Education:	High School or Less	441	25	73	3
	Some College	237	26	73	1
	College Graduate	317	22	77	1
Marital Status:	Married	538	27	71	2
	Not Married	461	20	78	2
Have Kids Under 18:	Yes	364	31	67	2
	No	633	20	78	2
Ethnicity:	White	743	24	74	1
	Black	124	38	59	3
	Hispanic	85	11	87	2
Region:	Northeast	222	16	82	2
	South	210	33	64	3
	Central	402	25	73	2
	West	170	22	78	0
Community Type:	Urban	411	23	75	1
	Suburban	212	23	74	3
	Rural	372	25	73	2
Voter Registration:	Not Registered	243	19	78	3
	Reg. Democrat	315	30	69	1
	Reg. Republican	244	26	72	2
	Reg. Independent	143	20	80	0
Denominational	Protestant	541	33	64	2
Affiliation:	Catholic	280	13	85	2
	Baptist	168	39	59	2
	Mainline Protestant	162	26	71	3
Churched:	Yes	774	30	68	2
	No	205	3	95	1
Born Again:	Yes	373	44	54	2
	No	630	13	86	2
	Evangelical	118	58	40	2

TABLE 46 211

During the past year have you "shared your religious faith with someone who had different beliefs and found that as a result that person changed their views and accepted the same beliefs as you for their own life"?

		N	Yes	No	Don't Know
Total Responding		1004	16%	80%	4%
Gender:	Male	492	15	82	3
	Female	512	18	78	5
Age:	18 to 27	188	22	75	3
	28-46	404	15	82	4
	47-65	223	17	80	3
	66-98	130	12	82	6
Income:	Under $20,000	213	20	78	2
	$20,000 to $40,000	349	21	74	5
	$40,000 to $60,000	163	12	86	2
	$60,000 or more	149	11	87	2
Education:	High School or Less	441	19	77	4
	Some College	237	15	82	3
	College Graduate	317	14	83	3
Marital Status:	Married	538	16	81	4
	Not Married	461	17	79	4
Have Kids Under 18:	Yes	364	17	79	4
	No	633	16	81	3
Ethnicity:	White	743	15	81	4
	Black	124	30	66	4
	Hispanic	85	18	82	0
Region:	Northeast	222	12	84	4
	South	210	24	69	7
	Central	402	16	81	3
	West	170	11	86	2
Community Type:	Urban	411	20	76	4
	Suburban	212	11	86	3
	Rural	372	16	80	4
Voter Registration:	Not Registered	243	19	76	5
	Reg. Democrat	315	18	80	2
	Reg. Republican	244	14	81	5
	Reg. Independent	143	16	81	4
Denominational Affiliation:	Protestant	541	20	75	4
	Catholic	280	12	85	2
	Baptist	168	26	73	2
	Mainline Protestant	162	10	82	8
Churched:	Yes	774	18	78	4
	No	205	7	92	1
Born Again:	Yes	373	25	70	6
	No	630	11	86	3
	Evangelical	118	31	62	7

TABLE 47

During the past year have you "participated in a small group that meets on a regular basis for Christian teaching, prayer or personal encouragement, other than a Sunday School class"?

		N	Yes	No	Don't Know
Total Responding		1004	28%	71%	0%
Gender:	Male	492	22	77	0
	Female	512	34	66	1
Age:	18 to 27	188	27	73	0
	28-46	404	28	72	0
	47-65	223	29	71	0
	66-98	130	28	70	2
Income:	Under $20,000	213	30	70	0
	$20,000 to $40,000	349	29	71	0
	$40,000 to $60,000	163	30	69	0
	$60,000 or more	149	22	78	0
Education:	High School or Less	441	27	72	1
	Some College	237	26	74	0
	College Graduate	317	31	69	0
Marital Status:	Married	538	29	70	0
	Not Married	461	27	73	0
Have Kids Under 18:	Yes	364	31	68	0
	No	633	26	74	0
Ethnicity:	White	743	28	72	0
	Black	124	40	59	1
	Hispanic	85	20	80	0
Region:	Northeast	222	19	80	0
	South	210	35	65	0
	Central	402	33	66	1
	West	170	19	81	0
Community Type:	Urban	411	28	71	0
	Suburban	212	28	72	0
	Rural	372	28	71	1
Voter Registration:	Not Registered	243	25	75	0
	Reg. Democrat	315	27	72	0
	Reg. Republican	244	39	60	1
	Reg. Independent	143	21	79	0
Denominational	Protestant	541	37	63	1
Affiliation:	Catholic	280	22	78	0
	Baptist	168	42	58	0
	Mainline Protestant	162	30	70	1
Churched:	Yes	774	35	65	0
	No	205	3	97	0
Born Again:	Yes	373	45	55	0
	No	630	18	81	1
	Evangelical	118	63	36	1

TABLE 48   213

When you meet for the religious mentoring or discipling process, do you usually spend time "praying together"?

		N	Yes	No	Don't Know
Total Responding		395	79%	20%	0%
Gender:	Male	170	75	25	0
	Female	225	82	17	0
Age:	18 to 27	83	67	33	0
	28-46	151	84	16	0
	47-65	86	83	17	0
	66-98	51	79	21	0
Income:	Under $20,000	85	82	18	0
	$20,000 to $40,000	150	76	24	0
	$40,000 to $60,000	61	83	17	0
	$60,000 or more	54	86	14	0
Education:	High School or Less	182	72	28	0
	Some College	92	86	14	0
	College Graduate	119	85	15	0
Marital Status:	Married	219	84	16	0
	Not Married	174	73	27	0
Have Kids Under 18:	Yes	176	81	19	0
	No	217	78	22	0
Ethnicity:	White	273	81	19	0
	Black	72	85	15	0
	Hispanic	26	60	40	0
Region:	Northeast	67	70	30	0
	South	96	85	15	0
	Central	171	82	18	0
	West	61	73	27	0
Community Type:	Urban	159	77	23	0
	Suburban	80	83	17	0
	Rural	153	79	21	0
Voter Registration:	Not Registered	90	72	27	1
	Reg. Democrat	144	77	23	0
	Reg. Republican	97	89	11	0
	Reg. Independent	47	78	22	0
Denominational	Protestant	261	85	15	0
Affiliation:	Catholic	95	64	36	0
	Baptist	94	86	14	0
	Mainline Protestant	66	80	18	1
Churched:	Yes	366	81	18	0
	No	24	51	49	0
Born Again:	Yes	234	89	11	0
	No	161	65	35	0
	Evangelical	89	98	1	1

TABLE 49

When you meet for the religious mentoring or discipling process, do you usually spend time "reading from the Bible together"?

		N	Yes	No
Total Responding		395	68%	32%
Gender:	Male	170	64	36
	Female	225	71	29
Age:	18 to 27	83	56	44
	28-46	151	71	29
	47-65	86	73	27
	66-98	51	73	27
Income:	Under $20,000	85	70	30
	$20,000 to $40,000	150	73	27
	$40,000 to $60,000	61	72	28
	$60,000 or more	54	63	37
Education:	High School or Less	182	66	34
	Some College	92	70	30
	College Graduate	119	70	30
Marital Status:	Married	219	72	28
	Not Married	174	63	37
Have Kids Under 18:	Yes	176	69	31
	No	217	67	33
Ethnicity:	White	273	67	33
	Black	72	80	20
	Hispanic	26	62	38
Region:	Northeast	67	58	42
	South	96	71	29
	Central	171	73	27
	West	61	62	38
Community Type:	Urban	159	68	32
	Suburban	80	63	37
	Rural	153	70	30
Voter Registration:	Not Registered	90	64	36
	Reg. Democrat	144	70	30
	Reg. Republican	97	73	27
	Reg. Independent	47	66	34
Denominational	Protestant	261	76	24
Affiliation:	Catholic	95	50	50
	Baptist	94	83	17
	Mainline Protestant	66	68	32
Churched:	Yes	366	71	29
	No	24	28	72
Born Again:	Yes	234	81	19
	No	161	50	50
	Evangelical	89	91	9

TABLE 50   215

When you meet for the religious mentoring or discipling process, do you usually spend time "discussing what is going on in your lives and how that relates to your faith"?

		N	Yes	No	Don't Know
Total Responding		395	75%	24%	1%
Gender:	Male	170	73	27	1
	Female	225	77	23	1
Age:	18 to 27	83	67	33	0
	28-46	151	80	19	1
	47-65	86	76	24	0
	66-98	51	72	27	2
Income:	Under $20,000	85	72	26	2
	$20,000 to $40,000	150	76	24	0
	$40,000 to $60,000	61	75	24	1
	$60,000 or more	54	83	17	0
Education:	High School or Less	182	71	28	1
	Some College	92	72	28	0
	College Graduate	119	84	15	1
Marital Status:	Married	219	78	21	1
	Not Married	174	71	29	0
Have Kids Under 18:	Yes	176	77	23	0
	No	217	73	26	1
Ethnicity:	White	273	76	23	1
	Black	72	82	18	0
	Hispanic	26	53	47	0
Region:	Northeast	67	70	28	2
	South	96	70	29	1
	Central	171	78	22	0
	West	61	79	20	1
Community Type:	Urban	159	80	19	1
	Suburban	80	83	16	1
	Rural	153	66	33	1
Voter Registration:	Not Registered	90	71	29	0
	Reg. Democrat	144	78	21	1
	Reg. Republican	97	79	20	1
	Reg. Independent	47	76	24	0
Denominational	Protestant	261	79	20	1
Affiliation:	Catholic	95	65	34	1
	Baptist	94	84	15	1
	Mainline Protestant	66	78	21	1
Churched:	Yes	366	76	24	1
	No	24	69	31	0
Born Again:	Yes	234	82	17	1
	No	161	64	35	0
	Evangelical	89	86	14	0

How many people usually meet together to participate in that mentoring or discipling process?

		N	1	2	3	4	5-9	10-14	15-19	20+	Don't Know
Total Responding		395	1%	11%	5%	7%	19%	16%	9%	16%	15%
Gender:	Male	170	1	13	5	9	19	16	10	13	15
	Female	225	2	10	6	6	19	16	8	18	16
Age:	18 to 27	83	2	16	5	6	10	20	11	17	13
	28 to 46	151	1	10	8	12	22	15	6	14	13
	47 to 65	86	2	10	4	2	24	13	14	19	13
	66 to 98	51	0	9	2	6	17	17	5	15	29
Income:	Under $20,000	85	2	7	4	12	15	11	9	17	24
	$20,000 to $40,000	150	1	15	7	3	18	20	9	14	13
	$40,000 to $60,000	61	1	12	4	6	21	19	11	14	11
	$60,000 or more	54	1	3	6	12	28	13	11	20	6
Education:	High School or Less	182	2	14	5	6	14	13	7	18	22
	Some College	92	1	11	7	7	25	17	10	11	11
	College Graduate	119	1	9	5	9	22	19	10	17	8
Marital Status:	Married	219	2	10	6	7	24	15	8	15	11
	Not Married	174	0	13	4	7	13	16	9	17	20
Have Kids Under 18:	Yes	176	2	12	7	10	18	14	8	18	12
	No	217	1	11	5	5	20	17	10	14	18
Ethnicity:	White	273	2	12	6	6	21	17	7	15	13
	Black	72	0	9	4	7	16	18	11	16	18
	Hispanic	26	0	0	0	18	18	0	13	19	31
Region:	Northeast	67	0	13	9	7	21	14	7	8	21
	South	96	0	11	4	6	21	13	8	21	16
	Central	171	2	10	6	7	17	20	11	15	14
	West	61	4	15	4	9	20	10	4	20	14
Community Type:	Urban	159	2	13	6	8	18	15	5	16	18
	Suburban	80	1	10	5	6	24	9	10	20	15
	Rural	153	1	11	5	7	17	19	11	14	13
Voter Registration:	Not Registered	90	1	12	6	7	11	12	10	21	19
	Democrat	144	2	12	4	9	23	14	7	13	16
	Republican	97	1	11	4	6	24	23	8	13	10
	Independent	47	0	12	10	5	16	17	10	18	11
Denominational Affiliation:	Protestant	261	2	13	5	6	20	16	9	16	13
	Catholic	95	1	8	8	8	21	18	6	11	19
	Baptist	94	0	8	2	6	20	21	13	15	13
	Mainline Protestant	66	2	13	3	6	20	16	12	13	15
Churched:	Yes	366	0	10	5	7	20	17	9	17	15
	No	24	14	27	14	13	8	5	5	0	14
Born Again	Yes	234	1	10	3	9	21	18	11	16	11
	No	161	2	13	9	5	16	13	5	16	22
	Evangelical	89	1	11	4	3	22	20	14	17	8

About how many hours a week, on average, do you spend involved in the mentoring or discipling process?

		N	One	Two	Three	Four	Five or More	Don't Know
Total Responding		395	33%	25%	11%	7%	14%	10%
Gender:	Male	170	30	21	17	8	17	7
	Female	225	35	28	8	6	12	13
Age:	18 to 27	83	24	22	14	8	19	14
	28 to 46	151	37	29	11	4	15	3
	47 to 65	86	39	20	14	7	11	9
	66 to 98	51	30	27	7	8	8	19
Income:	Under $20,000	85	26	23	11	7	19	13
	$20,000 to $40,000	150	28	30	12	7	14	9
	$40,000 to $60,000	61	35	24	18	7	11	4
	$60,000 or more	54	49	15	9	6	13	8
Education:	High School or Less	182	29	23	12	9	14	13
	Some College	92	39	31	8	4	8	10
	College Graduate	119	35	23	13	6	18	5
Marital Status:	Married	219	37	24	11	6	13	9
	Not Married	174	28	25	12	7	15	12
Have Kids Under 18:	Yes	176	34	25	10	7	16	7
	No	217	32	24	13	6	12	13
Ethnicity:	White	273	36	23	11	6	14	10
	Black	72	21	30	12	7	21	10
	Hispanic	26	38	25	0	22	0	16
Region:	Northeast	67	29	31	7	6	10	17
	South	96	38	17	5	8	22	10
	Central	171	35	29	14	5	10	6
	West	61	23	18	18	12	15	15
Community Type:	Urban	159	30	25	14	7	15	10
	Suburban	80	37	26	7	11	10	10
	Rural	153	34	24	12	4	16	11
Voter Registration:	Not Registered	90	26	27	6	9	19	12
	Democrat	144	34	21	10	7	16	13
	Republican	97	33	32	18	3	9	6
	Independent	47	38	20	14	6	10	12
Denominational Affiliation:	Protestant	261	33	29	9	5	16	7
	Catholic	95	34	19	19	9	6	13
	Baptist	94	29	34	5	7	17	8
	Mainline Protestant	66	49	28	9	2	3	8
Churched:	Yes	366	32	26	12	7	14	9
	No	24	44	8	10	3	13	22
Born Again	Yes	234	32	29	12	8	15	5
	No	161	34	19	11	5	12	18
	Evangelical	89	29	35	11	7	13	5

Table 53

Overall, how helpful have you found the mentoring or discipling process to be?

		N	Very Helpful to You	Somewhat Helpful	Not Too Helpful	Or Not at All Helpful to You	Don't Know
Total Responding		395	60%	33%	2%	3%	2%
Gender:	Male	170	54	36	5	3	3
	Female	225	64	31	1	3	2
Age:	18 to 27	83	52	40	1	5	2
	28 to 46	151	59	35	3	2	1
	47 to 65	86	63	27	3	4	3
	66 to 98	51	71	24	0	0	5
Income:	Under $20,000	85	61	32	3	1	3
	$20,000 to $40,000	150	64	31	0	5	1
	$40,000 to $60,000	61	52	40	5	3	1
	$60,000 or more	54	55	33	8	1	1
Education:	High School or Less	182	63	28	2	4	3
	Some College	92	56	37	2	2	3
	College Graduate	119	57	36	4	2	1
Marital Status:	Married	219	59	35	3	1	2
	Not Married	174	61	30	2	5	2
Have Kids Under 18:	Yes	176	62	31	3	2	1
	No	217	58	34	2	3	3
Ethnicity:	White	273	59	34	2	3	3
	Black	72	73	25	2	0	0
	Hispanic	26	44	40	0	16	0
Region:	Northeast	67	60	30	3	1	5
	South	96	69	27	1	0	3
	Central	171	55	38	1	3	2
	West	61	56	30	7	8	0
Community Type:	Urban	159	59	36	1	2	3
	Suburban	80	61	28	7	2	2
	Rural	153	59	33	2	4	2
Voter Registration:	Not Registered	90	62	30	1	4	3
	Democrat	144	62	31	1	3	3
	Republican	97	56	39	0	3	2
	Independent	47	54	29	14	2	2
Denominational Affiliation:	Protestant	261	64	33	2	0	2
	Catholic	95	46	41	2	7	4
	Baptist	94	68	31	1	0	0
	Mainline Protestant	66	57	38	3	0	2
Churched:	Yes	366	60	32	3	2	2
	No	24	51	37	0	8	5
Born Again	Yes	234	67	30	2	0	1
	No	161	49	37	3	6	4
	Evangelical	89	74	26	0	0	0

TABLE 54   219

On issues related to "finances and the economy," do you consider yourself to be mostly conservative, mostly liberal, or mostly in between?

		N	Mostly Conservative	In-Between	Mostly Liberal	Don't Know
Total Responding		761	47%	37%	12%	4%
Gender:	Male	369	50	34	13	3
	Female	392	45	40	11	5
Age:	18 to 27	100	32	45	21	2
	28-46	302	49	36	12	2
	47-65	195	52	37	8	3
	66-98	115	51	34	5	10
Income:	Under $20,000	146	35	48	13	4
	$20,000 to $40,000	248	49	37	13	2
	$40,000 to $60,000	136	47	38	10	4
	$60,000 or more	132	55	33	11	1
Education:	High School or Less	308	40	44	10	6
	Some College	183	52	34	13	2
	College Graduate	262	53	31	13	3
Marital Status:	Married	454	52	36	8	4
	Not Married	304	40	39	17	4
Have Kids Under 18:	Yes	275	47	38	13	2
	No	479	48	36	11	4
Ethnicity:	White	579	51	35	10	4
	Black	94	30	44	23	4
	Hispanic	52	48	44	8	0
Region:	Northeast	155	44	32	19	5
	South	154	52	34	9	5
	Central	318	47	39	10	4
	West	134	46	42	10	2
Community Type:	Urban	317	42	42	13	3
	Suburban	169	56	29	11	4
	Rural	268	49	36	10	5
Voter Registration:	Not Registered	0	0	0	0	0
	Reg. Democrat	315	35	42	18	5
	Reg. Republican	244	67	27	4	2
	Reg. Independent	143	46	40	12	2
Denominational Affiliation:	Protestant	430	53	34	9	4
	Catholic	208	39	46	11	3
	Baptist	132	48	37	11	4
	Mainline Protestant	141	51	36	10	3
Churched:	Yes	613	48	37	11	4
	No	135	45	38	14	3
Born Again:	Yes	306	51	37	8	4
	No	455	45	37	14	4
	Evangelical	98	66	26	5	3

TABLE 55

On issues related to "domestic and social policies," do you consider yourself to be mostly conservative, mostly liberal, or mostly in between?

		N	Mostly Conservative	In-Between	Mostly Liberal	Don't Know
Total Responding		761	35%	41%	20%	4%
Gender:	Male	369	40	34	24	2
	Female	392	31	47	17	6
Age:	18 to 27	100	19	50	28	2
	28-46	302	33	41	24	1
	47-65	195	43	35	18	5
	66-98	115	44	40	8	9
Income:	Under $20,000	146	29	48	16	7
	$20,000 to $40,000	248	39	41	19	2
	$40,000 to $60,000	136	36	37	25	2
	$60,000 or more	132	31	43	26	1
Education:	High School or Less	308	33	48	12	7
	Some College	183	38	39	21	2
	College Graduate	262	35	33	31	1
Marital Status:	Married	454	40	39	18	3
	Not Married	304	28	43	24	4
Have Kids Under 18:	Yes	275	35	45	18	2
	No	479	35	38	22	4
Ethnicity:	White	579	39	39	19	3
	Black	94	26	48	20	7
	Hispanic	52	21	41	35	3
Region:	Northeast	155	35	35	24	6
	South	154	38	38	20	4
	Central	318	33	45	17	5
	West	134	36	40	24	1
Community Type:	Urban	317	34	41	21	4
	Suburban	169	33	38	26	3
	Rural	268	38	42	16	4
Voter Registration:	Not Registered	0	0	0	0	0
	Reg. Democrat	315	22	45	28	5
	Reg. Republican	244	56	34	8	2
	Reg. Independent	143	31	41	28	1
Denominational Affiliation:	Protestant	430	42	39	14	5
	Catholic	208	29	48	21	3
	Baptist	132	41	42	12	5
	Mainline Protestant	141	37	43	16	4
Churched:	Yes	613	37	40	19	4
	No	135	30	42	27	1
Born Again:	Yes	306	44	38	13	5
	No	455	29	42	25	3
	Evangelical	98	62	32	5	2

TABLE 56   221

On issues related to "international and foreign policies," do you consider yourself to be mostly conservative, mostly liberal, or mostly in between?

		N	Mostly Conservative	In-Between	Mostly Liberal	Don't Know
Total Responding		761	39%	44%	12%	5%
Gender:	Male	369	39	43	15	3
	Female	392	38	45	10	8
Age:	18 to 27	100	30	49	19	1
	28-46	302	36	49	13	2
	47-65	195	43	39	11	7
	66-98	115	47	36	6	11
Income:	Under $20,000	146	31	49	13	7
	$20,000 to $40,000	248	34	48	14	3
	$40,000 to $60,000	136	43	43	10	4
	$60,000 or more	132	47	38	14	1
Education:	High School or Less	308	31	51	10	8
	Some College	183	44	43	11	3
	College Graduate	262	45	37	16	3
Marital Status:	Married	454	42	45	9	4
	Not Married	304	34	43	17	5
Have Kids Under 18:	Yes	275	36	50	10	3
	No	479	40	41	14	5
Ethnicity:	White	579	44	40	11	5
	Black	94	26	51	17	7
	Hispanic	52	13	68	16	3
Region:	Northeast	155	45	35	14	6
	South	154	35	46	11	8
	Central	318	38	47	11	5
	West	134	37	46	15	2
Community Type:	Urban	317	36	45	14	5
	Suburban	169	39	41	13	6
	Rural	268	42	45	9	4
Voter Registration:	Not Registered	0	0	0	0	0
	Reg. Democrat	315	27	49	18	7
	Reg. Republican	244	55	36	5	4
	Reg. Independent	143	37	48	13	2
Denominational Affiliation:	Protestant	430	47	38	9	6
	Catholic	208	33	52	12	3
	Baptist	132	39	42	12	8
	Mainline Protestant	141	53	33	10	5
Churched:	Yes	613	40	44	12	5
	No	135	37	42	15	5
Born Again:	Yes	306	46	41	8	5
	No	455	34	46	15	5
	Evangelical	98	55	35	3	6

(Asked in July 1992) If the presidential election were held today, would you vote for George Bush, the Republican; Bill Clinton, the Democrat; or Ross Perot, an Independent? How sure are you that in November you will vote for that same candidate?

		N	Absolutely Sure, Bush	Likely, Bush	Absolutely Sure, Clinton	Likely, Clinton
Total Responding		761	12%	15%	20%	18%
Gender:	Male	369	14	16	18	21
	Female	392	11	13	21	16
Age:	18 to 27	100	13	14	25	24
	28-46	302	10	17	19	18
	47-65	195	13	13	17	19
	66-98	115	17	12	24	12
Income:	Under $20,000	146	10	7	27	30
	$20,000 to $40,000	248	14	15	21	16
	$40,000 to $60,000	136	16	18	17	18
	$60,000 or more	132	9	23	18	18
Education:	High School or Less	308	12	11	23	21
	Some College	183	15	16	18	14
	College Graduate	262	12	18	18	19
Marital Status:	Married	454	14	16	16	17
	Not Married	304	10	13	26	21
Have Kids Under 18:	Yes	275	11	17	19	16
	No	479	13	14	21	20
Ethnicity:	White	579	15	16	16	18
	Black	94	5	5	40	20
	Hispanic	52	3	17	27	19
Region:	Northeast	155	12	15	19	19
	South	154	16	14	18	16
	Central	318	11	15	22	18
	West	134	12	16	17	22
Community Type:	Urban	317	13	11	23	21
	Suburban	169	11	23	19	7
	Rural	268	14	14	16	22
Voter Registration:	Not Registered	0	0	0	0	0
	Reg. Democrat	315	4	7	38	24
	Reg. Republican	244	30	25	3	9
	Reg. Independent	143	6	14	13	24
Denominational Affiliation:	Protestant	430	15	14	20	18
	Catholic	208	11	17	21	16
	Baptist	132	12	13	27	15
	Mainline Protestant	141	13	15	17	22
Churched:	Yes	613	14	15	20	17
	No	135	5	15	21	23
Born Again:	Yes	306	17	17	18	16
	No	455	9	13	21	20
	Evangelical	98	24	23	15	11

TABLE 57 (continued) 223

(Asked in July 1992) If the presidential election were held today, would you vote for George Bush, the Republican; Bill Clinton, the Democrat; or Ross Perot, an Independent? How sure are you that in November you will vote for that same candidate?

		N	Absolutely Sure, Perot	Likely, Perot	Other Candidate	Don't Know
Total Responding		761	2%	9%	1%	23%
Gender:	Male	369	3	10	1	16
	Female	392	1	8	1	29
Age:	18 to 27	100	2	9	2	11
	28-46	302	3	12	1	20
	47-65	195	2	8	0	27
	66-98	115	1	3	1	30
Income:	Under $20,000	146	2	4	1	19
	$20,000 to $40,000	248	1	11	1	20
	$40,000 to $60,000	136	0	8	1	22
	$60,000 or more	132	6	13	1	11
Education:	High School or Less	308	2	8	0	24
	Some College	183	1	9	1	25
	College Graduate	262	3	11	1	18
Marital Status:	Married	454	3	10	1	24
	Not Married	304	1	8	1	19
Have Kids Under 18:	Yes	275	2	12	1	23
	No	479	2	8	1	22
Ethnicity:	White	579	3	9	1	23
	Black	94	0	6	0	24
	Hispanic	52	0	22	0	11
Region:	Northeast	155	2	10	1	23
	South	154	2	11	1	22
	Central	318	2	7	1	25
	West	134	2	11	1	19
Community Type:	Urban	317	2	10	0	20
	Suburban	169	3	8	2	27
	Rural	268	1	9	0	23
Voter Registration:	Not Registered	0	0	0	0	0
	Reg. Democrat	315	2	7	1	18
	Reg. Republican	244	3	8	1	22
	Reg. Independent	143	2	16	1	24
Denominational Affiliation:	Protestant	430	1	8	0	25
	Catholic	208	3	11	2	18
	Baptist	132	0	11.	0	22
	Mainline Protestant	141	0	8	0	24
Churched:	Yes	613	2	9	1	23
	No	135	3	12	1	20
Born Again:	Yes	306	1	8	0	23
	No	455	3	10	1	22
	Evangelical	98	0	5	0	23

January 1993
Survey Tables

TABLE 58 227

In a typical weekday, from Monday through Friday, about how many hours a day do you watch television?

		N	None	Less Than One Hour	1 Hour to Less Than 2 Hours	2 Hours to Less Than 3 Hours	3 Hours to Less Than 4 Hours	4 Hours to Less Than 5 Hours	5 Hours or More	Don't Know
Total Responding		1186	2%	4%	10%	20%	19%	15%	29%	3%
Gender:	Male	570	1	5	10	24	20	13	25	2
	Female	617	2	3	10	17	17	17	32	3
Age:	18 to 27	206	1	4	10	20	17	10	34	4
	28 to 46	449	2	3	11	22	20	13	26	2
	47 to 65	247	2	4	9	21	25	17	20	2
	66 to 98	197	2	3	8	17	10	19	37	4
Income:	Under $20,000	268	2	2	7	16	13	23	35	1
	$20,000 to $40,000	386	2	4	10	20	20	15	28	2
	$40,000 to $60,000	211	2	3	9	23	25	11	25	2
	$60,000 or more	163	1	7	12	24	22	13	19	2
Education:	High School or Less	523	2	3	7	16	18	18	33	5
	Some College	258	2	3	11	21	18	12	31	3
	College Graduate	400	2	6	12	26	21	12	21	1
Marital Status:	Married	682	2	3	9	21	21	14	27	3
	Not Married	502	2	4	10	19	15	15	31	3
Have Kids Under 18:	Yes	463	2	3	10	18	21	15	29	3
	No	719	2	4	10	22	17	14	28	3
Ethnicity:	White	889	2	5	10	19	19	15	27	3
	Black	149	2	0	5	20	16	14	37	6
	Hispanic	88	2	0	9	23	19	15	29	2
Region:	Northeast	259	2	4	9	24	15	14	31	3
	South	260	2	3	7	21	19	15	29	4
	Central	475	1	4	11	16	22	16	28	3
	West	192	3	5	11	24	15	14	27	2
Community Type:	Urban	627	2	4	10	23	19	13	28	2
	Suburban	167	4	7	12	22	16	9	27	3
	Rural	380	1	3	8	15	19	19	31	4
Voter Registration:	Not Registered	199	3	7	5	18	15	11	37	4
	Democrat	390	1	3	8	21	18	15	32	3
	Republican	312	2	3	12	22	18	17	24	1
	Independent	207	2	4	14	17	26	13	22	3
Denominational Affiliation:	Protestant	488	2	4	9	20	19	15	29	3
	Catholic	338	1	2	8	21	20	17	29	2
	Baptist	121	0	5	4	27	19	11	31	3
	Mainline Protestant	203	2	4	8	17	19	19	29	2
Churched:	Yes	889	2	3	10	21	20	15	27	3
	No	266	3	7	9	18	16	13	31	4
Born Again	Yes	472	2	4	10	20	21	17	24	3
	No	714	2	4	10	20	17	13	31	3
	Evangelical	129	2	1	12	24	22	14	23	1

TABLE 59

Does your household subscribe to cable TV?

		N	Yes	No	Don't Know
Total Responding		1186	62%	38%	0%
Gender:	Male	570	63	37	0
	Female	617	62	38	0
Age:	18 to 27	206	61	39	0
	28-46	449	65	35	0
	47-65	247	63	37	0
	66-98	197	58	42	0
Income:	Under $20,000	268	51	48	0
	$20,000 to $40,000	386	61	39	0
	$40,000 to $60,000	211	73	27	0
	$60,000 or more	163	67	33	0
Education:	High School or Less	523	62	38	0
	Some College	258	63	37	0
	College Graduate	400	63	37	0
Marital Status:	Married	682	65	35	0
	Not Married	502	59	41	0
Have Kids Under 18:	Yes	463	65	35	0
	No	719	61	39	0
Ethnicity:	White	889	63	37	0
	Black	149	54	46	0
	Hispanic	88	72	28	0
Region:	Northeast	259	67	33	0
	South	260	68	32	0
	Central	475	59	41	0
	West	192	58	42	0
Community Type:	Urban	627	64	36	0
	Suburban	167	63	37	0
	Rural	380	60	40	0
Voter Registration:	Not Registered	199	53	47	0
	Reg. Democrat	390	67	33	0
	Reg. Republican	312	63	37	0
	Reg. Independent	207	61	39	0
Denominational	Protestant	488	61	39	0
Affiliation:	Catholic	338	71	29	0
	Baptist	121	61	39	0
	Mainline Protestant	203	60	40	0
Churched:	Yes	889	63	37	0
	No	266	61	39	0
Born Again:	Yes	472	61	39	0
	No	714	63	37	0
	Evangelical	129	54	46	0

TABLE 60 229

Does your household subscribe to any premium cable channels? (Channels you pay extra to receive.)

		N	Yes	No	Don't Know
Total Responding		740	40%	60%	0%
Gender:	Male	357	42	58	0
	Female	383	38	61	1
Age:	18 to 27	125	44	56	0
	28-46	291	45	54	1
	47-65	155	40	60	0
	66-98	114	23	76	1
Income:	Under $20,000	137	27	73	0
	$20,000 to $40,000	236	43	56	1
	$40,000 to $60,000	154	44	55	0
	$60,000 or more	109	52	48	0
Education:	High School or Less	323	40	60	0
	Some College	162	38	62	0
	College Graduate	253	42	57	1
Marital Status:	Married	445	38	62	0
	Not Married	294	43	56	1
Have Kids Under 18:	Yes	299	47	53	0
	No	439	35	64	1
Ethnicity:	White	560	38	61	0
	Black	81	54	46	0
	Hispanic	63	43	57	0
Region:	Northeast	173	43	56	1
	South	176	39	61	0
	Central	280	40	59	1
	West	111	35	65	0
Community Type:	Urban	401	40	59	0
	Suburban	106	42	57	1
	Rural	227	39	61	0
Voter Registration:	Not Registered	105	43	56	1
	Reg. Democrat	260	40	60	0
	Reg. Republican	195	37	63	0
	Reg. Independent	126	46	54	0
Denominational	Protestant	297	38	61	0
Affiliation:	Catholic	240	40	60	0
	Baptist	74	41	59	0
	Mainline Protestant	123	37	62	0
Churched:	Yes	558	39	61	0
	No	162	44	55	1
Born Again:	Yes	288	37	62	0
	No	452	42	58	1
	Evangelical	70	31	68	1

Rate your enjoyment of the programming you watched on "MTV, Music Television": very much, somewhat, not too much, or not at all.

		N	Very Much	Somewhat	Not Too Much	Not at All	Don't Know
Total Responding		233	33%	52%	10%	3%	3%
Gender:	Male	123	24	59	11	2	3
	Female	110	42	44	9	3	2
Age:	18 to 27	71	47	46	4	3	0
	28-46	98	18	61	17	2	1
	47-65	23	25	57	8	3	7
	66-98	24	61	28	0	0	12
Income:	Under $20,000	46	47	37	7	0	9
	$20,000 to $40,000	81	35	49	12	3	0
	$40,000 to $60,000	41	25	65	8	0	2
	$60,000 or more	43	20	58	12	6	4
Education:	High School or Less	100	40	45	8	3	4
	Some College	48	25	60	12	4	0
	College Graduate	84	28	55	12	2	3
Marital Status:	Married	118	28	53	12	3	4
	Not Married	114	37	50	8	2	2
Have Kids Under 18:	Yes	97	33	52	11	2	2
	No	136	32	51	10	3	4
Ethnicity:	White	175	33	52	11	3	2
	Black	28	29	47	12	0	12
	Hispanic	18	37	54	9	0	0
Region:	Northeast	71	39	50	7	4	0
	South	54	32	42	16	3	6
	Central	79	28	59	9	1	3
	West	28	31	54	9	3	3
Community Type:	Urban	139	34	53	7	3	3
	Suburban	27	22	59	13	0	6
	Rural	65	32	47	16	4	2
Voter Registration:	Not Registered	50	28	45	20	2	5
	Reg. Democrat	74	38	51	5	2	4
	Reg. Republican	50	25	62	8	5	0
	Reg. Independent	45	25	57	12	2	3
Denominational Affiliation:	Protestant	64	32	48	13	1	5
	Catholic	94	28	57	9	5	2
	Baptist	13	38	54	8	0	0
	Mainline Protestant	25	27	49	20	0	5
Churched:	Yes	168	32	53	10	3	2
	No	57	31	49	11	3	6
Born Again:	Yes	80	32	50	13	1	4
	No	153	33	52	9	3	2
	Evangelical	10	36	30	15	0	19

TABLE 62   231

**Rate your enjoyment of the programming you watched on "ESPN, the Sports Channel":
very much, somewhat, not too much, or not at all.**

		N	Very Much	Somewhat	Not Too Much	Not at All	Don't Know
Total Responding		476	63%	30%	4%	1%	1%
Gender:	Male	269	66	30	2	0	1
	Female	207	59	30	6	3	1
Age:	18 to 27	88	66	30	5	0	0
	28-46	200	60	34	3	2	1
	47-65	90	58	32	5	2	3
	66-98	60	71	17	7	2	3
Income:	Under $20,000	83	67	21	10	0	2
	$20,000 to $40,000	157	63	32	2	2	2
	$40,000 to $60,000	101	56	38	3	2	1
	$60,000 or more	78	73	25	0	1	1
Education:	High School or Less	201	64	29	4	2	1
	Some College	110	65	29	3	2	2
	College Graduate	163	60	33	4	1	2
Marital Status:	Married	302	61	33	3	2	2
	Not Married	173	67	27	5	1	1
Have Kids Under 18:	Yes	204	58	37	2	2	0
	No	270	66	25	5	1	2
Ethnicity:	White	359	61	33	3	2	2
	Black	55	80	15	6	0	0
	Hispanic	35	57	34	5	5	0
Region:	Northeast	105	64	33	2	0	1
	South	117	64	29	4	1	1
	Central	193	64	27	5	2	2
	West	60	56	37	4	3	0
Community Type:	Urban	256	62	31	3	2	2
	Suburban	65	69	25	2	2	1
	Rural	151	61	32	6	1	1
Voter Registration:	Not Registered	65	60	38	2	0	0
	Reg. Democrat	161	66	25	5	2	2
	Reg. Republican	121	63	32	2	2	2
	Reg. Independent	84	56	36	6	2	0
Denominational	Protestant	185	65	29	4	.0	2
Affiliation:	Catholic	165	60	34	2	3	2
	Baptist	51	68	26	7	0	0
	Mainline Protestant	78	66	32	2	0	1
Churched:	Yes	370	64	29	3	2	1
	No	89	59	33	6	0	2
Born Again:	Yes	188	64	29	4	2	1
	No	288	63	31	4	1	2
	Evangelical	42	66	23	5	3	2

TABLE 63

Rate your enjoyment of the programming you watched on "The USA Network": very much, somewhat, not too much, or not at all.

		N	Very Much	Somewhat	Not Too Much	Not at All	Don't Know
Total Responding		543	47%	44%	5%	1%	3%
Gender:	Male	278	40	49	7	1	3
	Female	265	55	38	3	1	3
Age:	18 to 27	104	48	47	4	1	0
	28-46	237	48	47	4	0	1
	47-65	97	48	39	7	2	4
	66-98	67	44	30	12	2	11
Income:	Under $20,000	96	49	42	2	2	4
	$20,000 to $40,000	188	52	39	6	0	2
	$40,000 to $60,000	110	46	47	7	0	1
	$60,000 or more	83	44	51	2	1	1
Education:	High School or Less	230	46	42	8	1	3
	Some College	123	55	37	4	1	3
	College Graduate	188	44	49	3	0	2
Marital Status:	Married	336	48	44	6	1	2
	Not Married	207	46	43	4	1	5
Have Kids Under 18:	Yes	239	50	46	3	0	1
	No	303	45	42	7	1	4
Ethnicity:	White	410	44	46	5	1	3
	Black	55	62	34	0	0	4
	Hispanic	51	60	31	9	0	0
Region:	Northeast	128	50	44	4	1	1
	South	132	40	46	6	1	7
	Central	204	49	45	4	0	2
	West	79	51	36	8	2	4
Community Type:	Urban	298	46	43	6	1	3
	Suburban	75	47	48	2	1	2
	Rural	166	50	43	5	1	1
Voter Registration:	Not Registered	78	42	48	4	1	4
	Reg. Democrat	187	51	37	6	2	4
	Reg. Republican	148	46	46	5	1	2
	Reg. Independent	93	48	48	3	0	1
Denominational Affiliation:	Protestant	205	43	43	7	1	5
	Catholic	192	51	42	5	1	2
	Baptist	55	44	38	7	0	10
	Mainline Protestant	79	44	45	8	2	1
Churched:	Yes	416	47	44	5	1	3
	No	110	46	43	7	1	4
Born Again:	Yes	214	47	44	4	1	3
	No	329	47	43	6	1	3
	Evangelical	53	44	43	8	0	5

Table 64   233

Rate your enjoyment of the programming you watched on "The Family Channel": very much, somewhat, not too much, or not at all.

		N	Very Much	Somewhat	Not Too Much	Not at All	Don't Know
Total Responding		455	58%	37%	4%	0%	2%
Gender:	Male	213	46	47	5	1	1
	Female	242	68	28	3	0	2
Age:	18 to 27	72	53	42	2	3	0
	28-46	190	56	39	4	0	1
	47-65	90	59	35	4	0	2
	66-98	67	66	26	6	0	2
Income:	Under $20,000	92	63	26	9	0	2
	$20,000 to $40,000	153	53	46	1	0	0
	$40,000 to $60,000	89	63	32	2	1	2
	$60,000 or more	67	55	38	4	2	1
Education:	High School or Less	203	57	35	4	1	2
	Some College	93	56	38	4	0	1
	College Graduate	156	59	37	2	0	2
Marital Status:	Married	297	60	34	4	0	2
	Not Married	156	54	41	3	1	2
Have Kids Under 18:	Yes	209	60	36	3	0	0
	No	243	56	36	4	0	3
Ethnicity:	White	341	56	38	3	1	2
	Black	50	71	29	0	0	0
	Hispanic	36	66	23	11	0	0
Region:	Northeast	98	57	38	4	0	1
	South	114	58	37	2	2	2
	Central	191	61	33	5	0	2
	West	51	48	48	2	0	1
Community Type:	Urban	257	56	39	2	1	2
	Suburban	61	63	31	1	0	4
	Rural	131	61	33	6	0	0
Voter Registration:	Not Registered	64	49	45	4	2	0
	Reg. Democrat	152	62	33	4	0	1
	Reg. Republican	126	56	39	2	0	3
	Reg. Independent	77	55	35	7	1	1
Denominational Affiliation:	Protestant	187	62	33	4	0	2
	Catholic	146	55	38	5	1	2
	Baptist	49	69	29	2	0	0
	Mainline Protestant	78	60	35	3	0	2
Churched:	Yes	362	61	33	4	0	2
	No	81	46	51	1	1	1
Born Again:	Yes	199	64	32	3	0	1
	No	256	53	40	4	1	2
	Evangelical	48	60	31	7	0	2

Rate your enjoyment of the programming you watched on "CNN, the Cable News Network": very much, somewhat, not too much, or not at all.

		N	Very Much	Somewhat	Not Too Much	Not at All	Don't Know
Total Responding		626	63%	32%	4%	1%	1%
Gender:	Male	314	61	34	5	1	0
	Female	312	66	30	2	1	2
Age:	18 to 27	101	51	40	8	0	1
	28-46	244	59	37	3	1	1
	47-65	132	67	30	3	0	0
	66-98	99	75	19	3	1	1
Income:	Under $20,000	107	60	32	7	1	0
	$20,000 to $40,000	202	65	30	3	1	0
	$40,000 to $60,000	130	66	31	3	0	0
	$60,000 or more	97	56	40	2	0	2
Education:	High School or Less	264	59	33	5	1	1
	Some College	136	68	28	3	0	1
	College Graduate	222	65	33	1	0	1
Marital Status:	Married	385	64	32	2	1	1
	Not Married	239	61	32	5	0	1
Have Kids Under 18:	Yes	245	58	37	4	0	1
	No	379	66	29	3	1	1
Ethnicity:	White	481	63	33	3	1	1
	Black	68	63	31	6	0	0
	Hispanic	46	67	29	4	0	0
Region:	Northeast	149	63	32	4	0	1
	South	148	62	34	3	1	0
	Central	243	67	27	4	1	1
	West	86	55	42	1	0	2
Community Type:	Urban	346	63	32	4	1	1
	Suburban	85	64	34	1	1	1
	Rural	188	63	32	3	0	1
Voter Registration:	Not Registered	79	54	35	10	0	1
	Reg. Democrat	214	67	30	2	0	1
	Reg. Republican	176	61	34	3	1	2
	Reg. Independent	111	63	34	2	1	0
Denominational Affiliation:	Protestant	258	65	29	4	0	1
	Catholic	199	63	33	2	1	1
	Baptist	62	72	25	1	2	0
	Mainline Protestant	114	68	27	4	0	1
Churched:	Yes	484	65	30	3	0	1
	No	126	57	37	4	1	0
Born Again:	Yes	249	61	33	4	1	1
	No	376	64	31	3	0	1
	Evangelical	60	47	44	6	2	1

TABLE 66   235

How enjoyable do you consider the TV programs that are available to be? Very enjoyable, somewhat, not too, or not at all enjoyable.

		N	Very Enjoyable	Somewhat Enjoyable	Not Too Enjoyable	Not at All Enjoyable	Don't Know
Total Responding		1186	16%	60%	16%	5%	3%
Gender:	Male	570	14	61	17	6	3
	Female	617	18	59	16	5	2
Age:	18 to 27	206	25	67	7	1	0
	28-46	449	11	65	19	4	2
	47-65	247	13	58	22	6	2
	66-98	197	16	47	16	11	10
Income:	Under $20,000	268	17	59	15	6	4
	$20,000 to $40,000	386	18	61	14	6	2
	$40,000 to $60,000	211	14	67	14	4	0
	$60,000 or more	163	7	62	23	4	3
Education:	High School or Less	523	17	60	14	6	3
	Some College	258	17	59	18	5	1
	College Graduate	400	12	60	19	5	3
Marital Status:	Married	682	14	59	19	6	2
	Not Married	502	18	61	13	5	4
Have Kids Under 18:	Yes	463	16	63	16	3	2
	No	719	16	58	16	6	3
Ethnicity:	White	889	15	59	19	6	2
	Black	149	21	65	10	1	3
	Hispanic	88	19	63	9	2	6
Region:	Northeast	259	16	64	14	5	1
	South	260	18	59	16	5	2
	Central	475	16	60	17	4	4
	West	192	13	56	19	8	3
Community Type:	Urban	627	15	62	14	6	3
	Suburban	167	11	65	15	4	4
	Rural	380	19	54	21	4	2
Voter Registration:	Not Registered	199	24	59	10	3	4
	Reg. Democrat	390	18	61	15	3	3
	Reg. Republican	312	12	57	20	9	2
	Reg. Independent	207	12	63	16	6	2
Denominational Affiliation:	Protestant	488	13	59	18	6	4
	Catholic	338	20	62	13	4	1
	Baptist	121	12	59	18	6	6
	Mainline Protestant	203	14	59	17	6	4
Churched:	Yes	889	16	61	16	5	2
	No	266	16	58	17	5	5
Born Again:	Yes	472	14	60	19	6	1
	No	714	17	60	15	5	4
	Evangelical	129	6	55	29	9	1

TABLE 67

In the last seven days did you "read all or part of a book for pleasure"?

		N	Yes	No	Don't Know
Total Responding		1205	62%	38%	0%
Gender:	Male	577	56	44	0
	Female	628	67	32	0
Age:	18 to 27	212	56	44	0
	28-46	453	62	38	0
	47-65	250	65	35	0
	66-98	201	63	36	1
Income:	Under $20,000	274	53	47	0
	$20,000 to $40,000	391	60	40	0
	$40,000 to $60,000	212	67	33	0
	$60,000 or more	166	76	24	0
Education:	High School or Less	532	50	49	0
	Some College	262	63	37	0
	College Graduate	403	76	24	0
Marital Status:	Married	689	65	35	0
	Not Married	512	57	42	0
Have Kids Under 18:	Yes	468	60	40	0
	No	731	63	37	0
Ethnicity:	White	903	63	37	0
	Black	150	61	38	2
	Hispanic	90	53	47	0
Region:	Northeast	264	58	42	0
	South	263	65	35	0
	Central	481	60	40	0
	West	197	67	33	0
Community Type:	Urban	638	64	36	0
	Suburban	169	59	41	0
	Rural	385	61	39	0
Voter Registration:	Not Registered	206	47	52	1
	Reg. Democrat	395	63	37	0
	Reg. Republican	315	70	30	0
	Reg. Independent	208	63	37	0
Denominational	Protestant	494	66	34	0
Affiliation:	Catholic	343	56	44	0
	Baptist	122	69	31	0
	Mainline Protestant	204	63	37	0
Churched:	Yes	902	64	36	0
	No	270	58	42	1
Born Again:	Yes	477	68	32	0
	No	728	57	42	0
	Evangelical	130	79	21	0

TABLE 68   237

In the last seven days did you "attend a meeting of a recovery group or 12-step program"?

		N	Yes	No	Don't Know
Total Responding		1205	4%	96%	1%
Gender:	Male	577	3	96	1
	Female	628	4	95	0
Age:	18 to 27	212	5	95	0
	28-46	453	3	97	0
	47-65	250	3	96	0
	66-98	201	5	93	3
Income:	Under $20,000	274	5	94	1
	$20,000 to $40,000	391	4	96	0
	$40,000 to $60,000	212	2	98	0
	$60,000 or more	166	3	97	0
Education:	High School or Less	532	4	95	1
	Some College	262	5	95	0
	College Graduate	403	3	97	0
Marital Status:	Married	689	2	97	1
	Not Married	512	6	94	0
Have Kids Under 18:	Yes	468	4	96	0
	No	731	4	95	1
Ethnicity:	White	903	3	97	0
	Black	150	7	91	2
	Hispanic	90	4	96	0
Region:	Northeast	264	3	97	0
	South	263	5	94	1
	Central	481	3	96	1
	West	197	5	95	0
Community Type:	Urban	638	4	95	1
	Suburban	169	3	96	1
	Rural	385	3	97	0
Voter Registration:	Not Registered	206	3	97	1
	Reg. Democrat	395	5	93	1
	Reg. Republican	315	2	98	0
	Reg. Independent	208	5	95	0
Denominational	Protestant	494	3	97	0
Affiliation:	Catholic	343	3	97	0
	Baptist	122	2	98	0
	Mainline Protestant	204	3	97	0
Churched:	Yes	902	4	95	0
	No	270	2	98	0
Born Again:	Yes	477	4	96	0
	No	728	3	96	1
	Evangelical	130	5	95	0

TABLE 69

In the last seven days did you "read from the Book of Mormon"?

		N	Yes	No	Don't Know
Total Responding		1205	2%	98%	0%
Gender:	Male	577	1	99	0
	Female	628	2	98	0
Age:	18 to 27	212	3	97	0
	28-46	453	1	99	0
	47-65	250	2	97	0
	66-98	201	1	99	0
Income:	Under $20,000	274	2	98	0
	$20,000 to $40,000	391	1	99	0
	$40,000 to $60,000	212	2	98	0
	$60,000 or more	166	2	98	0
Education:	High School or Less	532	2	97	0
	Some College	262	2	98	0
	College Graduate	403	1	99	0
Marital Status:	Married	689	1	99	0
	Not Married	512	2	98	0
Have Kids Under 18:	Yes	468	1	99	0
	No	731	2	98	0
Ethnicity:	White	903	2	98	0
	Black	150	1	99	0
	Hispanic	90	4	96	0
Region:	Northeast	264	2	98	0
	South	263	0	99	0
	Central	481	2	98	0
	West	197	4	96	0
Community Type:	Urban	638	1	98	0
	Suburban	169	2	98	0
	Rural	385	2	98	0
Voter Registration:	Not Registered	206	2	98	0
	Reg. Democrat	395	2	98	0
	Reg. Republican	315	2	98	0
	Reg. Independent	208	1	98	0
Denominational	Protestant	494	1	99	0
Affiliation:	Catholic	343	2	98	0
	Baptist	122	1	99	0
	Mainline Protestant	204	0	99	1
Churched:	Yes	902	2	98	0
	No	270	0	100	0
Born Again:	Yes	477	2	98	0
	No	728	2	98	0
	Evangelical	130	1	98	1

TABLE 70   239

In the last seven days did you "rent a prerecorded videocassette"?

		N	Yes	No	Don't Know
Total Responding		1205	31%	68%	0%
Gender:	Male	577	32	68	0
	Female	628	31	69	0
Age:	18 to 27	212	48	52	0
	28-46	453	39	61	0
	47-65	250	19	81	0
	66-98	201	11	88	1
Income:	Under $20,000	274	22	77	0
	$20,000 to $40,000	391	33	67	0
	$40,000 to $60,000	212	36	64	0
	$60,000 or more	166	42	58	0
Education:	High School or Less	532	26	74	0
	Some College	262	33	67	0
	College Graduate	403	37	63	0
Marital Status:	Married	689	33	67	0
	Not Married	512	30	70	0
Have Kids Under 18:	Yes	468	41	59	0
	No	731	26	74	0
Ethnicity:	White	903	32	68	0
	Black	150	23	77	0
	Hispanic	90	40	60	0
Region:	Northeast	264	33	67	0
	South	263	31	69	0
	Central	481	30	70	0
	West	197	33	67	0
Community Type:	Urban	638	33	67	0
	Suburban	169	29	71	0
	Rural	385	32	68	0
Voter Registration:	Not Registered	206	34	66	0
	Reg. Democrat	395	28	72	0
	Reg. Republican	315	35	65	0
	Reg. Independent	208	33	66	1
Denominational Affiliation:	Protestant	494	28	71	0
	Catholic	343	35	65	0
	Baptist	122	29	71	0
	Mainline Protestant	204	28	72	0
Churched:	Yes	902	32	68	0
	No	270	31	69	0
Born Again:	Yes	477	32	68	0
	No	728	31	69	0
	Evangelical	130	32	68	0

In the last seven days did you "read from the Bible, not including when you were at a church or synagogue"?

		N	Yes	No
Total Responding		1205	34%	66%
Gender:	Male	577	28	72
	Female	628	40	60
Age:	18 to 27	212	27	73
	28-46	453	31	69
	47-65	250	39	61
	66-98	201	45	55
Income:	Under $20,000	274	38	62
	$20,000 to $40,000	391	35	65
	$40,000 to $60,000	212	35	65
	$60,000 or more	166	22	78
Education:	High School or Less	532	35	65
	Some College	262	35	65
	College Graduate	403	33	67
Marital Status:	Married	689	37	63
	Not Married	512	31	69
Have Kids Under 18:	Yes	468	35	65
	No	731	33	67
Ethnicity:	White	903	33	67
	Black	150	40	60
	Hispanic	90	33	67
Region:	Northeast	264	18	82
	South	263	45	55
	Central	481	38	62
	West	197	32	68
Community Type:	Urban	638	35	65
	Suburban	169	24	76
	Rural	385	36	64
Voter Registration:	Not Registered	206	30	70
	Reg. Democrat	395	34	66
	Reg. Republican	315	40	60
	Reg. Independent	208	31	69
Denominational	Protestant	494	47	53
Affiliation:	Catholic	343	22	78
	Baptist	122	57	43
	Mainline Protestant	204	38	62
Churched:	Yes	902	41	59
	No	270	10	90
Born Again:	Yes	477	57	43
	No	728	19	81
	Evangelical	130	82	18

TABLE 72   241

In the last seven days did you "attend a church service, not including a wedding, funeral or other special event"?

		N	Yes	No	Don't Know
Total Responding		1205	45%	55%	0%
Gender:	Male	577	37	63	0
	Female	628	53	47	0
Age:	18 to 27	212	38	62	0
	28-46	453	43	57	0
	47-65	250	50	49	1
	66-98	201	52	48	0
Income:	Under $20,000	274	45	55	1
	$20,000 to $40,000	391	42	58	0
	$40,000 to $60,000	212	49	51	0
	$60,000 or more	166	47	53	0
Education:	High School or Less	532	47	53	0
	Some College	262	47	53	0
	College Graduate	403	43	57	0
Marital Status:	Married	689	52	48	0
	Not Married	512	36	64	0
Have Kids Under 18:	Yes	468	49	51	0
	No	731	43	57	0
Ethnicity:	White	903	47	53	0
	Black	150	40	59	1
	Hispanic	90	37	63	0
Region:	Northeast	264	37	63	0
	South	263	49	50	1
	Central	481	51	49	0
	West	197	38	62	0
Community Type:	Urban	638	42	58	0
	Suburban	169	46	54	0
	Rural	385	52	48	0
Voter Registration:	Not Registered	206	31	68	1
	Reg. Democrat	395	48	52	0
	Reg. Republican	315	55	45	0
	Reg. Independent	208	42	58	0
Denominational	Protestant	494	52	48	0
Affiliation:	Catholic	343	51	49	0
	Baptist	122	56	44	0
	Mainline Protestant	204	49	51	0
Churched:	Yes	902	60	40	0
	No	270	0	99	1
Born Again:	Yes	477	67	32	0
	No	728	31	69	0
	Evangelical	130	86	14	0

TABLE 73

In the last seven days did you "use a computer"?

		N	Yes	No	Don't Know
Total Responding		1205	46%	54%	0%
Gender:	Male	577	48	52	0
	Female	628	44	56	0
Age:	18 to 27	212	53	47	0
	28-46	453	59	41	0
	47-65	250	43	57	0
	66-98	201	10	90	1
Income:	Under $20,000	274	23	77	0
	$20,000 to $40,000	391	45	55	0
	$40,000 to $60,000	212	63	37	0
	$60,000 or more	166	74	26	0
Education:	High School or Less	532	26	74	0
	Some College	262	54	45	0
	College Graduate	403	68	32	0
Marital Status:	Married	689	49	51	0
	Not Married	512	43	57	0
Have Kids Under 18:	Yes	468	54	46	0
	No	731	41	59	0
Ethnicity:	White	903	44	56	0
	Black	150	47	53	0
	Hispanic	90	51	49	0
Region:	Northeast	264	47	53	0
	South	263	44	55	0
	Central	481	43	57	0
	West	197	54	46	0
Community Type:	Urban	638	50	50	0
	Suburban	169	60	40	0
	Rural	385	34	66	0
Voter Registration:	Not Registered	206	41	59	0
	Reg. Democrat	395	45	55	0
	Reg. Republican	315	52	48	0
	Reg. Independent	208	50	49	0
Denominational	Protestant	494	43	57	0
Affiliation:	Catholic	343	47	53	0
	Baptist	122	44	56	0
	Mainline Protestant	204	41	59	0
Churched:	Yes	902	48	52	0
	No	270	42	58	0
Born Again:	Yes	477	49	51	0
	No	728	44	56	0
	Evangelical	130	52	48	0

TABLE 74   243

In the last seven days did you "volunteer some of your free time to help a nonprofit organization, not including a church"?

		N	Yes	No	Don't Know
Total Responding		1205	27%	72%	0%
Gender:	Male	577	24	76	0
	Female	628	30	69	1
Age:	18 to 27	212	24	76	0
	28-46	453	28	72	0
	47-65	250	29	70	1
	66-98	201	27	72	1
Income:	Under $20,000	274	29	69	2
	$20,000 to $40,000	391	26	74	0
	$40,000 to $60,000	212	25	75	0
	$60,000 or more	166	33	67	0
Education:	High School or Less	532	23	77	0
	Some College	262	33	67	0
	College Graduate	403	31	69	0
Marital Status:	Married	689	29	71	0
	Not Married	512	26	74	1
Have Kids Under 18:	Yes	468	27	72	0
	No	731	27	72	1
Ethnicity:	White	903	29	71	0
	Black	150	19	81	0
	Hispanic	90	29	71	0
Region:	Northeast	264	29	71	0
	South	263	25	74	1
	Central	481	27	73	0
	West	197	31	69	0
Community Type:	Urban	638	28	71	1
	Suburban	169	28	72	0
	Rural	385	26	73	0
Voter Registration:	Not Registered	206	22	78	0
	Reg. Democrat	395	28	72	1
	Reg. Republican	315	28	72	0
	Reg. Independent	208	30	70	0
Denominational	Protestant	494	27	72	0
Affiliation:	Catholic	343	26	74	0
	Baptist	122	24	76	1
	Mainline Protestant	204	32	68	0
Churched:	Yes	902	29	71	0
	No	270	23	77	0
Born Again:	Yes	477	27	73	1
	No	728	28	72	0
	Evangelical	130	26	73	1

TABLE 75

In the last seven days did you "volunteer some of your free time to help a church"?

		N	Yes	No	Don't Know
Total Responding		1205	24%	76%	0%
Gender:	Male	577	18	82	0
	Female	628	29	71	0
Age:	18 to 27	212	13	87	0
	28-46	453	23	77	0
	47-65	250	31	69	0
	66-98	201	28	72	0
Income:	Under $20,000	274	21	79	0
	$20,000 to $40,000	391	24	76	0
	$40,000 to $60,000	212	27	73	0
	$60,000 or more	166	23	77	0
Education:	High School or Less	532	21	79	0
	Some College	262	27	73	0
	College Graduate	403	25	74	0
Marital Status:	Married	689	28	72	0
	Not Married	512	18	82	0
Have Kids Under 18:	Yes	468	25	75	0
	No	731	23	77	0
Ethnicity:	White	903	25	75	0
	Black	150	22	78	0
	Hispanic	90	22	78	0
Region:	Northeast	264	16	84	0
	South	263	26	74	0
	Central	481	27	73	0
	West	197	23	77	0
Community Type:	Urban	638	23	76	0
	Suburban	169	20	80	0
	Rural	385	26	74	0
Voter Registration:	Not Registered	206	12	88	0
	Reg. Democrat	395	25	75	0
	Reg. Republican	315	31	68	0
	Reg. Independent	208	22	78	0
Denominational Affiliation:	Protestant	494	33	67	0
	Catholic	343	18	82	0
	Baptist	122	32	68	0
	Mainline Protestant	204	32	68	0
Churched:	Yes	902	31	69	0
	No	270	1	99	0
Born Again:	Yes	477	39	61	0
	No	728	14	86	0
	Evangelical	130	59	41	0

TABLE 76 (continued on next page) 245

When you, personally, have to make a decision on a moral or ethical matter, what would you be most likely to base your decision on?

		N	Available Choices & Likely Outcomes	Your Past Experience	The Advice of Friends & Family
Total Responding		594	13%	28%	6%
Gender:	Male	286	11	34	6
	Female	308	16	22	7
Age:	18 to 27	114	15	31	13
	28 to 46	249	14	26	5
	47 to 65	123	11	28	4
	66 to 98	71	11	27	5
Income:	Under $20,000	128	11	27	9
	$20,000 to $40,000	189	12	27	7
	$40,000 to $60,000	106	14	30	2
	$60,000 or more	93	17	30	9
Education:	High School or Less	261	8	27	9
	Some College	134	17	28	5
	College Graduate	193	18	27	4
Marital Status:	Married	337	13	26	5
	Not Married	255	14	29	9
Have Kids Under 18:	Yes	239	12	25	9
	No	353	14	29	5
Ethnicity:	White	444	13	31	6
	Black	74	6	18	4
	Hispanic	44	18	11	15
Region:	Northeast	135	16	29	6
	South	134	10	31	5
	Central	223	12	24	5
	West	103	17	30	12
Community Type:	Urban	304	15	26	6
	Suburban	92	11	33	5
	Rural	191	13	27	8
Voter Registration:	Not Registered	113	12	23	9
	Democrat	173	13	22	6
	Republican	149	11	28	7
	Independent	114	16	38	3
Denominational Affiliation:	Protestant	227	10	27	4
	Catholic	177	19	29	11
	Baptist	54	8	27	0
	Mainline Protestant	85	13	31	6
Churched:	Yes	449	11	27	7
	No	130	20	32	4
Born Again	Yes	231	14	20	5
	No	362	13	33	7
	Evangelical	64	3	9	0

When you, personally, have to make a decision on a moral or ethical matter, what would you be most likely to base your decision on?

		The Common Wisdom	The Bible	Or Just Let Whatever Happens, Happen	Combination of Several	Don't Know
Total Responding		12%	20%	8%	10%	3%
Gender:	Male	13	15	9	11	2
	Female	11	25	7	10	3
Age:	18 to 27	7	11	10	12	1
	28 to 46	13	23	6	9	3
	47 to 65	14	18	7	15	3
	66 to 98	10	26	11	8	3
Income:	Under $20,000	8	24	14	5	3
	$20,000 to $40,000	12	15	9	15	3
	$40,000 to $60,000	17	28	3	6	0
	$60,000 or more	11	18	1	11	2
Education:	High School or Less	10	21	15	7	3
	Some College	12	19	3	13	3
	College Graduate	14	20	2	13	1
Marital Status:	Married	12	25	7	10	3
	Not Married	11	14	9	12	2
Have Kids Under 18:	Yes	11	23	7	9	4
	No	12	18	8	11	2
Ethnicity:	White	10	19	8	11	2
	Black	18	29	11	13	2
	Hispanic	9	20	10	10	6
Region:	Northeast	7	11	13	12	5
	South	9	31	8	5	1
	Central	13	24	7	13	3
	West	18	11	3	9	1
Community Type:	Urban	14	19	9	9	2
	Suburban	12	13	9	16	2
	Rural	8	24	6	10	4
Voter Registration:	Not Registered	7	21	12	12	3
	Democrat	18	19	10	9	2
	Republican	10	29	3	10	2
	Independent	8	14	5	12	3
Denominational Affiliation:	Protestant	11	30	4	14	1
	Catholic	13	8	9	8	3
	Baptist	4	36	5	19	0
	Mainline Protestant	14	18	4	12	3
Churched:	Yes	9	25	7	10	3
	No	17	6	10	11	1
Born Again	Yes	9	35	4	11	1
	No	13	11	10	10	4
	Evangelical	3	69	3	11	2

TABLE 77   247

When it comes to your most important views and beliefs about life, which influences have had a greater impact on your life?

		N	Gov't Laws & Regu- lations	Attitudes & Opinion of Friends & Family	Your Religious Views	The Views of Public Leaders	Or Info. & Suggest. Made by Media	Combi- nation of Several	Don't Know
Total Responding		594	7%	32%	41%	2%	5%	7%	7%
Gender:	Male	286	9	35	31	3	6	7	10
	Female	308	5	30	51	1	3	7	4
Age:	18 to 27	114	13	48	26	2	3	3	5
	28 to 46	249	4	32	43	2	5	8	7
	47 to 65	123	7	28	45	2	2	10	6
	66 to 98	71	4	23	50	1	5	8	9
Income:	Under $20,000	128	13	24	42	1	6	7	6
	$20,000 to $40,000	189	6	37	37	2	6	7	6
	$40,000 to $60,000	106	3	34	49	3	2	7	2
	$60,000 or more	93	6	41	33	0	5	8	7
Education:	High School or Less	261	10	32	38	2	7	4	7
	Some College	134	5	30	43	3	3	10	7
	College Graduate	193	4	35	42	0	3	8	6
Marital Status:	Married	337	5	32	47	1	4	6	5
	Not Married	255	9	33	34	2	5	8	9
Have Kids Under 18:	Yes	239	6	30	49	2	3	5	4
	No	353	7	34	36	2	5	8	8
Ethnicity:	White	444	5	34	40	1	6	7	7
	Black	74	9	20	51	2	2	11	4
	Hispanic	44	5	50	34	6	0	0	6
Region:	Northeast	135	6	37	31	4	4	9	8
	South	134	6	31	48	1	6	4	4
	Central	223	5	26	46	1	5	10	7
	West	103	10	41	33	2	3	3	7
Community Type:	Urban	304	8	34	40	1	4	5	8
	Suburban	92	5	29	40	1	5	14	5
	Rural	191	6	32	42	2	6	7	5
Voter Registration:	Not Registered	113	8	32	33	0	10	6	11
	Democrat	173	7	32	39	2	5	7	8
	Republican	149	1	31	54	3	0	8	2
	Independent	114	12	33	35	2	6	9	5
Denominational Affiliation:	Protestant	227	5	26	52	1	4	8	4
	Catholic	177	8	39	34	2	4	6	7
	Baptist	54	2	16	61	2	2	15	4
	Mainline Protestant	85	6	29	52	0	6	4	4
Churched:	Yes	449	6	31	47	1	3	7	6
	No	130	9	39	22	3	11	7	9
Born Again	Yes	231	3	28	58	0	1	6	4
	No	362	9	35	30	2	7	8	9
	Evangelical	64	2	10	78	2	1	7	1

248 TABLE 78

Do you agree strongly, agree somewhat, disagree somewhat, or disagree strongly with the following statement: "Things will be better for you five years from now than they are today"?

		N	Agree Strongly	Agree Somewhat	Disagree Somewhat	Disagree Strongly	Don't Know
Total Responding		617	37%	26%	11%	12%	15%
Gender:	Male	298	42	26	9	11	13
	Female	318	33	26	12	12	17
Age:	18 to 27	120	59	13	13	12	3
	28-46	234	44	30	6	7	13
	47-65	116	20	28	14	18	19
	66-98	93	15	24	15	16	31
Income:	Under $20,000	138	36	24	10	10	19
	$20,000 to $40,000	205	41	24	13	11	12
	$40,000 to $60,000	116	38	28	6	16	11
	$60,000 or more	79	41	32	11	6	10
Education:	High School or Less	268	33	24	11	14	18
	Some College	129	35	24	19	11	10
	College Graduate	217	43	29	5	10	13
Marital Status:	Married	353	34	29	11	13	13
	Not Married	262	41	22	10	9	18
Have Kids Under 18:	Yes	254	45	29	6	11	9
	No	359	31	24	14	12	19
Ethnicity:	White	458	30	30	11	13	16
	Black	80	58	11	9	7	15
	Hispanic	45	54	14	12	14	6
Region:	Northeast	135	34	27	8	12	19
	South	136	41	23	8	14	14
	Central	250	39	27	15	8	10
	West	96	30	24	7	16	23
Community Type:	Urban	339	40	21	10	14	15
	Suburban	75	37	31	11	2	20
	Rural	199	33	32	12	11	12
Voter Registration:	Not Registered	103	48	21	8	11	11
	Reg. Democrat	218	41	24	10	10	15
	Reg. Republican	163	26	33	12	16	13
	Reg. Independent	97	44	26	6	7	18
Denominational Affiliation:	Protestant	251	25	32	15	12	16
	Catholic	174	47	23	7	11	13
	Baptist	64	25	32	18	13	11
	Mainline Protestant	114	26	31	12	11	21
Churched:	Yes	456	37	26	11	12	14
	No	144	38	28	11	10	14
Born Again:	Yes	247	35	27	14	11	13
	No	369	38	25	9	12	16
	Evangelical	68	29	26	12	17	16

TABLE 79   249

Overall, how often, if ever, do you consciously think of yourself as a representative of "the United States": always, often, sometimes, rarely, or never?

		N	Always	Often	Sometimes	Rarely	Never	Don't Know
Total Responding		594	31%	16%	22%	16%	13%	2%
Gender:	Male	286	30	18	22	16	12	2
	Female	308	32	14	22	16	14	2
Age:	18 to 27	114	24	23	22	21	8	2
	28 to 46	249	30	13	24	18	14	0
	47 to 65	123	36	12	23	9	14	5
	66 to 98	71	40	19	15	7	12	6
Income:	Under $20,000	128	28	14	19	19	15	5
	$20,000 to $40,000	189	36	17	20	14	12	1
	$40,000 to $60,000	106	24	18	29	18	11	1
	$60,000 or more	93	28	18	27	15	11	1
Education:	High School or Less	261	30	18	16	14	18	4
	Some College	134	31	17	25	18	9	1
	College Graduate	193	33	12	30	15	9	1
Marital Status:	Married	337	32	17	22	16	12	2
	Not Married	255	31	14	23	16	14	2
Have Kids Under 18:	Yes	239	27	15	26	18	12	1
	No	353	34	16	20	14	13	3
Ethnicity:	White	444	32	16	24	14	12	3
	Black	74	23	13	26	17	21	0
	Hispanic	44	38	20	10	27	5	0
Region:	Northeast	135	21	16	32	15	14	1
	South	134	34	16	21	13	12	3
	Central	223	36	16	21	13	11	3
	West	103	29	15	15	25	16	2
Community Type:	Urban	304	31	16	20	16	16	1
	Suburban	92	24	18	32	15	9	3
	Rural	191	34	14	22	16	10	3
Voter Registration:	Not Registered	113	25	11	21	22	18	2
	Democrat	173	28	21	19	18	12	1
	Republican	149	31	16	25	12	14	2
	Independent	114	38	14	24	12	7	3
Denominational Affiliation:	Protestant	227	32	13	26	13	14	2
	Catholic	177	32	15	21	21	9	2
	Baptist	54	38	14	20	10	13	5
	Mainline Protestant	85	24	17	30	12	17	0
Churched:	Yes	449	32	16	24	16	10	2
	No	130	28	15	20	16	19	2
Born Again	Yes	231	35	15	26	15	7	3
	No	362	29	17	20	16	16	2
	Evangelical	64	37	11	30	15	5	1

TABLE 80

Overall, how often, if ever, do you consciously think of yourself as a representative of "your church or synagogue": always, often, sometimes, rarely, or never?

		N	Always	Often	Sometimes	Rarely	Never	Don't Know
Total Responding		594	15%	14%	25%	16%	28%	2%
Gender:	Male	286	11	10	25	19	35	1
	Female	308	19	17	25	13	22	3
Age:	18 to 27	114	10	11	25	27	27	0
	28 to 46	249	11	16	28	14	30	1
	47 to 65	123	21	12	20	13	30	4
	66 to 98	71	28	19	16	9	22	6
Income:	Under $20,000	128	22	15	20	9	28	6
	$20,000 to $40,000	189	16	12	26	18	26	1
	$40,000 to $60,000	106	10	20	33	18	20	0
	$60,000 or more	93	11	10	20	17	42	0
Education:	High School or Less	261	18	13	26	14	26	3
	Some College	134	14	19	23	16	28	1
	College Graduate	193	13	12	25	17	31	2
Marital Status:	Married	337	13	19	29	14	24	2
	Not Married	255	18	8	20	19	34	3
Have Kids Under 18:	Yes	239	11	17	34	16	21	1
	No	353	18	12	19	16	33	3
Ethnicity:	White	444	16	14	24	15	29	2
	Black	74	20	10	32	8	27	2
	Hispanic	44	5	18	31	26	20	0
Region:	Northeast	135	8	11	29	19	32	2
	South	134	19	17	29	13	19	2
	Central	223	20	16	23	14	24	3
	West	103	8	8	18	21	44	1
Community Type:	Urban	304	16	15	21	16	31	1
	Suburban	92	8	12	34	21	23	2
	Rural	191	17	13	27	13	27	4
Voter Registration:	Not Registered	113	9	16	18	19	34	3
	Democrat	173	14	10	31	14	28	2
	Republican	149	21	21	24	13	19	1
	Independent	114	16	8	22	19	34	1
Denominational Affiliation:	Protestant	227	21	17	22	13	24	3
	Catholic	177	10	11	35	24	20	0
	Baptist	54	31	16	16	7	27	4
	Mainline Protestant	85	18	18	25	16	21	2
Churched:	Yes	449	19	18	29	16	17	1
	No	130	4	1	9	15	67	4
Born Again	Yes	231	22	25	27	10	14	2
	No	362	11	7	23	20	37	2
	Evangelical	64	30	36	21	6	7	1

TABLE 81   251

Overall, how often, if ever, do you consciously think of yourself as a representative of "your ethnic heritage": always, often, sometimes, rarely, or never?

		N	Always	Often	Sometimes	Rarely	Never	Don't Know
Total Responding		594	21%	15%	22%	17%	23%	2%
Gender:	Male	286	20	16	22	17	23	1
	Female	308	21	14	21	17	23	3
Age:	18 to 27	114	24	20	23	23	10	0
	28 to 46	249	19	15	23	16	26	1
	47 to 65	123	24	9	24	13	24	5
	66 to 98	71	20	17	18	15	26	5
Income:	Under $20,000	128	23	17	19	18	20	3
	$20,000 to $40,000	189	22	15	28	14	18	2
	$40,000 to $60,000	106	17	11	22	20	29	1
	$60,000 or more	93	20	15	15	18	32	1
Education:	High School or Less	261	20	14	24	14	25	3
	Some College	134	26	12	21	22	18	1
	College Graduate	193	19	17	20	18	24	2
Marital Status:	Married	337	17	14	23	18	27	2
	Not Married	255	26	17	21	16	18	3
Have Kids Under 18:	Yes	239	20	11	25	18	25	1
	No	353	22	17	19	16	22	3
Ethnicity:	White	444	15	12	22	20	28	3
	Black	74	48	21	23	4	4	0
	Hispanic	44	25	26	25	10	14	0
Region:	Northeast	135	14	16	28	21	19	3
	South	134	25	17	22	13	18	4
	Central	223	24	13	18	18	25	1
	West	103	19	15	21	15	29	1
Community Type:	Urban	304	23	18	19	17	22	2
	Suburban	92	18	12	24	15	29	3
	Rural	191	18	11	27	19	22	3
Voter Registration:	Not Registered	113	22	23	19	14	18	3
	Democrat	173	24	17	23	16	18	2
	Republican	149	16	14	22	14	31	2
	Independent	114	22	5	23	23	25	2
Denominational Affiliation:	Protestant	227	19	13	18	18	28	4
	Catholic	177	17	21	24	18	19	1
	Baptist	54	29	11	22	10	21	7
	Mainline Protestant	85	11	17	17	19	32	4
Churched:	Yes	449	22	14	23	17	21	2
	No	130	16	17	17	15	32	3
Born Again	Yes	231	21	16	22	15	24	2
	No	362	21	14	22	18	23	2
	Evangelical	64	23	12	18	15	29	3

TABLE 82

Overall, how often, if ever, do you consciously think of yourself as a representative of "your parents": always, often, sometimes, rarely, or never?

		N	Always	Often	Sometimes	Rarely	Never	Don't Know
Total Responding		594	23%	20%	26%	12%	15%	3%
Gender:	Male	286	24	24	24	10	16	2
	Female	308	23	17	27	15	14	4
Age:	18 to 27	114	20	28	30	17	6	0
	28 to 46	249	22	19	27	13	18	1
	47 to 65	123	29	14	26	10	16	4
	66 to 98	71	21	22	18	6	17	15
Income:	Under $20,000	128	28	18	14	14	19	7
	$20,000 to $40,000	189	30	22	26	9	11	2
	$40,000 to $60,000	106	16	18	38	15	12	1
	$60,000 or more	93	14	20	30	12	24	0
Education:	High School or Less	261	28	21	21	11	13	5
	Some College	134	26	15	34	12	13	1
	College Graduate	193	15	22	27	15	19	2
Marital Status:	Married	337	23	19	28	12	14	3
	Not Married	255	24	21	22	13	16	4
Have Kids Under 18:	Yes	239	23	21	26	14	16	0
	No	353	23	20	26	12	14	5
Ethnicity:	White	444	22	19	27	13	16	3
	Black	74	29	23	17	12	15	4
	Hispanic	44	29	37	30	5	0	0
Region:	Northeast	135	19	26	31	10	12	3
	South	134	32	14	30	12	9	3
	Central	223	23	21	21	14	15	5
	West	103	18	17	24	13	26	2
Community Type:	Urban	304	22	21	25	14	16	2
	Suburban	92	17	21	28	15	16	3
	Rural	191	28	19	26	9	12	5
Voter Registration:	Not Registered	113	20	19	32	14	11	4
	Democrat	173	25	20	20	12	17	4
	Republican	149	22	21	24	13	18	3
	Independent	114	26	17	31	12	11	2
Denominational Affiliation:	Protestant	227	21	20	29	11	15	4
	Catholic	177	22	27	27	13	9	3
	Baptist	54	28	16	31	5	17	3
	Mainline Protestant	85	23	23	28	12	12	3
Churched:	Yes	449	26	21	28	12	12	2
	No	130	15	18	18	16	26	6
Born Again	Yes	231	26	17	29	12	14	2
	No	362	22	22	24	13	15	4
	Evangelical	64	25	9	32	15	17	1

TABLE 83   253

Overall, how often, if ever, do you consciously think of yourself as a representative of "Jesus Christ": always, often, sometimes, rarely, or never?

		N	Always	Often	Sometimes	Rarely	Never	Don't Know
Total Responding		594	27%	17%	26%	12%	17%	2%
Gender:	Male	286	20	14	24	20	21	1
	Female	308	33	20	28	5	12	2
Age:	18 to 27	114	22	15	29	16	18	1
	28 to 46	249	26	18	29	12	14	0
	47 to 65	123	29	15	20	12	24	1
	66 to 98	71	35	20	17	5	12	11
Income:	Under $20,000	128	31	27	20	7	13	2
	$20,000 to $40,000	189	31	17	26	11	14	0
	$40,000 to $60,000	106	22	16	30	15	17	1
	$60,000 or more	93	22	11	21	18	29	0
Education:	High School or Less	261	30	18	26	10	13	3
	Some College	134	29	18	22	14	16	2
	College Graduate	193	20	16	29	13	22	1
Marital Status:	Married	337	28	18	26	13	13	2
	Not Married	255	24	16	25	11	21	2
Have Kids Under 18:	Yes	239	27	19	30	12	10	1
	No	353	26	16	23	12	21	2
Ethnicity:	White	444	24	18	28	11	18	2
	Black	74	47	17	18	7	9	2
	Hispanic	44	23	20	18	28	10	0
Region:	Northeast	135	21	9	28	19	20	3
	South	134	37	21	20	10	11	1
	Central	223	30	19	29	11	10	2
	West	103	13	19	24	9	35	1
Community Type:	Urban	304	24	17	25	14	18	1
	Suburban	92	22	13	33	13	16	3
	Rural	191	33	19	25	8	14	1
Voter Registration:	Not Registered	113	20	12	31	15	20	3
	Democrat	173	27	20	24	10	18	1
	Republican	149	34	21	21	13	10	1
	Independent	114	22	12	31	14	19	3
Denominational Affiliation:	Protestant	227	35	20	22	9	12	2
	Catholic	177	20	16	34	18	10	1
	Baptist	54	45	21	15	5	13	2
	Mainline Protestant	85	33	21	27	9	7	3
Churched:	Yes	449	30	20	27	13	9	2
	No	130	12	6	25	10	45	2
Born Again	Yes	231	38	28	23	6	4	1
	No	362	19	10	27	16	25	2
	Evangelical	64	50	36	12	2	0	0

TABLE 84

Do you agree strongly, agree somewhat, disagree somewhat, or disagree strongly with the following statement: "Overall, the mass media seem to be biased against Christian beliefs"?

		N	Agree Strongly	Agree Somewhat	Disagree Somewhat	Disagree Strongly	Don't Know
Total Responding		617	21%	17%	28%	24%	9%
Gender:	Male	298	20	19	31	21	9
	Female	318	22	15	25	27	10
Age:	18 to 27	120	15	17	32	29	7
	28-46	234	19	20	31	21	9
	47-65	116	29	17	23	24	7
	66-98	93	32	17	16	21	14
Income:	Under $20,000	138	23	20	21	28	7
	$20,000 to $40,000	205	21	17	29	26	6
	$40,000 to $60,000	116	24	11	33	22	9
	$60,000 or more	79	19	24	26	18	13
Education:	High School or Less	268	25	18	26	23	8
	Some College	129	16	21	28	26	9
	College Graduate	217	19	14	30	25	12
Marital Status:	Married	353	23	19	26	21	11
	Not Married	262	19	15	31	28	7
Have Kids Under 18:	Yes	254	19	20	27	22	12
	No	359	23	15	28	26	8
Ethnicity:	White	458	21	16	30	24	9
	Black	80	29	15	22	27	7
	Hispanic	45	24	26	19	24	7
Region:	Northeast	135	17	13	31	27	13
	South	136	28	17	25	20	10
	Central	250	19	20	24	27	9
	West	96	22	16	40	18	3
Community Type:	Urban	339	22	16	25	26	10
	Suburban	75	20	14	29	25	13
	Rural	199	21	21	32	20	6
Voter Registration:	Not Registered	103	16	20	25	21	17
	Reg. Democrat	218	17	14	30	31	8
	Reg. Republican	163	38	14	28	17	4
	Reg. Independent	97	8	27	30	24	10
Denominational Affiliation:	Protestant	251	29	15	26	20	10
	Catholic	174	9	22	34	25	10
	Baptist	64	46	17	20	12	6
	Mainline Protestant	114	19	13	34	26	7
Churched:	Yes	456	25	19	27	22	7
	No	144	9	14	33	30	14
Born Again:	Yes	247	36	22	22	14	7
	No	369	12	14	32	31	11
	Evangelical	68	71	18	6	4	1

TABLE 85   255

Do you agree strongly, agree somewhat, disagree somewhat, or disagree strongly with the following statement: "Overall, the mass media seem to favor liberal views on politics and issues"?

		N	Agree Strongly	Agree Somewhat	Disagree Somewhat	Disagree Strongly	Don't Know
Total Responding		617	33%	32%	20%	8%	8%
Gender:	Male	298	36	32	20	6	5
	Female	318	29	31	20	10	10
Age:	18 to 27	120	26	33	25	13	4
	28-46	234	33	37	19	6	6
	47-65	116	42	23	22	7	7
	66-98	93	38	26	11	7	17
Income:	Under $20,000	138	36	32	18	5	9
	$20,000 to $40,000	205	32	31	19	11	6
	$40,000 to $60,000	116	31	32	26	5	6
	$60,000 or more	79	35	34	21	7	3
Education:	High School or Less	268	33	31	21	6	9
	Some College	129	40	29	12	10	10
	College Graduate	217	29	34	24	8	5
Marital Status:	Married	353	33	31	20	6	9
	Not Married	262	32	32	20	11	5
Have Kids Under 18:	Yes	254	29	36	22	6	7
	No	359	36	29	19	9	8
Ethnicity:	White	458	34	31	19	8	8
	Black	80	28	31	34	3	4
	Hispanic	45	42	38	11	3	7
Region:	Northeast	135	35	32	23	7	3
	South	136	36	31	16	6	11
	Central	250	29	35	19	7	10
	West	96	36	22	26	13	2
Community Type:	Urban	339	33	31	19	9	7
	Suburban	75	32	38	18	8	5
	Rural	199	32	30	23	5	10
Voter Registration:	Not Registered	103	31	30	18	10	11
	Reg. Democrat	218	24	41	24	6	5
	Reg. Republican	163	49	23	14	8	6
	Reg. Independent	97	28	31	26	7	8
Denominational Affiliation:	Protestant	251	38	27	19	8	8
	Catholic	174	25	44	18	9	3
	Baptist	64	47	24	17	5	8
	Mainline Protestant	114	36	27	20	9	8
Churched:	Yes	456	36	33	17	8	5
	No	144	25	28	27	8	12
Born Again:	Yes	247	41	30	17	6	6
	No	369	27	32	22	9	9
	Evangelical	68	66	23	7	3	1

TABLE 86

Do you agree strongly, agree somewhat, disagree somewhat, or disagree strongly with the following statement: "The mass media should report information on the moral behavior of political candidates and leaders"?

		N	Agree Strongly	Agree Somewhat	Disagree Somewhat	Disagree Strongly	Don't Know
Total Responding		617	39%	26%	16%	15%	4%
Gender:	Male	298	41	27	15	13	4
	Female	318	37	25	17	17	5
Age:	18 to 27	120	38	23	29	9	1
	28-46	234	33	32	16	16	3
	47-65	116	49	20	10	13	8
	66-98	93	49	22	4	17	8
Income:	Under $20,000	138	43	21	12	15	9
	$20,000 to $40,000	205	36	28	18	16	2
	$40,000 to $60,000	116	39	31	16	13	2
	$60,000 or more	79	34	28	20	14	3
Education:	High School or Less	268	38	23	16	16	6
	Some College	129	45	28	13	10	4
	College Graduate	217	35	29	18	17	2
Marital Status:	Married	353	41	27	13	16	3
	Not Married	262	36	25	20	14	6
Have Kids Under 18:	Yes	254	36	28	18	15	3
	No	359	40	25	15	15	5
Ethnicity:	White	458	40	25	15	15	4
	Black	80	42	27	13	14	4
	Hispanic	45	23	19	24	23	11
Region:	Northeast	135	37	26	14	18	5
	South	136	50	23	9	16	3
	Central	250	33	29	21	14	4
	West	96	41	24	16	14	5
Community Type:	Urban	339	38	25	17	15	5
	Suburban	75	35	22	16	21	7
	Rural	199	40	30	15	13	2
Voter Registration:	Not Registered	103	40	20	22	11	7
	Reg. Democrat	218	30	23	18	23	6
	Reg. Republican	163	52	27	10	9	2
	Reg. Independent	97	34	33	16	15	2
Denominational Affiliation:	Protestant	251	43	25	12	15	5
	Catholic	174	31	27	21	18	3
	Baptist	64	46	18	9	16	10
	Mainline Protestant	114	44	22	11	20	3
Churched:	Yes	456	40	26	15	15	4
	No	144	34	27	18	15	6
Born Again:	Yes	247	49	23	11	12	4
	No	369	32	28	19	17	5
	Evangelical	68	71	17	4	4	4

TABLE 87   257

Do you agree strongly, agree somewhat, disagree somewhat, or disagree strongly with the following statement: "Overall, the mass media are objective; that is, they do not interpret events and information, they just report them without any type of bias"?

		N	Agree Strongly	Agree Somewhat	Disagree Somewhat	Disagree Strongly	Don't Know
Total Responding		617	12%	21%	27%	35%	6%
Gender:	Male	298	12	19	30	35	4
	Female	318	12	22	25	34	8
Age:	18 to 27	120	16	17	35	30	2
	28-46	234	9	24	28	35	3
	47-65	116	12	18	27	38	6
	66-98	93	15	23	14	34	14
Income:	Under $20,000	138	17	23	24	30	6
	$20,000 to $40,000	205	15	24	29	29	4
	$40,000 to $60,000	116	7	18	28	44	2
	$60,000 or more	79	7	15	32	44	3
Education:	High School or Less	268	14	24	23	30	9
	Some College	129	12	20	28	37	3
	College Graduate	217	8	17	32	40	3
Marital Status:	Married	353	9	21	28	36	6
	Not Married	262	15	21	27	33	5
Have Kids Under 18:	Yes	254	12	20	28	34	5
	No	359	11	21	26	35	6
Ethnicity:	White	458	10	20	27	37	6
	Black	80	23	20	28	26	3
	Hispanic	45	20	25	32	19	4
Region:	Northeast	135	10	20	35	32	3
	South	136	13	14	24	38	10
	Central	250	12	23	28	33	5
	West	96	12	26	19	39	4
Community Type:	Urban	339	13	22	25	34	5
	Suburban	75	3	19	23	52	4
	Rural	199	12	19	32	29	7
Voter Registration:	Not Registered	103	12	16	34	27	10
	Reg. Democrat	218	16	28	26	23	6
	Reg. Republican	163	6	11	29	50	4
	Reg. Independent	97	12	27	19	40	2
Denominational Affiliation:	Protestant	251	12	18	23	41	6
	Catholic	174	11	28	30	25	6
	Baptist	64	18	13	17	44	8
	Mainline Protestant	114	10	22	23	40	5
Churched:	Yes	456	12	21	28	34	5
	No	144	11	18	25	39	7
Born Again:	Yes	247	11	18	26	39	7
	No	369	12	23	28	32	5
	Evangelical	68	9	11	31	43	6

TABLE 88

In the past 30 days, did you make a contribution to any type of charitable organization, including a church or synagogue?

		N	Yes	No	Don't Know
Total Responding		1205	67%	33%	0%
Gender:	Male	577	62	38	0
	Female	628	72	28	0
Age:	18 to 27	212	51	49	0
	28-46	453	69	31	0
	47-65	250	75	25	0
	66-98	201	67	33	0
Income:	Under $20,000	274	52	48	0
	$20,000 to $40,000	391	66	34	0
	$40,000 to $60,000	212	75	25	0
	$60,000 or more	166	81	19	0
Education:	High School or Less	532	59	41	0
	Some College	262	70	30	0
	College Graduate	403	75	24	0
Marital Status:	Married	689	76	24	0
	Not Married	512	55	45	0
Have Kids Under 18:	Yes	468	68	32	0
	No	731	67	33	0
Ethnicity:	White	903	70	30	0
	Black	150	56	44	0
	Hispanic	90	64	36	0
Region:	Northeast	264	61	39	0
	South	263	65	35	0
	Central	481	71	28	0
	West	197	68	32	0
Community Type:	Urban	638	66	34	0
	Suburban	169	70	30	0
	Rural	385	69	31	0
Voter Registration:	Not Registered	206	46	54	0
	Reg. Democrat	395	69	31	0
	Reg. Republican	315	75	25	0
	Reg. Independent	208	70	30	0
Denominational	Protestant	494	75	25	0
Affiliation:	Catholic	343	69	31	0
	Baptist	122	74	26	0
	Mainline Protestant	204	78	22	0
Churched:	Yes	902	75	25	0
	No	270	43	57	0
Born Again:	Yes	477	79	21	0
	No	728	59	40	0
	Evangelical	130	89	11	0

TABLE 89   259

Overall, how trustworthy are the leaders of nonprofit organizations and charities in America? In general, do you feel they are very, somewhat, not too, or not at all trustworthy?

		N	Very	Somewhat	Not Too	Or Not At All	Don't Know
Total Responding		1205	8%	58%	19%	8%	6%
Gender:	Male	577	8	57	19	8	8
	Female	628	8	58	20	8	5
Age:	18 to 27	212	10	68	15	6	1
	28-46	453	9	65	15	5	6
	47-65	250	9	48	24	12	7
	66-98	201	6	44	27	12	11
Income:	Under $20,000	274	8	54	20	11	7
	$20,000 to $40,000	391	7	63	18	8	4
	$40,000 to $60,000	212	9	62	18	7	4
	$60,000 or more	166	10	58	20	6	7
Education:	High School or Less	532	6	54	21	11	8
	Some College	262	10	61	19	6	3
	College Graduate	403	10	61	17	6	6
Marital Status:	Married	689	8	57	21	7	7
	Not Married	512	8	60	17	10	6
Have Kids Under 18:	Yes	468	8	63	14	8	6
	No	731	8	54	22	8	7
Ethnicity:	White	903	8	59	20	8	5
	Black	150	5	59	24	6	7
	Hispanic	90	17	58	4	8	12
Region:	Northeast	264	11	62	14	9	4
	South	263	6	60	18	9	7
	Central	481	8	55	22	7	7
	West	197	8	56	21	8	7
Community Type:	Urban	638	9	59	18	8	6
	Suburban	169	8	53	24	11	4
	Rural	385	8	59	19	7	7
Voter Registration:	Not Registered	206	7	57	19	7	10
	Reg. Democrat	395	9	56	19	9	7
	Reg. Republican	315	9	59	20	8	4
	Reg. Independent	208	7	60	22	8	2
Denominational Affiliation:	Protestant	494	8	59	19	8	7
	Catholic	343	11	59	20	6	4
	Baptist	122	3	57	21	8	11
	Mainline Protestant	204	9	56	19	10	7
Churched:	Yes	902	9	59	18	8	6
	No	270	7	56	20	9	8
Born Again:	Yes	477	9	60	18	7	6
	No	728	8	56	20	9	7
	Evangelical	130	12	60	17	6	5

TABLE 90

In the next six months, will you probably give more money or the same amount of money to nonprofit organizations and charities as you did in the last six months?

		N	More Money	Same Amount	Less Money	Don't Know
Total Responding		1205	13%	70%	11%	5%
Gender:	Male	577	14	70	12	4
	Female	628	12	71	11	6
Age:	18 to 27	212	19	66	9	6
	28-46	453	19	70	9	3
	47-65	250	7	77	13	4
	66-98	201	4	67	17	12
Income:	Under $20,000	274	11	61	16	12
	$20,000 to $40,000	391	12	72	11	4
	$40,000 to $60,000	212	14	76	9	1
	$60,000 or more	166	14	78	8	0
Education:	High School or Less	532	12	67	14	7
	Some College	262	12	72	12	4
	College Graduate	403	15	74	8	3
Marital Status:	Married	689	13	73	11	3
	Not Married	512	13	67	11	8
Have Kids Under 18:	Yes	468	19	68	9	5
	No	731	9	72	13	6
Ethnicity:	White	903	10	75	11	4
	Black	150	25	52	13	9
	Hispanic	90	22	59	12	7
Region:	Northeast	264	8	71	15	6
	South	263	13	69	12	6
	Central	481	16	70	10	5
	West	197	11	73	10	6
Community Type:	Urban	638	13	70	11	6
	Suburban	169	11	75	12	2
	Rural	385	13	70	12	5
Voter Registration:	Not Registered	206	15	65	13	6
	Reg. Democrat	395	13	69	13	6
	Reg. Republican	315	13	74	10	3
	Reg. Independent	208	10	75	11	3
Denominational Affiliation:	Protestant	494	13	71	11	5
	Catholic	343	12	73	11	4
	Baptist	122	15	68	11	5
	Mainline Protestant	204	8	76	11	5
Churched:	Yes	902	15	70	11	4
	No	270	7	74	13	6
Born Again:	Yes	477	16	72	7	4
	No	728	11	69	14	6
	Evangelical	130	21	71	5	4

TABLE 91   261

In the next six months, will you probably give money to more nonprofit organizations and charities, fewer organizations, or the same number of organizations as you did in the last six months?

		N	More Organizations	Same Number	Fewer Organizations	Don't Know
Total Responding		1205	5%	77%	12%	6%
Gender:	Male	577	4	78	12	6
	Female	628	7	76	11	6
Age:	18 to 27	212	9	77	11	4
	28-46	453	7	79	10	4
	47-65	250	2	78	14	6
	66-98	201	0	71	14	15
Income:	Under $20,000	274	5	70	12	12
	$20,000 to $40,000	391	5	79	12	4
	$40,000 to $60,000	212	6	84	9	1
	$60,000 or more	166	5	84	10	1
Education:	High School or Less	532	5	73	13	8
	Some College	262	5	77	12	6
	College Graduate	403	5	81	10	4
Marital Status:	Married	689	4	81	11	5
	Not Married	512	7	71	13	8
Have Kids Under 18:	Yes	468	7	79	9	4
	No	731	4	75	13	7
Ethnicity:	White	903	4	79	12	5
	Black	150	11	68	9	12
	Hispanic	90	8	68	14	10
Region:	Northeast	264	5	73	15	7
	South	263	3	77	13	7
	Central	481	6	78	9	7
	West	197	5	78	13	3
Community Type:	Urban	638	6	76	12	6
	Suburban	169	4	80	12	4
	Rural	385	4	79	11	6
Voter Registration:	Not Registered	206	10	70	12	8
	Reg. Democrat	395	4	75	13	8
	Reg. Republican	315	5	79	12	4
	Reg. Independent	208	3	84	9	4
Denominational	Protestant	494	4	79	11	6
Affiliation:	Catholic	343	4	77	13	6
	Baptist	122	8	74	9	9
	Mainline Protestant	204	3	81	12	5
Churched:	Yes	902	5	78	12	5
	No	270	5	75	12	8
Born Again:	Yes	477	6	80	9	4
	No	728	5	75	13	7
	Evangelical	130	5	84	8	3

TABLE 92

Do you agree strongly, agree somewhat, disagree somewhat, or disagree strongly with the following statement: "Allowing homosexuals in the military will make our armed forces more effective in combat"?

		N	Agree Strongly	Agree Somewhat	Disagree Somewhat	Disagree Strongly	Don't Know
Total Responding		1205	8%	7%	21%	47%	17%
Gender:	Male	577	7	5	18	57	12
	Female	628	9	9	23	38	22
Age:	18 to 27	212	10	14	26	36	14
	28-46	453	7	7	23	47	16
	47-65	250	6	5	17	54	18
	66-98	201	9	5	17	51	19
Income:	Under $20,000	274	13	8	23	43	14
	$20,000 to $40,000	391	8	8	18	51	15
	$40,000 to $60,000	212	5	6	28	46	15
	$60,000 or more	166	7	5	20	47	21
Education:	High School or Less	532	8	10	17	47	18
	Some College	262	10	8	23	46	13
	College Graduate	403	7	3	23	47	19
Marital Status:	Married	689	6	6	19	52	17
	Not Married	512	10	9	23	41	18
Have Kids Under 18:	Yes	468	8	9	21	44	17
	No	731	8	6	20	49	18
Ethnicity:	White	903	6	7	20	52	16
	Black	150	21	6	22	31	20
	Hispanic	90	9	8	27	42	14
Region:	Northeast	264	5	10	22	46	17
	South	263	9	4	18	52	18
	Central	481	7	6	22	48	17
	West	197	12	10	20	41	17
Community Type:	Urban	638	9	7	20	48	16
	Suburban	169	4	7	25	42	22
	Rural	385	7	8	19	48	18
Voter Registration:	Not Registered	206	6	10	19	50	16
	Reg. Democrat	395	12	8	21	39	20
	Reg. Republican	315	6	7	16	61	11
	Reg. Independent	208	7	4	29	40	20
Denominational Affiliation:	Protestant	494	7	4	19	55	15
	Catholic	343	6	11	24	46	13
	Baptist	122	12	1	18	58	11
	Mainline Protestant	204	6	5	22	52	15
Churched:	Yes	902	8	7	21	49	15
	No	270	8	9	20	41	22
Born Again:	Yes	477	8	5	19	56	12
	No	728	8	8	22	41	21
	Evangelical	130	4	2	11	73	10

TABLE 93   263

Do you agree strongly, agree somewhat, disagree somewhat, or disagree strongly with the following statement: "Allowing homosexuals in the military will make it more difficult for some soldiers who are not homosexual to concentrate on their job duties"?

		N	Agree Strongly	Agree Somewhat	Disagree Somewhat	Disagree Strongly	Don't Know
Total Responding		1205	38%	20%	12%	20%	10%
Gender:	Male	577	44	22	10	18	7
	Female	628	32	19	15	22	12
Age:	18 to 27	212	41	20	14	18	6
	28-46	453	36	23	12	21	7
	47-65	250	35	19	13	22	11
	66-98	201	42	19	10	15	14
Income:	Under $20,000	274	44	14	14	16	12
	$20,000 to $40,000	391	37	22	14	20	7
	$40,000 to $60,000	212	37	24	11	22	6
	$60,000 or more	166	35	21	10	26	8
Education:	High School or Less	532	43	19	13	14	10
	Some College	262	36	20	13	21	9
	College Graduate	403	32	22	11	27	8
Marital Status:	Married	689	38	22	12	21	9
	Not Married	512	38	19	13	19	11
Have Kids Under 18:	Yes	468	37	22	15	19	7
	No	731	38	19	11	21	11
Ethnicity:	White	903	39	22	12	19	8
	Black	150	33	10	16	29	13
	Hispanic	90	38	19	9	25	9
Region:	Northeast	264	37	23	13	19	8
	South	263	47	16	11	19	6
	Central	481	34	23	13	20	11
	West	197	36	16	12	23	13
Community Type:	Urban	638	37	19	12	23	9
	Suburban	169	36	22	13	19	10
	Rural	385	39	23	13	17	9
Voter Registration:	Not Registered	206	41	20	10	20	9
	Reg. Democrat	395	29	18	14	30	9
	Reg. Republican	315	50	22	10	10	8
	Reg. Independent	208	34	24	16	17	9
Denominational Affiliation:	Protestant	494	44	20	11	17	8
	Catholic	343	33	25	11	24	8
	Baptist	122	54	12	12	14	8
	Mainline Protestant	204	35	23	13	22	8
Churched:	Yes	902	40	21	12	20	8
	No	270	32	19	15	21	12
Born Again:	Yes	477	45	20	13	15	7
	No	728	33	20	12	24	11
	Evangelical	130	63	15	9	7	7

TABLE 94

Do you agree strongly, agree somewhat, disagree somewhat, or disagree strongly with the following statement: "Acknowledged homosexuals should not be prohibited from serving in the military solely because of their sexual orientation"?

		N	Agree Strongly	Agree Somewhat	Disagree Somewhat	Disagree Strongly	Don't Know
Total Responding		1205	41%	16%	8%	26%	8%
Gender:	Male	577	38	17	7	32	6
	Female	628	43	16	9	21	10
Age:	18 to 27	212	50	14	8	25	4
	28-46	453	40	19	8	28	5
	47-65	250	36	14	10	28	12
	66-98	201	37	16	9	25	13
Income:	Under $20,000	274	40	13	11	26	11
	$20,000 to $40,000	391	41	17	10	25	7
	$40,000 to $60,000	212	46	17	8	25	4
	$60,000 or more	166	45	20	3	29	4
Education:	High School or Less	532	36	15	10	28	11
	Some College	262	41	17	9	23	9
	College Graduate	403	47	17	6	25	5
Marital Status:	Married	689	38	19	8	26	9
	Not Married	512	45	13	8	26	8
Have Kids Under 18:	Yes	468	40	18	9	28	5
	No	731	41	15	8	25	10
Ethnicity:	White	903	38	17	10	27	8
	Black	150	46	14	4	27	9
	Hispanic	90	53	11	4	28	4
Region:	Northeast	264	45	18	9	21	7
	South	263	35	14	9	30	11
	Central	481	39	18	8	27	8
	West	197	49	14	8	24	6
Community Type:	Urban	638	45	15	7	26	7
	Suburban	169	40	21	10	21	8
	Rural	385	35	17	10	28	9
Voter Registration:	Not Registered	206	36	16	7	26	14
	Reg. Democrat	395	50	17	7	21	6
	Reg. Republican	315	32	14	10	38	6
	Reg. Independent	208	45	21	10	16	8
Denominational Affiliation:	Protestant	494	37	18	8	29	8
	Catholic	343	41	15	12	24	8
	Baptist	122	36	12	7	36	8
	Mainline Protestant	204	39	23	6	25	6
Churched:	Yes	902	39	17	9	27	8
	No	270	51	15	5	20	8
Born Again:	Yes	477	36	16	11	31	7
	No	728	44	17	7	23	9
	Evangelical	130	26	9	10	47	9

Do you agree strongly, agree somewhat, disagree somewhat, or disagree strongly with the following statement: "The government should have the right to deny admission to the military to homosexuals if there is proof that their presence would jeopardize the effectiveness of the armed forces in times of combat"?

		N	Agree Strongly	Agree Somewhat	Disagree Somewhat	Disagree Strongly	Don't Know
Total Responding		1205	51%	17%	6%	17%	8%
Gender:	Male	577	57	17	6	14	6
	Female	628	46	18	7	20	10
Age:	18 to 27	212	49	23	8	16	4
	28-46	453	50	18	8	18	5
	47-65	250	52	16	5	16	11
	66-98	201	54	13	2	18	13
Income:	Under $20,000	274	53	15	6	18	9
	$20,000 to $40,000	391	53	18	7	17	5
	$40,000 to $60,000	212	53	20	5	16	6
	$60,000 or more	166	51	18	4	17	9
Education:	High School or Less	532	54	17	7	14	8
	Some College	262	52	16	8	19	6
	College Graduate	403	48	18	5	20	9
Marital Status:	Married	689	52	17	6	16	9
	Not Married	512	50	18	7	19	6
Have Kids Under 18:	Yes	468	50	20	9	15	6
	No	731	52	16	5	18	9
Ethnicity:	White	903	53	18	5	15	8
	Black	150	51	15	4	23	7
	Hispanic	90	45	11	17	27	0
Region:	Northeast	264	46	22	6	18	7
	South	263	59	12	6	14	9
	Central	481	52	18	7	15	8
	West	197	46	17	6	23	7
Community Type:	Urban	638	51	17	7	18	7
	Suburban	169	45	20	9	17	9
	Rural	385	55	17	4	15	8
Voter Registration:	Not Registered	206	50	16	9	14	10
	Reg. Democrat	395	44	17	7	25	7
	Reg. Republican	315	63	15	4	11	7
	Reg. Independent	208	49	23	8	13	7
Denominational Affiliation:	Protestant	494	59	16	4	13	8
	Catholic	343	46	20	10	19	5
	Baptist	122	64	10	3	16	6
	Mainline Protestant	204	51	20	7	14	8
Churched:	Yes	902	53	18	6	16	7
	No	270	47	17	7	18	12
Born Again:	Yes	477	62	15	6	12	6
	No	728	45	19	7	20	9
	Evangelical	130	82	9	1	3	5

Do you agree strongly, agree somewhat, disagree somewhat, or disagree strongly with the following statement: "If you were serving in the armed forces, you would not want to be forced to serve with homosexuals"?

		N	Agree Strongly	Agree Somewhat	Disagree Somewhat	Disagree Strongly	Don't Know
Total Responding		1205	38%	11%	14%	28%	9%
Gender:	Male	577	48	10	14	22	7
	Female	628	28	12	14	34	12
Age:	18 to 27	212	33	12	17	33	5
	28-46	453	37	12	14	32	5
	47-65	250	38	8	13	26	15
	66-98	201	43	10	12	18	17
Income:	Under $20,000	274	42	11	11	22	15
	$20,000 to $40,000	391	37	10	15	29	9
	$40,000 to $60,000	212	38	12	17	31	3
	$60,000 or more	166	36	8	12	37	7
Education:	High School or Less	532	41	11	15	22	11
	Some College	262	36	11	15	29	9
	College Graduate	403	34	9	12	37	8
Marital Status:	Married	689	39	11	14	27	9
	Not Married	512	36	10	14	31	10
Have Kids Under 18:	Yes	468	36	14	15	28	6
	No	731	38	8	13	29	11
Ethnicity:	White	903	41	11	13	26	9
	Black	150	26	6	14	41	14
	Hispanic	90	31	16	18	32	2
Region:	Northeast	264	33	13	16	30	8
	South	263	43	10	12	27	8
	Central	481	38	10	14	25	11
	West	197	34	10	10	37	9
Community Type:	Urban	638	36	11	13	31	9
	Suburban	169	38	13	18	24	8
	Rural	385	41	9	13	26	11
Voter Registration:	Not Registered	206	40	11	16	26	7
	Reg. Democrat	395	27	9	15	39	11
	Reg. Republican	315	55	12	9	18	6
	Reg. Independent	208	31	13	18	27	11
Denominational Affiliation:	Protestant	494	48	8	12	22	10
	Catholic	343	31	15	15	32	7
	Baptist	122	59	8	9	13	11
	Mainline Protestant	204	40	8	15	29	8
Churched:	Yes	902	39	12	15	26	8
	No	270	33	8	11	38	11
Born Again:	Yes	477	45	11	13	22	9
	No	728	32	11	14	33	10
	Evangelical	130	69	9	7	6	8

TABLE 97 267

Do you agree strongly, agree somewhat, disagree somewhat, or disagree strongly with the following statement: "Whether a person is homosexual or not is a private matter that is nobody else's business"?

		N	Agree Strongly	Agree Somewhat	Disagree Somewhat	Disagree Strongly	Don't Know
Total Responding		1205	61%	20%	4%	10%	5%
Gender:	Male	577	58	21	6	12	3
	Female	628	65	18	3	9	6
Age:	18 to 27	212	62	19	5	12	2
	28-46	453	64	20	5	9	3
	47-65	250	59	21	2	13	5
	66-98	201	55	20	3	11	12
Income:	Under $20,000	274	59	21	3	14	3
	$20,000 to $40,000	391	61	21	4	9	5
	$40,000 to $60,000	212	64	19	6	9	2
	$60,000 or more	166	65	16	6	11	1
Education:	High School or Less	532	58	20	4	13	5
	Some College	262	57	24	2	10	7
	College Graduate	403	68	16	5	8	3
Marital Status:	Married	689	60	21	4	11	4
	Not Married	512	63	18	4	10	6
Have Kids Under 18:	Yes	468	61	21	5	10	3
	No	731	62	19	3	11	6
Ethnicity:	White	903	60	20	5	11	5
	Black	150	62	21	2	10	5
	Hispanic	90	76	10	0	12	2
Region:	Northeast	264	65	21	3	7	3
	South	263	54	20	5	17	4
	Central	481	61	20	4	9	6
	West	197	66	16	4	11	4
Community Type:	Urban	638	63	17	4	11	5
	Suburban	169	61	28	4	4	3
	Rural	385	59	20	5	11	4
Voter Registration:	Not Registered	206	61	19	6	10	5
	Reg. Democrat	395	71	18	3	6	2
	Reg. Republican	315	48	21	6	18	7
	Reg. Independent	208	64	22	2	8	3
Denominational Affiliation:	Protestant	494	54	21	5	15	5
	Catholic	343	69	18	3	6	3
	Baptist	122	50	20	4	19	7
	Mainline Protestant	204	64	17	5	9	4
Churched:	Yes	902	59	21	5	12	4
	No	270	71	15	2	6	5
Born Again:	Yes	477	50	23	6	16	4
	No	728	69	17	3	7	5
	Evangelical	130	30	22	7	35	7

TABLE 98

Do you agree strongly, agree somewhat, disagree somewhat, or disagree strongly with the following statement: "In your view, homosexuality is immoral"?

		N	Agree Strongly	Agree Somewhat	Disagree Somewhat	Disagree Strongly	Don't Know
Total Responding		1205	44%	11%	14%	21%	10%
Gender:	Male	577	50	10	15	16	9
	Female	628	39	12	14	25	11
Age:	18 to 27	212	42	9	19	24	5
	28-46	453	42	13	15	24	6
	47-65	250	46	9	13	20	12
	66-98	201	55	12	7	7	19
Income:	Under $20,000	274	52	12	11	17	8
	$20,000 to $40,000	391	46	11	14	19	10
	$40,000 to $60,000	212	42	11	19	24	4
	$60,000 or more	166	37	10	17	28	8
Education:	High School or Less	532	52	12	14	13	10
	Some College	262	40	12	13	22	12
	College Graduate	403	36	10	15	31	9
Marital Status:	Married	689	47	11	14	18	10
	Not Married	512	40	11	15	25	9
Have Kids Under 18:	Yes	468	46	12	17	19	7
	No	731	43	11	13	22	11
Ethnicity:	White	903	45	12	14	20	9
	Black	150	41	12	10	21	15
	Hispanic	90	43	8	13	31	5
Region:	Northeast	264	35	13	14	29	9
	South	263	50	11	15	17	8
	Central	481	47	12	14	17	10
	West	197	42	7	14	24	13
Community Type:	Urban	638	46	10	12	23	8
	Suburban	169	30	15	18	23	14
	Rural	385	47	11	15	16	10
Voter Registration:	Not Registered	206	47	11	17	18	7
	Reg. Democrat	395	38	11	14	27	10
	Reg. Republican	315	54	9	13	15	9
	Reg. Independent	208	35	15	16	23	11
Denominational Affiliation:	Protestant	494	53	10	12	15	10
	Catholic	343	36	15	17	22	11
	Baptist	122	69	7	9	8	8
	Mainline Protestant	204	39	14	16	20	10
Churched:	Yes	902	47	12	14	18	9
	No	270	33	9	16	33	10
Born Again:	Yes	477	60	10	11	11	8
	No	728	33	12	16	27	11
	Evangelical	130	88	4	2	4	3

TABLE 99   269

Do you agree strongly, agree somewhat, disagree somewhat, or disagree strongly with the following statement: "You would prefer that the government keep its existing policy, which does not allow acknowledged homosexuals to serve in the armed forces"?

		N	Agree Strongly	Agree Somewhat	Disagree Somewhat	Disagree Strongly	Don't Know
Total Responding		1205	37%	10%	15%	29%	9%
Gender:	Male	577	44	10	12	26	8
	Female	628	30	10	18	31	11
Age:	18 to 27	212	28	14	25	30	4
	28-46	453	37	12	13	30	8
	47-65	250	34	7	19	30	10
	66-98	201	48	5	12	18	17
Income:	Under $20,000	274	40	7	19	24	10
	$20,000 to $40,000	391	39	12	14	28	7
	$40,000 to $60,000	212	34	12	16	32	6
	$60,000 or more	166	36	8	10	39	7
Education:	High School or Less	532	41	9	18	21	11
	Some College	262	35	12	15	30	8
	College Graduate	403	33	9	12	39	8
Marital Status:	Married	689	38	10	14	27	10
	Not Married	512	35	9	17	31	8
Have Kids Under 18:	Yes	468	36	13	18	25	8
	No	731	38	8	14	31	10
Ethnicity:	White	903	40	10	15	27	9
	Black	150	27	13	11	38	10
	Hispanic	90	39	6	18	33	5
Region:	Northeast	264	35	10	15	31	8
	South	263	45	7	15	23	10
	Central	481	36	12	14	28	9
	West	197	29	8	19	35	9
Community Type:	Urban	638	35	11	17	31	7
	Suburban	169	34	11	14	30	10
	Rural	385	41	8	14	26	12
Voter Registration:	Not Registered	206	34	12	14	28	11
	Reg. Democrat	395	27	8	17	39	9
	Reg. Republican	315	55	9	12	18	6
	Reg. Independent	208	32	12	19	27	10
Denominational Affiliation:	Protestant	494	46	10	12	24	9
	Catholic	343	31	10	19	32	8
	Baptist	122	60	9	6	19	5
	Mainline Protestant	204	37	9	15	32	7
Churched:	Yes	902	39	11	16	26	8
	No	270	30	7	13	38	12
Born Again:	Yes	477	45	10	15	22	7
	No	728	31	9	16	33	11
	Evangelical	130	70	10	5	9	6

TABLE 100

Do you agree strongly, agree somewhat, disagree somewhat, or disagree strongly with the following statement: "The Bible is totally accurate in all of its teachings"?

		N	Agree Strongly	Agree Somewhat	Disagree Somewhat	Disagree Strongly	Don't Know
Total Responding		1205	42%	18%	19%	15%	6%
Gender:	Male	577	36	20	21	18	5
	Female	628	47	17	16	12	7
Age:	18 to 27	212	38	22	19	18	3
	28-46	453	39	21	21	13	5
	47-65	250	42	13	19	18	7
	66-98	201	53	14	12	11	9
Income:	Under $20,000	274	54	16	14	11	4
	$20,000 to $40,000	391	41	22	18	13	6
	$40,000 to $60,000	212	36	19	23	18	4
	$60,000 or more	166	29	16	24	26	4
Education:	High School or Less	532	50	19	17	8	6
	Some College	262	42	15	20	16	6
	College Graduate	403	31	20	20	24	5
Marital Status:	Married	689	45	18	18	13	5
	Not Married	512	37	18	19	18	7
Have Kids Under 18:	Yes	468	43	22	20	10	5
	No	731	41	16	18	18	6
Ethnicity:	White	903	40	19	19	16	7
	Black	150	60	7	16	13	3
	Hispanic	90	42	20	20	12	6
Region:	Northeast	264	28	22	24	18	8
	South	263	56	15	17	9	4
	Central	481	46	19	17	13	5
	West	197	32	16	19	25	9
Community Type:	Urban	638	41	15	20	18	6
	Suburban	169	33	23	22	15	7
	Rural	385	45	21	16	11	6
Voter Registration:	Not Registered	206	41	18	19	15	8
	Reg. Democrat	395	42	18	19	17	5
	Reg. Republican	315	49	17	19	9	6
	Reg. Independent	208	34	20	19	20	7
Denominational Affiliation:	Protestant	494	52	14	19	11	4
	Catholic	343	28	29	23	13	9
	Baptist	122	70	9	12	5	4
	Mainline Protestant	204	42	20	22	13	4
Churched:	Yes	902	47	19	17	12	5
	No	270	22	17	24	26	10
Born Again:	Yes	477	67	14	12	3	3
	No	728	25	21	23	23	8
	Evangelical	130	100	0	0	0	0

TABLE 101   271

Do you agree strongly, agree somewhat, disagree somewhat, or disagree strongly with the following statement: "If a person is generally good, or does enough good things for others during their life, they will earn a place in heaven"?

		N	Agree Strongly	Agree Somewhat	Disagree Somewhat	Disagree Strongly	Don't Know
Total Responding		1205	39%	18%	8%	26%	9%
Gender:	Male	577	37	19	8	26	10
	Female	628	41	16	9	27	8
Age:	18 to 27	212	37	27	12	19	5
	28-46	453	38	18	9	26	9
	47-65	250	38	14	8	30	10
	66-98	201	46	9	5	29	11
Income:	Under $20,000	274	40	16	9	27	7
	$20,000 to $40,000	391	38	21	9	24	7
	$40,000 to $60,000	212	40	17	7	30	7
	$60,000 or more	166	35	20	9	26	10
Education:	High School or Less	532	47	17	7	24	6
	Some College	262	33	21	8	30	9
	College Graduate	403	33	17	11	27	12
Marital Status:	Married	689	39	18	7	28	8
	Not Married	512	39	18	10	24	9
Have Kids Under 18:	Yes	468	41	19	8	25	6
	No	731	38	16	9	27	10
Ethnicity:	White	903	39	17	8	28	8
	Black	150	35	15	17	21	13
	Hispanic	90	57	15	2	22	4
Region:	Northeast	264	51	18	6	16	8
	South	263	28	18	10	37	6
	Central	481	39	17	9	26	9
	West	197	38	18	7	26	11
Community Type:	Urban	638	38	17	9	26	9
	Suburban	169	42	20	8	22	8
	Rural	385	40	17	8	27	8
Voter Registration:	Not Registered	206	41	23	9	19	9
	Reg. Democrat	395	45	14	8	25	7
	Reg. Republican	315	34	16	6	37	7
	Reg. Independent	208	36	21	9	22	12
Denominational Affiliation:	Protestant	494	31	14	9	39	6
	Catholic	343	61	23	6	5	4
	Baptist	122	23	12	9	54	2
	Mainline Protestant	204	38	18	11	27	5
Churched:	Yes	902	39	16	8	30	6
	No	270	37	23	9	15	16
Born Again:	Yes	477	30	11	10	46	3
	No	728	45	22	7	13	12
	Evangelical	130	0	0	0	100	0

TABLE 102

Do you agree strongly, agree somewhat, disagree somewhat, or disagree strongly with the following statement: "Jesus Christ was crucified, died, and rose from the dead and is spiritually alive today"?

		N	Agree Strongly	Agree Somewhat	Disagree Somewhat	Disagree Strongly	Don't Know
Total Responding		1205	74%	11%	3%	6%	6%
Gender:	Male	577	70	13	4	7	6
	Female	628	79	9	2	5	5
Age:	18 to 27	212	69	16	5	7	3
	28-46	453	75	11	3	4	7
	47-65	250	73	11	3	7	5
	66-98	201	82	5	2	7	5
Income:	Under $20,000	274	80	9	5	4	2
	$20,000 to $40,000	391	76	10	3	7	4
	$40,000 to $60,000	212	71	16	3	5	6
	$60,000 or more	166	69	12	4	9	7
Education:	High School or Less	532	80	10	2	4	4
	Some College	262	74	12	4	6	4
	College Graduate	403	67	12	4	9	8
Marital Status:	Married	689	77	10	2	5	6
	Not Married	512	71	12	5	7	5
Have Kids Under 18:	Yes	468	76	12	3	5	5
	No	731	74	10	4	7	6
Ethnicity:	White	903	74	11	3	7	5
	Black	150	80	9	1	5	5
	Hispanic	90	83	6	5	2	4
Region:	Northeast	264	68	13	4	9	5
	South	263	82	8	1	5	4
	Central	481	78	9	4	4	5
	West	197	63	16	3	8	10
Community Type:	Urban	638	71	11	4	7	6
	Suburban	169	76	11	3	6	4
	Rural	385	79	11	2	4	4
Voter Registration:	Not Registered	206	67	17	5	5	5
	Reg. Democrat	395	77	8	2	8	6
	Reg. Republican	315	81	10	2	3	4
	Reg. Independent	208	71	10	6	7	6
Denominational Affiliation:	Protestant	494	82	10	2	3	3
	Catholic	343	80	10	2	4	4
	Baptist	122	90	5	1	2	2
	Mainline Protestant	204	80	12	2	4	2
Churched:	Yes	902	82	10	2	4	3
	No	270	49	15	8	13	14
Born Again:	Yes	477	93	5	0	2	1
	No	728	62	15	5	8	9
	Evangelical	130	100	0	0	0	0

TABLE 103   273

Do you agree strongly, agree somewhat, disagree somewhat, or disagree strongly with the following statement: "You, personally, have a responsibility to tell other people your religious beliefs"?

		N	Agree Strongly	Agree Somewhat	Disagree Somewhat	Disagree Strongly	Don't Know
Total Responding		1205	31%	14%	18%	34%	2%
Gender:	Male	577	30	14	20	36	1
	Female	628	33	14	17	33	3
Age:	18 to 27	212	30	14	19	37	0
	28-46	453	27	17	21	33	2
	47-65	250	38	11	14	36	1
	66-98	201	39	12	18	26	6
Income:	Under $20,000	274	41	13	12	31	3
	$20,000 to $40,000	391	31	16	24	28	2
	$40,000 to $60,000	212	28	14	16	40	1
	$60,000 or more	166	20	15	22	43	0
Education:	High School or Less	532	39	15	17	26	3
	Some College	262	29	13	17	40	1
	College Graduate	403	23	14	20	42	1
Marital Status:	Married	689	32	15	20	31	2
	Not Married	512	31	13	16	39	1
Have Kids Under 18:	Yes	468	30	16	21	33	1
	No	731	33	13	17	35	2
Ethnicity:	White	903	30	15	19	35	2
	Black	150	51	11	12	26	0
	Hispanic	90	24	8	27	38	4
Region:	Northeast	264	22	16	16	45	1
	South	263	43	14	17	24	2
	Central	481	31	14	21	31	2
	West	197	29	12	17	41	2
Community Type:	Urban	638	33	14	16	35	2
	Suburban	169	26	11	22	39	1
	Rural	385	30	16	21	31	2
Voter Registration:	Not Registered	206	34	17	17	30	2
	Reg. Democrat	395	32	10	18	39	1
	Reg. Republican	315	34	17	20	27	1
	Reg. Independent	208	27	14	17	41	2
Denominational Affiliation:	Protestant	494	39	17	15	27	2
	Catholic	343	17	14	26	40	3
	Baptist	122	58	15	9	16	2
	Mainline Protestant	204	30	21	17	29	3
Churched:	Yes	902	36	16	19	28	2
	No	270	17	8	18	56	1
Born Again:	Yes	477	50	18	15	15	2
	No	728	19	11	21	47	2
	Evangelical	130	100	0	0	0	0

TABLE 104

Do you agree strongly, agree somewhat, disagree somewhat, or disagree strongly with the following statement: "Religion is very important in your life"?

		N	Agree Strongly	Agree Somewhat	Disagree Somewhat	Disagree Strongly	Don't Know
Total Responding		1205	65%	19%	9%	7%	1%
Gender:	Male	577	53	23	13	10	1
	Female	628	75	15	5	4	1
Age:	18 to 27	212	53	27	11	9	0
	28-46	453	61	21	11	7	1
	47-65	250	64	19	7	9	1
	66-98	201	84	6	4	3	3
Income:	Under $20,000	274	76	11	7	5	1
	$20,000 to $40,000	391	61	22	11	4	2
	$40,000 to $60,000	212	60	21	8	11	1
	$60,000 or more	166	54	25	9	12	0
Education:	High School or Less	532	71	17	7	4	1
	Some College	262	62	19	12	6	1
	College Graduate	403	58	21	8	11	1
Marital Status:	Married	689	68	18	8	4	1
	Not Married	512	60	20	10	10	1
Have Kids Under 18:	Yes	468	66	20	8	5	0
	No	731	63	18	9	8	1
Ethnicity:	White	903	63	20	9	7	1
	Black	150	77	17	2	4	0
	Hispanic	90	70	11	15	5	0
Region:	Northeast	264	54	25	14	6	0
	South	263	75	14	7	5	0
	Central	481	67	19	6	5	2
	West	197	58	16	10	15	2
Community Type:	Urban	638	66	16	8	9	2
	Suburban	169	62	21	11	6	0
	Rural	385	63	23	9	4	1
Voter Registration:	Not Registered	206	57	22	14	7	1
	Reg. Democrat	395	70	16	5	9	1
	Reg. Republican	315	68	17	9	4	2
	Reg. Independent	208	54	26	11	8	1
Denominational Affiliation:	Protestant	494	72	17	7	3	1
	Catholic	343	65	20	9	4	1
	Baptist	122	80	13	4	2	1
	Mainline Protestant	204	70	19	8	2	2
Churched:	Yes	902	74	17	6	2	1
	No	270	33	23	19	23	2
Born Again:	Yes	477	85	12	2	1	1
	No	728	51	23	13	11	1
	Evangelical	130	99	1	0	0	0

TABLE 105   275

Do you agree strongly, agree somewhat, disagree somewhat, or disagree strongly with the following statement: "It is perfectly acceptable to you for a woman to be the pastor or head minister of a church"?

		N	Agree Strongly	Agree Somewhat	Disagree Somewhat	Disagree Strongly	Don't Know
Total Responding		1205	57%	19%	6%	14%	5%
Gender:	Male	577	58	20	6	12	4
	Female	628	56	18	6	15	5
Age:	18 to 27	212	65	16	7	10	2
	28-46	453	58	19	6	13	5
	47-65	250	55	14	5	21	5
	66-98	201	48	26	5	14	7
Income:	Under $20,000	274	57	18	5	15	5
	$20,000 to $40,000	391	55	19	6	16	4
	$40,000 to $60,000	212	62	20	4	13	1
	$60,000 or more	166	59	19	8	9	4
Education:	High School or Less	532	50	21	6	17	6
	Some College	262	63	15	5	15	2
	College Graduate	403	62	19	6	9	4
Marital Status:	Married	689	56	18	6	15	5
	Not Married	512	59	19	5	12	4
Have Kids Under 18:	Yes	468	58	17	6	14	4
	No	731	57	19	5	14	5
Ethnicity:	White	903	57	21	6	13	4
	Black	150	57	11	6	19	8
	Hispanic	90	56	10	4	21	8
Region:	Northeast	264	63	18	3	11	5
	South	263	56	16	6	17	5
	Central	481	53	22	7	14	4
	West	197	60	16	6	14	4
Community Type:	Urban	638	58	17	6	15	4
	Suburban	169	62	16	5	11	6
	Rural	385	54	24	5	13	4
Voter Registration:	Not Registered	206	53	16	6	16	8
	Reg. Democrat	395	59	17	5	15	3
	Reg. Republican	315	54	18	8	15	4
	Reg. Independent	208	64	20	4	9	3
Denominational Affiliation:	Protestant	494	56	19	8	15	3
	Catholic	343	51	25	6	14	4
	Baptist	122	39	21	10	28	3
	Mainline Protestant	204	69	17	5	6	3
Churched:	Yes	902	54	19	7	16	3
	No	270	66	18	3	6	6
Born Again:	Yes	477	47	21	9	22	2
	No	728	64	18	3	9	6
	Evangelical	130	31	14	14	40	1

TABLE 106

Do you agree strongly, agree somewhat, disagree somewhat, or disagree strongly with the following statement: "Eventually all people will be personally judged by God"?

		N	Agree Strongly	Agree Somewhat	Disagree Somewhat	Disagree Strongly	Don't Know
Total Responding		1205	74%	11%	4%	6%	4%
Gender:	Male	577	70	14	4	7	5
	Female	628	78	9	4	5	4
Age:	18 to 27	212	67	15	8	5	5
	28-46	453	75	11	4	6	5
	47-65	250	75	10	4	7	4
	66-98	201	80	9	2	6	2
Income:	Under $20,000	274	80	10	4	4	3
	$20,000 to $40,000	391	75	13	4	5	4
	$40,000 to $60,000	212	71	11	5	9	3
	$60,000 or more	166	67	12	5	11	5
Education:	High School or Less	532	81	9	3	3	3
	Some College	262	73	14	3	7	4
	College Graduate	403	65	13	6	10	6
Marital Status:	Married	689	77	11	3	5	4
	Not Married	512	70	12	6	8	5
Have Kids Under 18:	Yes	468	77	12	3	4	4
	No	731	72	11	5	8	5
Ethnicity:	White	903	73	12	4	7	4
	Black	150	82	7	4	2	5
	Hispanic	90	79	9	2	5	5
Region:	Northeast	264	68	13	6	7	6
	South	263	80	10	3	5	2
	Central	481	78	10	3	4	4
	West	197	64	16	5	12	4
Community Type:	Urban	638	72	11	5	8	4
	Suburban	169	74	14	2	5	6
	Rural	385	77	12	3	5	3
Voter Registration:	Not Registered	206	73	12	6	6	4
	Reg. Democrat	395	74	10	4	8	4
	Reg. Republican	315	80	11	2	4	4
	Reg. Independent	208	68	14	6	7	5
Denominational Affiliation:	Protestant	494	82	10	3	2	2
	Catholic	343	78	13	3	4	3
	Baptist	122	90	4	3	0	2
	Mainline Protestant	204	79	12	4	3	3
Churched:	Yes	902	81	10	3	4	2
	No	270	49	16	9	16	10
Born Again:	Yes	477	92	6	1	1	1
	No	728	62	15	6	10	6
	Evangelical	130	97	1	0	1	1

TABLE 107   277

Do you agree strongly, agree somewhat, disagree somewhat, or disagree strongly with the following statement: "There are some crimes, sins, or other things people might do, which cannot be forgiven by God"?

		N	Agree Strongly	Agree Somewhat	Disagree Somewhat	Disagree Strongly	Don't Know
Total Responding		1205	23%	9%	12%	49%	8%
Gender:	Male	577	25	10	12	45	8
	Female	628	20	8	12	52	8
Age:	18 to 27	212	24	12	14	46	4
	28-46	453	21	10	12	52	6
	47-65	250	25	7	11	48	10
	66-98	201	25	9	10	43	12
Income:	Under $20,000	274	28	12	11	41	7
	$20,000 to $40,000	391	25	10	11	48	6
	$40,000 to $60,000	212	19	8	11	57	5
	$60,000 or more	166	13	6	14	60	6
Education:	High School or Less	532	28	11	11	43	7
	Some College	262	20	6	12	54	7
	College Graduate	403	17	9	13	52	9
Marital Status:	Married	689	21	9	12	51	8
	Not Married	512	25	10	12	46	8
Have Kids Under 18:	Yes	468	22	10	12	51	6
	No	731	23	8	12	47	9
Ethnicity:	White	903	22	9	13	48	8
	Black	150	30	7	5	49	9
	Hispanic	90	23	4	12	61	0
Region:	Northeast	264	23	9	15	45	8
	South	263	23	10	10	51	6
	Central	481	23	8	11	50	8
	West	197	20	9	13	48	9
Community Type:	Urban	638	25	9	11	47	8
	Suburban	169	16	7	18	50	9
	Rural	385	22	10	10	51	7
Voter Registration:	Not Registered	206	35	6	12	42	6
	Reg. Democrat	395	22	10	11	50	7
	Reg. Republican	315	19	8	12	54	7
	Reg. Independent	208	20	13	11	47	9
Denominational Affiliation:	Protestant	494	19	9	11	56	6
	Catholic	343	21	11	14	50	4
	Baptist	122	24	8	6	57	4
	Mainline Protestant	204	17	7	14	58	4
Churched:	Yes	902	21	8	12	54	5
	No	270	28	12	12	33	14
Born Again:	Yes	477	19	8	9	60	4
	No	728	25	10	14	41	10
	Evangelical	130	19	6	3	68	4

TABLE 108

In a typical month, how many times would you attend services at a church, synagogue, or other religious meeting place?

		N	Four or More Times	Three Times	Two Times	Once	Less Than Once a Month	None	Don't Know
Total Responding		1205	44%	5%	8%	9%	2%	28%	3%
Gender:	Male	577	35	6	9	9	4	34	3
	Female	628	52	5	7	9	1	23	2
Age:	18 to 27	212	38	8	7	17	1	26	2
	28 to 46	453	40	7	11	9	2	30	1
	47 to 65	250	44	4	8	8	3	29	3
	66 to 98	201	59	1	4	4	4	25	4
Income:	Under $20,000	274	49	6	6	7	2	24	5
	$20,000 to $40,000	391	43	5	7	10	3	30	1
	$40,000 to $60,000	212	45	6	8	11	2	29	0
	$60,000 or more	166	41	6	10	9	3	31	1
Education:	High School or Less	532	47	5	8	7	2	26	5
	Some College	262	41	8	8	10	2	31	1
	College Graduate	403	43	5	8	10	2	30	1
Marital Status:	Married	689	49	6	9	7	2	24	3
	Not Married	512	38	5	6	12	3	34	3
Have Kids Under 18:	Yes	468	45	8	11	9	1	24	2
	No	731	44	4	6	9	4	31	3
Ethnicity:	White	903	44	5	8	9	2	30	2
	Black	150	43	9	8	6	5	24	5
	Hispanic	90	49	4	11	17	0	15	3
Region:	Northeast	264	35	7	7	12	2	34	2
	South	263	49	6	11	9	3	20	3
	Central	481	48	5	8	8	3	24	3
	West	197	39	5	5	6	0	41	3
Community Type:	Urban	638	44	5	7	9	2	30	3
	Suburban	169	42	7	7	12	2	27	2
	Rural	385	45	6	9	7	4	27	2
Voter Registration:	Not Registered	206	34	5	6	13	1	39	2
	Democrat	395	48	5	8	9	2	25	4
	Republican	315	51	6	9	7	2	24	1
	Independent	208	41	6	7	9	5	31	1
Denominational Affiliation:	Protestant	494	51	5	8	6	4	24	2
	Catholic	343	52	5	10	11	1	18	3
	Baptist	122	54	6	5	4	6	21	4
	Mainline Protestant	204	47	5	12	8	3	24	1
Churched:	Yes	902	59	7	11	12	2	9	0
	No	270	0	0	0	0	4	96	0
Born Again	Yes	477	66	7	7	6	1	12	2
	No	728	30	5	8	11	3	39	3
	Evangelical	130	87	2	5	1	0	3	2

TABLE 109   279

Have you attended a church service during the past six months, not including a special service such as a wedding or funeral?

		N	Yes	No
Total Responding		369	27%	73%
Gender:	Male	218	30	70
	Female	151	22	78
Age:	18 to 27	58	36	64
	28-46	146	25	75
	47-65	81	25	75
	66-98	57	30	70
Income:	Under $20,000	73	28	72
	$20,000 to $40,000	128	23	77
	$40,000 to $60,000	65	23	77
	$60,000 or more	55	34	66
Education:	High School or Less	150	23	77
	Some College	87	31	69
	College Graduate	132	29	71
Marital Status:	Married	180	30	70
	Not Married	189	24	76
Have Kids Under 18:	Yes	118	20	80
	No	251	30	70
Ethnicity:	White	291	26	74
	Black	44	27	73
	Hispanic	14	50	50
Region:	Northeast	96	34	66
	South	60	20	80
	Central	132	29	71
	West	81	20	80
Community Type:	Urban	198	26	74
	Suburban	50	33	67
	Rural	118	26	74
Voter Registration:	Not Registered	81	31	69
	Reg. Democrat	108	26	74
	Reg. Republican	81	30	70
	Reg. Independent	75	21	79
Denominational	Protestant	139	30	70
Affiliation:	Catholic	66	36	64
	Baptist	33	24	76
	Mainline Protestant	55	27	73
Churched:	Yes	99	100	0
	No	270	0	100
Born Again:	Yes	59	35	65
	No	310	25	75
	Evangelical	4	61	39

TABLE 110

If a friend or family member who regularly attends a Christian church in your area were to invite you to attend their church with them, how likely is that you would attend with them? Would you definitely attend, probably attend, probably not attend, or definitely not attend?

		N	Definitely Attend	Probably Attend	Probably Not Attend	Definitely Not Attend	Don't Know/ Depends
Total Responding		369	7%	42%	31%	17%	3%
Gender:	Male	218	5	39	35	19	3
	Female	151	10	47	26	14	3
Age:	18 to 27	58	12	55	17	15	2
	28-46	146	8	41	36	14	2
	47-65	81	5	38	35	17	4
	66-98	57	5	38	25	27	5
Income:	Under $20,000	73	4	60	23	8	5
	$20,000 to $40,000	128	6	41	31	21	1
	$40,000 to $60,000	65	11	29	44	14	1
	$60,000 or more	55	12	34	28	22	4
Education:	High School or Less	150	6	48	28	16	2
	Some College	87	10	41	37	12	0
	College Graduate	132	7	36	31	21	5
Marital Status:	Married	180	8	40	34	13	4
	Not Married	189	6	44	28	20	2
Have Kids Under 18:	Yes	118	8	40	35	15	2
	No	251	7	43	29	18	3
Ethnicity:	White	291	8	39	34	17	3
	Black	44	10	53	15	22	0
	Hispanic	14	0	77	23	0	0
Region:	Northeast	96	13	41	30	15	2
	South	60	6	45	26	20	3
	Central	132	4	46	29	17	4
	West	81	7	35	40	16	2
Community Type:	Urban	198	7	46	28	17	1
	Suburban	50	8	41	28	19	5
	Rural	118	7	37	38	13	5
Voter Registration:	Not Registered	81	9	52	21	15	4
	Reg. Democrat	108	7	41	32	19	1
	Reg. Republican	81	11	34	36	14	5
	Reg. Independent	75	2	42	34	18	3
Denominational Affiliation:	Protestant	139	9	46	28	12	5
	Catholic	66	7	42	42	9	0
	Baptist	33	8	50	25	11	5
	Mainline Protestant	55	8	53	21	13	5
Churched:	Yes	99	12	46	28	11	4
	No	270	6	41	33	19	2
Born Again:	Yes	59	10	62	22	4	3
	No	310	7	38	33	19	3
	Evangelical	4	0	100	0	0	0

TABLE 111   281

Suppose a friend or family member invited you to attend a Bible study group of 6 to 12 people from your community, meeting for 2 hours a week at someone's home. How likely is that you would attend with them? Would you definitely attend, probably attend, probably not attend, or definitely not attend?

		N	Definitely Attend	Probably Attend	Probably Not Attend	Definitely Not Attend	Don't Know/ Depends
Total Responding		369	4%	12%	38%	43%	3%
Gender:	Male	218	2	12	40	45	2
	Female	151	6	14	35	41	5
Age:	18 to 27	58	5	20	34	41	0
	28-46	146	3	12	44	40	1
	47-65	81	1	12	33	50	3
	66-98	57	9	8	32	41	11
Income:	Under $20,000	73	8	26	32	30	4
	$20,000 to $40,000	128	4	9	46	38	3
	$40,000 to $60,000	65	2	14	39	45	0
	$60,000 or more	55	3	4	30	61	1
Education:	High School or Less	150	4	19	37	36	4
	Some College	87	6	12	38	42	1
	College Graduate	132	1	6	39	52	2
Marital Status:	Married	180	3	10	42	43	2
	Not Married	189	5	15	35	43	3
Have Kids Under 18:	Yes	118	2	11	43	43	1
	No	251	5	13	36	43	4
Ethnicity:	White	291	2	11	40	44	3
	Black	44	16	12	28	39	5
	Hispanic	14	0	47	38	15	0
Region:	Northeast	96	4	10	36	47	2
	South	60	1	11	44	39	4
	Central	132	6	14	36	41	3
	West	81	1	13	39	45	1
Community Type:	Urban	198	5	14	37	42	2
	Suburban	50	0	7	32	59	2
	Rural	118	4	12	43	39	2
Voter Registration:	Not Registered	81	5	19	32	40	4
	Reg. Democrat	108	5	13	38	42	1
	Reg. Republican	81	4	11	41	39	5
	Reg. Independent	75	0	9	42	48	1
Denominational Affiliation:	Protestant	139	4	12	43	37	3
	Catholic	66	1	8	45	43	3
	Baptist	33	13	19	45	21	2
	Mainline Protestant	55	3	7	35	48	7
Churched:	Yes	99	5	16	44	33	2
	No	270	3	11	36	47	3
Born Again:	Yes	59	6	32	40	18	4
	No	310	3	9	38	48	3
	Evangelical	4	0	81	0	19	0

TABLE 112

Do you consider yourself to be Protestant, Catholic, Jewish, or of some other religious faith?

		N	Protestant	Catholic	Jewish	Other Faith	Atheist/ No Faith	Christian	Don't Know
Total Responding		1205	41%	28%	1%	23%	3%	1%	2%
Gender:	Male	577	40	29	1	23	5	0	2
	Female	628	42	28	1	23	2	1	2
Age:	18 to 27	212	19	38	2	38	2	0	1
	28 to 46	453	31	33	2	27	4	2	3
	47 to 65	250	52	22	1	17	4	1	3
	66 to 98	201	67	21	1	8	2	1	0
Income:	Under $20,000	274	40	25	0	29	3	1	1
	$20,000 to $40,000	391	39	30	1	25	3	1	1
	$40,000 to $60,000	212	42	28	2	22	3	1	2
	$60,000 or more	166	44	33	3	12	6	0	0
Education:	High School or Less	532	40	30	1	26	2	1	2
	Some College	262	38	27	2	25	3	2	2
	College Graduate	403	44	27	2	18	5	1	3
Marital Status:	Married	689	45	29	1	19	3	1	2
	Not Married	512	36	28	2	28	4	0	2
Have Kids Under 18:	Yes	468	32	31	1	30	2	1	2
	No	731	47	27	1	18	4	1	2
Ethnicity:	White	903	47	26	2	18	4	1	2
	Black	150	29	13	0	54	1	0	3
	Hispanic	90	12	74	0	12	0	2	0
Region:	Northeast	264	32	40	3	20	2	1	2
	South	263	48	15	1	34	2	0	1
	Central	481	44	29	1	19	3	1	3
	West	197	36	30	2	21	8	2	2
Community Type:	Urban	638	38	30	1	24	4	1	2
	Suburban	169	41	36	2	17	3	0	2
	Rural	385	47	24	1	23	1	1	2
Voter Registration:	Not Registered	206	27	31	0	36	3	1	2
	Democrat	395	36	32	1	25	3	1	2
	Republican	315	60	24	0	11	3	1	1
	Independent	208	36	29	4	23	4	1	3
Denominational Affiliation:	Protestant	494	100	0	0	0	0	0	0
	Catholic	343	0	100	0	0	0	0	0
	Baptist	122	99	0	0	0	0	1	0
	Mainline Protestant	204	99	0	0	0	0	1	0
Churched:	Yes	902	43	32	1	20	1	1	1
	No	270	36	16	3	32	11	0	3
Born Again	Yes	477	59	18	0	20	0	2	1
	No	728	29	35	2	25	5	0	3
	Evangelical	130	75	0	0	20	0	6	0

TABLE 113   283

There are many different beliefs about God or a higher power. Which one of the following descriptions comes closest to what you personally believe about God?

		N	Everyone is God.	God Is All-Powerful, All-Knowing, Creator	God Is Total Realization of Pers., Human Pot.	There Are Many Gods, Each with Power/Auth.	God Is Higher State of Consciousness	There is no such thing as God.	Don't Know
Total Responding		1205	3%	68%	6%	3%	10%	2%	7%
Gender:	Male	577	5	62	7	3	12	4	9
	Female	628	2	74	6	3	9	1	6
Age:	18 to 27	212	4	67	7	4	11	2	6
	28 to 46	453	4	66	8	3	12	2	5
	47 to 65	250	3	69	4	4	11	3	6
	66 to 98	201	3	74	5	1	4	2	12
Income:	Under $20,000	274	3	74	5	2	7	3	6
	$20,000 to $40,000	391	4	70	6	4	11	2	4
	$40,000 to $60,000	212	4	69	8	2	9	3	5
	$60,000 or more	166	3	63	8	2	16	3	6
Education:	High School or Less	532	3	73	5	3	9	1	5
	Some College	262	4	66	9	3	10	3	6
	College Graduate	403	3	62	6	2	13	4	10
Marital Status:	Married	689	3	70	7	2	10	2	6
	Not Married	512	4	66	6	3	11	3	8
Have Kids Under 18:	Yes	468	4	71	7	3	9	1	5
	No	731	3	66	6	3	11	3	8
Ethnicity:	White	903	3	68	6	2	10	3	8
	Black	150	7	71	1	2	12	0	7
	Hispanic	90	0	76	10	0	11	0	2
Region:	Northeast	264	3	59	8	6	16	3	5
	South	263	3	75	4	2	8	1	7
	Central	481	3	73	6	1	9	2	7
	West	197	4	59	8	3	11	4	10
Community Type:	Urban	638	4	66	7	3	9	3	8
	Suburban	169	4	61	6	3	15	3	7
	Rural	385	2	75	5	2	11	1	4
Voter Registration:	Not Registered	206	4	61	7	4	15	1	7
	Democrat	395	4	71	5	2	9	3	6
	Republican	315	2	76	4	2	9	1	6
	Independent	208	5	60	11	4	13	2	5
Denominational Affiliation:	Protestant	494	3	75	5	2	8	0	6
	Catholic	343	4	73	7	2	10	0	4
	Baptist	122	3	86	2	0	5	1	4
	Mainline Protestant	204	4	73	7	2	8	0	5
Churched:	Yes	902	3	76	6	2	9	1	5
	No	270	6	43	9	5	16	8	12
Born Again	Yes	477	1	91	2	0	3	0	2
	No	728	5	53	9	4	15	4	10
	Evangelical	130	0	100	0	0	0	0	0

In a typical week, on how many days, if any, would you read the Bible, not including times when you are at a church?

		N	One	Two	Three	Four	Five	Six	Seven	None	Don't Know
Total Responding		594	12%	9%	5%	4%	4%	1%	9%	50%	4%
Gender:	Male	286	10	11	5	2	3	1	4	59	4
	Female	308	15	7	6	5	6	1	14	42	5
Age:	18 to 27	114	15	9	7	2	5	1	5	51	3
	28 to 46	249	13	10	6	4	3	2	5	54	2
	47 to 65	123	12	7	4	5	4	0	15	48	5
	66 to 98	71	8	6	3	1	7	2	19	41	12
Income:	Under $20,000	128	12	11	5	3	7	1	16	40	6
	$20,000 to $40,000	189	16	9	6	6	4	1	8	49	2
	$40,000 to $60,000	106	9	8	9	7	6	1	7	52	2
	$60,000 or more	93	10	8	3	0	2	2	6	70	0
Education:	High School or Less	261	12	10	3	4	4	1	11	48	6
	Some College	134	18	9	8	3	6	1	5	47	3
	College Graduate	193	9	9	7	3	4	2	8	55	3
Marital Status:	Married	337	14	9	6	4	3	2	9	50	3
	Not Married	255	10	9	5	4	5	1	10	52	5
Have Kids Under 18:	Yes	239	14	8	8	5	5	2	7	47	4
	No	353	11	10	4	3	4	1	11	52	5
Ethnicity:	White	444	12	8	5	3	5	1	10	53	4
	Black	74	12	18	10	6	2	2	10	37	4
	Hispanic	44	10	15	9	0	0	0	5	56	6
Region:	Northeast	135	10	5	4	2	5	1	6	64	3
	South	134	17	15	7	8	5	1	11	32	5
	Central	223	11	9	4	3	4	2	12	51	4
	West	103	10	6	8	3	3	2	5	55	7
Community Type:	Urban	304	12	10	6	5	5	2	8	50	3
	Suburban	92	8	6	4	2	6	0	8	60	7
	Rural	191	15	9	6	3	3	1	11	47	4
Voter Registration:	Not Registered	113	14	10	7	3	3	2	5	52	4
	Democrat	173	14	8	5	4	4	1	10	52	3
	Republican	149	12	10	5	2	6	2	14	43	5
	Independent	114	9	7	7	6	4	0	7	57	3
Denominational Affiliation:	Protestant	227	14	9	7	5	6	2	17	36	5
	Catholic	177	15	8	4	1	1	0	4	62	5
	Baptist	54	12	13	14	10	8	1	12	28	2
	Mainline Protestant	85	18	7	4	4	6	2	11	41	6
Churched:	Yes	449	14	11	6	5	5	1	11	42	4
	No	130	7	2	1	1	1	1	2	83	2
Born Again	Yes	231	16	13	9	6	6	3	18	25	3
	No	362	10	6	3	2	3	0	4	66	5
	Evangelical	64	13	11	13	11	14	6	26	5	2

TABLE 115 285

Have you ever made a personal commitment to Jesus Christ that is still important in your life today?

		N	Yes	No/Don't Know
Total Responding		1205	66%	34%
Gender:	Male	577	60	40
	Female	628	70	30
Age:	18 to 27	212	54	46
	28-46	453	66	34
	47-65	250	66	34
	66-98	201	75	25
Income:	Under $20,000	274	68	32
	$20,000 to $40,000	391	67	33
	$40,000 to $60,000	212	64	36
	$60,000 or more	166	57	43
Education:	High School or Less	532	68	32
	Some College	262	61	39
	College Graduate	403	65	35
Marital Status:	Married	689	69	31
	Not Married	512	61	39
Have Kids Under 18:	Yes	468	67	33
	No	731	65	35
Ethnicity:	White	903	65	35
	Black	150	75	25
	Hispanic	90	67	33
Region:	Northeast	264	53	47
	South	263	73	27
	Central	481	71	29
	West	197	58	42
Community Type:	Urban	638	64	36
	Suburban	169	60	40
	Rural	385	69	31
Voter Registration:	Not Registered	206	52	48
	Reg. Democrat	395	68	32
	Reg. Republican	315	77	23
	Reg. Independent	208	58	42
Denominational Affiliation:	Protestant	494	79	21
	Catholic	343	59	41
	Baptist	122	91	9
	Mainline Protestant	204	74	26
Churched:	Yes	902	74	26
	No	270	37	63
Born Again:	Yes	477	91	9
	No	728	49	51
	Evangelical	130	100	0

TABLE 116

Please tell me which one of the following statements best describes your own belief about what will happen to you after you die.

		N	Heaven; Tried to Obey 10 Command- ments	Heaven; Basi- cally a Good Person	Heaven; Confess Sins/ Accept Christ	Heaven; God Loves All/ Not Let Perish	When You Die You Won't Go to Heaven	You Don't Know What Happens When You Die	Other	Don't Know
Total Responding		1205	7%	13%	40%	7%	2%	25%	3%	3%
Gender:	Male	577	6	14	35	7	3	30	3	3
	Female	628	8	13	44	8	1	20	3	3
Age:	18 to 27	212	7	16	33	9	3	29	2	2
	28 to 46	453	6	16	39	7	1	26	2	3
	47 to 65	250	8	8	44	9	2	22	2	4
	66 to 98	201	9	14	·40	4	2	20	7	4
Income:	Under $20,000	274	9	12	39	5	3	26	5	2
	$20,000 to $40,000	391	6	15	42	9	1	22	2	2
	$40,000 to $60,000	212	6	13	43	9	2	24	2	1
	$60,000 or more	166	8	16	33	5	1	31	1	4
Education:	High School or Less	532	11	14	38	8	2	21	4	3
	Some College	262	3	11	45	9	2	26	2	2
	College Graduate	403	4	15	39	5	2	29	3	4
Marital Status:	Married	689	7	11	45	7	2	22	2	4
	Not Married	512	7	16	32	8	2	29	4	3
Have Kids Under 18:	Yes	468	7	14	42	8	2	22	2	3
	No	731	7	13	38	6	2	26	4	3
Ethnicity:	White	903	7	14	41	8	2	22	3	3
	Black	150	9	7	46	2	0	29	5	2
	Hispanic	90	9	13	27	13	3	31	0	5
Region:	Northeast	264	8	22	23	10	0	32	2	3
	South	263	6	9	53	5	2	18	3	4
	Central	481	8	13	43	7	2	22	3	3
	West	197	7	9	35	7	3	31	4	3
Community Type:	Urban	638	7	12	40	7	2	26	3	3
	Suburban	169	10	18	28	10	2	26	1	4
	Rural	385	7	13	44	7	1	22	3	3
Voter Registration:	Not Registered	206	4	14	27	11	3	32	5	4
	Democrat	395	8	12	40	6	2	26	2	3
	Republican	315	6	15	52	5	1	15	2	4
	Independent	208	7	15	32	10	2	31	2	1
Denominational Affiliation:	Protestant	494	5	9	57	6	1	18	2	2
	Catholic	343	12	24	25	12	1	20	1	3
	Baptist	122	1	1	79	1	0	15	4	0
	Mainline Protestant	204	6	14	49	7	0	20	2	2
Churched:	Yes	902	8	13	48	7	1	18	3	3
	No	270	4	15	14	8	3	47	3	5
Born Again	Yes	477	0	0	100	0	0	0	0	0
	No	728	12	22	0	12	3	41	5	5
	Evangelical	130	0	0	100	0	0	0	0	0

TABLE 117   287

Are you currently actively involved in "a recovery or 12-step group associated with a local church"?

		N	Yes	No	Don't Know
Total Responding		1205	6%	93%	1%
Gender:	Male	577	5	94	1
	Female	628	7	92	1
Age:	18 to 27	212	6	94	0
	28-46	453	3	96	0
	47-65	250	4	95	1
	66-98	201	12	84	4
Income:	Under $20,000	274	11	88	2
	$20,000 to $40,000	391	4	95	1
	$40,000 to $60,000	212	4	96	1
	$60,000 or more	166	3	97	0
Education:	High School or Less	532	8	91	1
	Some College	262	6	92	2
	College Graduate	403	4	95	1
Marital Status:	Married	689	5	94	1
	Not Married	512	7	92	1
Have Kids Under 18:	Yes	468	5	94	1
	No	731	7	92	1
Ethnicity:	White	903	5	94	1
	Black	150	16	83	1
	Hispanic	90	4	96	0
Region:	Northeast	264	5	95	0
	South	263	7	91	2
	Central	481	5	93	2
	West	197	8	92	1
Community Type:	Urban	638	8	91	1
	Suburban	169	2	97	1
	Rural	385	5	94	1
Voter Registration:	Not Registered	206	4	96	1
	Reg. Democrat	395	6	93	1
	Reg. Republican	315	6	94	0
	Reg. Independent	208	6	92	2
Denominational	Protestant	494	8	90	2
Affiliation:	Catholic	343	4	96	0
	Baptist	122	3	94	3
	Mainline Protestant	204	8	91	1
Churched:	Yes	902	7	92	1
	No	270	1	99	0
Born Again:	Yes	477	10	88	2
	No	728	3	96	1
	Evangelical	130	8	90	2

　TABLE 118

Are you currently actively involved in "a small group that meets regularly for Bible study, prayer or Christian fellowship, not including a Sunday School or 12-step group"?

		N	Yes	No	Don't Know
Total Responding		1205	16%	83%	1%
Gender:	Male	577	11	88	1
	Female	628	22	78	1
Age:	18 to 27	212	15	85	0
	28-46	453	14	85	1
	47-65	250	16	83	1
	66-98	201	24	75	1
Income:	Under $20,000	274	17	81	2
	$20,000 to $40,000	391	16	84	0
	$40,000 to $60,000	212	16	84	0
	$60,000 or more	166	16	84	0
Education:	High School or Less	532	17	82	1
	Some College	262	17	82	0
	College Graduate	403	15	84	0
Marital Status:	Married	689	17	82	1
	Not Married	512	15	84	1
Have Kids Under 18:	Yes	468	16	84	1
	No	731	17	82	1
Ethnicity:	White	903	15	84	1
	Black	150	24	76	0
	Hispanic	90	15	83	2
Region:	Northeast	264	9	90	1
	South	263	20	79	0
	Central	481	18	82	1
	West	197	19	81	1
Community Type:	Urban	638	16	83	1
	Suburban	169	11	89	0
	Rural	385	19	80	1
Voter Registration:	Not Registered	206	11	87	2
	Reg. Democrat	395	18	82	0
	Reg. Republican	315	22	78	0
	Reg. Independent	208	11	89	0
Denominational	Protestant	494	23	77	1
Affiliation:	Catholic	343	8	91	1
	Baptist	122	22	77	1
	Mainline Protestant	204	22	78	0
Churched:	Yes	902	22	78	1
	No	270	0	100	0
Born Again:	Yes	477	29	70	1
	No	728	8	91	1
	Evangelical	130	46	54	0

TABLE 119 289

Are you currently actively involved in "a formal leadership position in a church, such as an elder, deacon or staff role"?

		N	Yes	No	Don't Know
Total Responding		1205	9%	91%	1%
Gender:	Male	577	9	90	1
	Female	628	8	91	1
Age:	18 to 27	212	5	95	0
	28-46	453	7	92	1
	47-65	250	13	87	0
	66-98	201	10	90	1
Income:	Under $20,000	274	7	92	1
	$20,000 to $40,000	391	7	92	1
	$40,000 to $60,000	212	11	89	0
	$60,000 or more	166	10	88	2
Education:	High School or Less	532	9	90	1
	Some College	262	9	91	0
	College Graduate	403	8	91	1
Marital Status:	Married	689	10	89	1
	Not Married	512	7	93	0
Have Kids Under 18:	Yes	468	8	91	1
	No	731	9	90	1
Ethnicity:	White	903	8	92	1
	Black	150	15	84	1
	Hispanic	90	12	88	0
Region:	Northeast	264	8	91	0
	South	263	9	90	1
	Central	481	9	90	1
	West	197	8	92	0
Community Type:	Urban	638	9	90	0
	Suburban	169	6	92	2
	Rural	385	9	90	1
Voter Registration:	Not Registered	206	5	93	2
	Reg. Democrat	395	10	89	0
	Reg. Republican	315	10	90	0
	Reg. Independent	208	7	92	1
Denominational	Protestant	494	12	88	0
Affiliation:	Catholic	343	7	93	0
	Baptist	122	16	84	0
	Mainline Protestant	204	12	87	1
Churched:	Yes	902	10	90	0
	No	270	4	95	1
Born Again:	Yes	477	13	86	1
	No	728	6	93	1
	Evangelical	130	20	80	0

Are you currently actively involved in "teaching Sunday School or a Christian education class at a church"?

		N	Yes	No	Don't Know
Total Responding		1205	10%	90%	0%
Gender:	Male	577	7	93	0
	Female	628	12	87	1
Age:	18 to 27	212	8	92	0
	28-46	453	11	89	0
	47-65	250	9	91	0
	66-98	201	8	91	1
Income:	Under $20,000	274	9	90	1
	$20,000 to $40,000	391	9	91	0
	$40,000 to $60,000	212	14	86	0
	$60,000 or more	166	7	93	0
Education:	High School or Less	532	9	90	0
	Some College	262	10	90	0
	College Graduate	403	10	90	0
Marital Status:	Married	689	11	89	0
	Not Married	512	8	92	0
Have Kids Under 18:	Yes	468	13	87	0
	No	731	8	92	0
Ethnicity:	White	903	9	90	0
	Black	150	14	86	0
	Hispanic	90	10	90	0
Region:	Northeast	264	7	93	0
	South	263	13	87	0
	Central	481	9	90	0
	West	197	9	90	1
Community Type:	Urban	638	8	91	1
	Suburban	169	8	92	0
	Rural	385	13	87	0
Voter Registration:	Not Registered	206	6	94	0
	Reg. Democrat	395	10	89	0
	Reg. Republican	315	13	87	0
	Reg. Independent	208	6	94	0
Denominational	Protestant	494	13	87	0
Affiliation:	Catholic	343	5	94	0
	Baptist	122	20	80	0
	Mainline Protestant	204	8	92	0
Churched:	Yes	902	13	87	0
	No	270	0	100	0
Born Again:	Yes	477	18	82	0
	No	728	4	95	0
	Evangelical	130	38	62	0

TABLE 121   291

Do you ever pray to God?

		N	Yes	No	Don't Know
Total Responding		617	89%	10%	1%
Gender:	Male	298	83	16	1
	Female	318	95	5	0
Age:	18 to 27	120	87	12	1
	28-46	234	88	12	0
	47-65	116	90	10	0
	66-98	93	92	7	2
Income:	Under $20,000	138	94	6	0
	$20,000 to $40,000	205	87	13	1
	$40,000 to $60,000	116	87	12	1
	$60,000 or more	79	89	10	1
Education:	High School or Less	268	93	7	0
	Some College	129	88	10	2
	College Graduate	217	86	14	0
Marital Status:	Married	353	92	8	0
	Not Married	262	86	13	1
Have Kids Under 18:	Yes	254	89	11	0
	No	359	90	10	1
Ethnicity:	White	458	88	11	1
	Black	80	94	6	0
	Hispanic	45	97	3	0
Region:	Northeast	135	87	13	0
	South	136	93	6	1
	Central	250	91	8	1
	West	96	83	17	0
Community Type:	Urban	339	90	10	0
	Suburban	75	83	17	0
	Rural	199	91	8	1
Voter Registration:	Not Registered	103	88	10	1
	Reg. Democrat	218	92	8	0
	Reg. Republican	163	90	10	0
	Reg. Independent	97	83	16	1
Denominational Affiliation:	Protestant	251	95	5	0
	Catholic	174	96	4	0
	Baptist	64	100	0	0
	Mainline Protestant	114	95	5	0
Churched:	Yes	456	97	3	0
	No	144	65	33	3
Born Again:	Yes	247	99	0	1
	No	369	83	17	1
	Evangelical	68	100	0	0

TABLE 122

In a typical week, during how many days would you pray?

		N	One	Two	Three	Four	Five	Six	Seven	None	Don't Know
Total Responding		551	8%	7%	7%	5%	5%	2%	58%	1%	7%
Gender:	Male	248	11	10	8	6	5	1	50	2	7
	Female	303	5	4	7	3	6	3	65	1	7
Age:	18 to 27	105	7	9	9	7	10	3	51	0	5
	28 to 46	206	12	6	7	5	7	1	56	2	5
	47 to 65	105	7	6	12	6	4	2	58	2	4
	66 to 98	85	0	5	3	1	0	1	75	0	14
Income:	Under $20,000	129	2	5	5	6	5	1	69	3	4
	$20,000 to $40,000	178	10	7	11	5	4	1	54	0	5
	$40,000 to $60,000	101	8	4	9	5	9	2	59	2	4
	$60,000 or more	70	13	15	4	2	8	1	55	0	3
Education:	High School or Less	248	6	5	5	6	5	2	62	2	7
	Some College	113	6	10	11	3	6	2	50	1	11
	College Graduate	187	10	7	9	4	5	2	58	0	4
Marital Status:	Married	325	7	8	8	5	4	1	60	1	6
	Not Married	224	9	5	7	3	8	3	56	2	8
Have Kids Under 18:	Yes	225	9	7	8	4	4	2	59	2	6
	No	322	7	6	7	5	6	2	57	1	8
Ethnicity:	White	405	8	6	7	5	5	2	56	1	9
	Black	75	8	4	6	6	8	0	62	3	2
	Hispanic	44	3	6	8	4	9	0	66	3	0
Region:	Northeast	116	12	4	8	6	8	3	46	2	10
	South	127	3	7	7	2	5	2	64	0	10
	Central	227	9	8	6	5	6	1	60	1	3
	West	79	5	5	9	4	2	1	62	2	8
Community Type:	Urban	305	9	5	9	4	4	2	58	2	8
	Suburban	62	9	19	4	4	9	0	49	1	4
	Rural	180	5	5	6	6	6	2	62	0	7
Voter Registration:	Not Registered	91	11	12	5	11	9	2	41	3	5
	Democrat	199	7	4	9	3	4	1	64	1	7
	Republican	147	6	4	5	5	5	2	62	2	9
	Independent	81	10	10	12	2	6	2	54	0	4
Denominational Affiliation:	Protestant	238	6	5	8	5	3	2	63	0	8
	Catholic	168	10	9	7	5	7	2	53	1	6
	Baptist	64	3	4	11	4	4	0	68	0	6
	Mainline Protestant	108	9	5	9	6	2	4	56	0	9
Churched:	Yes	443	6	5	7	5	5	2	64	1	6
	No	93	19	10	12	3	7	2	34	4	10
Born Again	Yes	245	2	4	7	4	4	2	74	0	4
	No	306	12	9	8	5	7	2	46	2	9
	Evangelical	68	0	0	3	1	3	0	91	0	2

TABLE 123   293

On those days when you pray, do you usually pray one time or several times?

		N	Once	Several Times	Varies	Don't Know
Total Responding		551	38%	52%	8%	3%
Gender:	Male	248	46	47	6	1
	Female	303	31	55	9	4
Age:	18 to 27	105	48	46	4	2
	28-46	206	41	50	5	4
	47-65	105	39	52	9	1
	66-98	85	17	66	15	3
Income:	Under $20,000	129	29	61	8	2
	$20,000 to $40,000	178	40	52	6	2
	$40,000 to $60,000	101	46	47	6	1
	$60,000 or more	70	43	45	10	2
Education:	High School or Less	248	33	58	7	2
	Some College	113	42	49	7	2
	College Graduate	187	41	46	9	4
Marital Status:	Married	325	35	52	9	3
	Not Married	224	40	51	5	3
Have Kids Under 18:	Yes	225	41	49	6	4
	No	322	35	54	9	3
Ethnicity:	White	405	39	50	8	3
	Black	75	25	66	6	3
	Hispanic	44	42	51	4	3
Region:	Northeast	116	51	38	7	4
	South	127	24	63	10	3
	Central	227	37	54	7	2
	West	79	43	48	5	3
Community Type:	Urban	305	37	52	6	4
	Suburban	62	33	62	3	2
	Rural	180	38	49	12	2
Voter Registration:	Not Registered	91	36	58	5	1
	Reg. Democrat	199	39	49	9	3
	Reg. Republican	147	37	51	9	3
	Reg. Independent	81	38	52	7	2
Denominational Affiliation:	Protestant	238	30	60	9	2
	Catholic	168	50	42	4	4
	Baptist	64	18	71	8	2
	Mainline Protestant	108	39	54	5	1
Churched:	Yes	443	35	56	7	2
	No	93	54	35	6	5
Born Again:	Yes	245	24	67	8	1
	No	306	48	39	8	5
	Evangelical	68	3	93	5	0

TABLE 124

When you pray, how long do you usually spend in prayer?

		N	One Minute or Less	One Minute to Less Than 5 Minutes	5 Min. to Less Than 10 Minutes	10 Min. to Less Than 15 Minutes	15 Min. to Less Than 30 Minutes	30 Minutes or More	Don't Know
Total Responding		551	9%	33%	20%	10%	7%	6%	16%
Gender:	Male	248	13	38	21	7	5	5	11
	Female	303	5	30	19	12	9	7	19
Age:	18 to 27	105	6	33	29	8	13	6	4
	28 to 46	206	10	38	17	8	5	7	14
	47 to 65	105	12	32	18	8	6	6	20
	66 to 98	85	3	28	16	18	9	5	21
Income:	Under $20,000	129	6	32	24	12	5	8	12
	$20,000 to $40,000	178	7	34	20	12	9	4	14
	$40,000 to $60,000	101	11	35	23	9	7	7	8
	$60,000 or more	70	14	44	20	5	0	6	12
Education:	High School or Less	248	8	27	22	13	9	8	14
	Some College	113	8	39	21	8	5	3	15
	College Graduate	187	10	39	17	6	6	5	18
Marital Status:	Married	325	10	33	20	9	6	5	16
	Not Married	224	7	33	19	10	8	7	14
Have Kids Under 18:	Yes	225	12	34	20	8	8	7	12
	No	322	7	33	20	11	6	5	18
Ethnicity:	White	405	9	35	18	10	7	6	16
	Black	75	8	27	29	10	3	8	16
	Hispanic	44	4	33	25	13	5	6	14
Region:	Northeast	116	7	25	23	13	9	6	16
	South	127	6	29	25	9	6	7	17
	Central	227	9	37	19	8	7	5	15
	West	79	12	41	9	10	5	8	16
Community Type:	Urban	305	11	33	16	9	8	6	18
	Suburban	62	9	30	28	17	3	5	8
	Rural	180	6	36	24	8	7	5	14
Voter Registration:	Not Registered	91	8	28	21	9	14	6	14
	Democrat	199	8	35	21	14	5	4	14
	Republican	147	9	36	21	7	7	7	13
	Independent	81	13	32	20	8	5	5	18
Denominational Affiliation:	Protestant	238	9	37	17	9	5	3	19
	Catholic	168	8	31	22	9	10	7	12
	Baptist	64	11	37	20	11	5	4	12
	Mainline Protestant	108	8	40	14	12	7	4	14
Churched:	Yes	443	7	34	20	11	7	6	14
	No	93	19	37	15	3	7	2	18
Born Again	Yes	245	7	32	22	11	8	6	14
	No	306	10	35	18	9	6	6	17
	Evangelical	68	3	22	27	12	5	13	18

TABLE 125   295

When you pray, do you usually spend time "acknowledging God's unique qualities"?

		N	Yes	No	Don't Know
Total Responding		551	68%	27%	5%
Gender:	Male	248	65	31	4
	Female	303	70	24	6
Age:	18 to 27	105	73	23	4
	28-46	206	67	30	4
	47-65	105	75	21	4
	66-98	85	64	26	10
Income:	Under $20,000	129	77	20	2
	$20,000 to $40,000	178	72	23	5
	$40,000 to $60,000	101	60	37	3
	$60,000 or more	70	60	34	6
Education:	High School or Less	248	70	23	6
	Some College	113	71	24	5
	College Graduate	187	62	34	4
Marital Status:	Married	325	67	26	6
	Not Married	224	68	28	4
Have Kids Under 18:	Yes	225	72	23	5
	No	322	64	30	6
Ethnicity:	White	405	67	28	5
	Black	75	77	17	6
	Hispanic	44	59	34	7
Region:	Northeast	116	58	36	6
	South	127	75	20	6
	Central	227	67	27	6
	West	79	71	26	3
Community Type:	Urban	305	68	26	6
	Suburban	62	62	33	5
	Rural	180	67	28	4
Voter Registration:	Not Registered	91	66	27	7
	Reg. Democrat	199	67	29	5
	Reg. Republican	147	69	26	5
	Reg. Independent	81	66	30	4
Denominational Affiliation:	Protestant	238	68	26	6
	Catholic	168	63	30	7
	Baptist	64	74	20	6
	Mainline Protestant	108	63	36	1
Churched:	Yes	443	71	24	5
	No	93	53	43	4
Born Again:	Yes	245	84	13	3
	No	306	54	38	8
	Evangelical	68	91	5	4

When you pray, do you usually spend time "asking God to forgive you for specific sins"?

		N	Yes	No	Don't Know
Total Responding		551	76%	23%	1%
Gender:	Male	248	77	23	0
	Female	303	75	23	2
Age:	18 to 27	105	77	23	0
	28-46	206	77	22	2
	47-65	105	73	27	0
	66-98	85	81	19	0
Income:	Under $20,000	129	89	10	1
	$20,000 to $40,000	178	70	30	0
	$40,000 to $60,000	101	72	27	1
	$60,000 or more	70	77	23	0
Education:	High School or Less	248	81	18	1
	Some College	113	73	27	1
	College Graduate	187	71	27	2
Marital Status:	Married	325	78	20	1
	Not Married	224	72	26	2
Have Kids Under 18:	Yes	225	78	21	2
	No	322	74	25	1
Ethnicity:	White	405	75	23	1
	Black	75	84	14	2
	Hispanic	44	70	27	3
Region:	Northeast	116	69	30	1
	South	127	82	17	1
	Central	227	77	21	1
	West	79	70	28	2
Community Type:	Urban	305	74	24	2
	Suburban	62	80	20	0
	Rural	180	78	22	0
Voter Registration:	Not Registered	91	73	26	1
	Reg. Democrat	199	79	20	1
	Reg. Republican	147	75	24	1
	Reg. Independent	81	72	27	2
Denominational	Protestant	238	80	19	1
Affiliation:	Catholic	168	75	23	2
	Baptist	64	90	10	0
	Mainline Protestant	108	81	18	1
Churched:	Yes	443	77	22	1
	No	93	68	32	1
Born Again:	Yes	245	85	14	0
	No	306	68	30	2
	Evangelical	68	94	6	0

TABLE 127   297

When you pray, do you usually spend time "thanking God for what He has done for you"?

		N	Yes	No	Don't Know
Total Responding		551	94%	4%	1%
Gender:	Male	248	94	6	0
	Female	303	95	3	2
Age:	18 to 27	105	91	9	0
	28-46	206	95	4	1
	47-65	105	97	3	0
	66-98	85	97	1	1
Income:	Under $20,000	129	95	4	1
	$20,000 to $40,000	178	99	1	0
	$40,000 to $60,000	101	94	6	0
	$60,000 or more	70	91	8	2
Education:	High School or Less	248	96	3	1
	Some College	113	92	7	1
	College Graduate	187	94	4	1
Marital Status:	Married	325	95	3	1
	Not Married	224	93	6	0
Have Kids Under 18:	Yes	225	94	4	2
	No	322	95	5	1
Ethnicity:	White	405	94	5	1
	Black	75	95	5	0
	Hispanic	44	97	0	3
Region:	Northeast	116	92	7	1
	South	127	96	3	1
	Central	227	94	5	1
	West	79	96	3	1
Community Type:	Urban	305	95	4	1
	Suburban	62	92	5	3
	Rural	180	95	5	0
Voter Registration:	Not Registered	91	92	6	1
	Reg. Democrat	199	97	2	1
	Reg. Republican	147	94	5	1
	Reg. Independent	81	92	8	0
Denominational	Protestant	238	97	3	0
Affiliation:	Catholic	168	89	8	3
	Baptist	64	98	2	0
	Mainline Protestant	108	98	2	0
Churched:	Yes	443	95	4	1
	No	93	90	9	1
Born Again:	Yes	245	97	3	0
	No	306	92	6	2
	Evangelical	68	100	0	0

When you pray, do you usually spend time "asking God to grant specific needs or desires"?

		N	Yes	No	Don't Know
Total Responding		551	61%	36%	2%
Gender:	Male	248	61	37	1
	Female	303	61	36	3
Age:	18 to 27	105	58	42	0
	28-46	206	62	36	2
	47-65	105	62	34	3
	66-98	85	67	31	1
Income:	Under $20,000	129	68	31	1
	$20,000 to $40,000	178	61	37	2
	$40,000 to $60,000	101	57	43	0
	$60,000 or more	70	63	37	0
Education:	High School or Less	248	61	37	2
	Some College	113	60	38	1
	College Graduate	187	62	35	2
Marital Status:	Married	325	61	37	2
	Not Married	224	61	37	3
Have Kids Under 18:	Yes	225	58	40	2
	No	322	64	34	2
Ethnicity:	White	405	61	37	2
	Black	75	69	26	4
	Hispanic	44	43	54	3
Region:	Northeast	116	58	41	1
	South	127	67	30	2
	Central	227	58	39	3
	West	79	67	32	1
Community Type:	Urban	305	61	36	3
	Suburban	62	65	34	1
	Rural	180	59	39	2
Voter Registration:	Not Registered	91	57	41	2
	Reg. Democrat	199	62	36	2
	Reg. Republican	147	63	36	1
	Reg. Independent	81	63	36	2
Denominational	Protestant	238	63	35	2
Affiliation:	Catholic	168	59	37	3
	Baptist	64	57	40	3
	Mainline Protestant	108	68	31	1
Churched:	Yes	443	61	37	2
	No	93	57	39	4
Born Again:	Yes	245	69	29	2
	No	306	55	42	3
	Evangelical	68	83	17	0

TABLE 129   299

When you pray, do you usually spend time "silently listening for God's response to you"?

		N	Yes	No	Don't Know
Total Responding		551	46%	51%	2%
Gender:	Male	248	41	58	1
	Female	303	50	46	3
Age:	18 to 27	105	34	66	0
	28-46	206	46	51	3
	47-65	105	51	48	1
	66-98	85	60	37	3
Income:	Under $20,000	129	56	43	2
	$20,000 to $40,000	178	46	52	2
	$40,000 to $60,000	101	38	60	2
	$60,000 or more	70	39	61	0
Education:	High School or Less	248	49	49	2
	Some College	113	45	53	1
	College Graduate	187	43	54	2
Marital Status:	Married	325	49	49	2
	Not Married	224	43	55	3
Have Kids Under 18:	Yes	225	50	48	2
	No	322	43	54	3
Ethnicity:	White	405	46	52	2
	Black	75	50	46	4
	Hispanic	44	48	49	3
Region:	Northeast	116	41	59	1
	South	127	47	48	5
	Central	227	46	52	2
	West	79	53	46	1
Community Type:	Urban	305	49	49	2
	Suburban	62	31	66	2
	Rural	180	47	50	3
Voter Registration:	Not Registered	91	36	62	1
	Reg. Democrat	199	46	52	2
	Reg. Republican	147	53	44	3
	Reg. Independent	81	40	59	2
Denominational	Protestant	238	48	48	3
Affiliation:	Catholic	168	39	59	2
	Baptist	64	40	54	6
	Mainline Protestant	108	52	46	2
Churched:	Yes	443	48	50	2
	No	93	38	61	1
Born Again:	Yes	245	55	42	3
	No	306	39	59	2
	Evangelical	68	69	27	4

When you pray, do you usually spend time "speaking in tongues or a spiritual language"?

		N	Yes	No	Don't Know
Total Responding		551	12%	85%	3%
Gender:	Male	248	14	85	1
	Female	303	11	85	4
Age:	18 to 27	105	13	87	0
	28-46	206	12	84	4
	47-65	105	10	89	1
	66-98	85	14	85	1
Income:	Under $20,000	129	15	82	3
	$20,000 to $40,000	178	11	88	1
	$40,000 to $60,000	101	9	89	1
	$60,000 or more	70	9	90	1
Education:	High School or Less	248	15	82	3
	Some College	113	11	88	1
	College Graduate	187	10	87	3
Marital Status:	Married	325	12	85	3
	Not Married	224	13	86	2
Have Kids Under 18:	Yes	225	13	83	4
	No	322	11	87	2
Ethnicity:	White	405	11	87	2
	Black	75	15	83	2
	Hispanic	44	12	79	9
Region:	Northeast	116	13	82	5
	South	127	12	87	1
	Central	227	11	87	2
	West	79	15	82	3
Community Type:	Urban	305	13	84	3
	Suburban	62	7	87	7
	Rural	180	13	87	0
Voter Registration:	Not Registered	91	18	80	1
	Reg. Democrat	199	9	87	4
	Reg. Republican	147	14	84	1
	Reg. Independent	81	9	90	2
Denominational Affiliation:	Protestant	238	11	88	1
	Catholic	168	11	84	5
	Baptist	64	6	94	0
	Mainline Protestant	108	13	86	1
Churched:	Yes	443	12	86	2
	No	93	14	85	2
Born Again:	Yes	245	12	88	0
	No	306	12	83	5
	Evangelical	68	15	85	0

TABLE 131   301

How positive are you that prayer really makes a difference in your life? Are you absolutely certain, somewhat certain, hopeful, not sure one way or the other, or pretty doubtful?

		N	Absolutely Certain	Somewhat Certain	Hopeful, Not Sure One Way or the Other	Pretty Doubtful	Don't Know
Total Responding		551	56%	23%	19%	1%	1%
Gender:	Male	248	47	26	23	2	1
	Female	303	64	20	15	1	1
Age:	18 to 27	105	56	20	23	1	0
	28-46	206	51	25	22	2	1
	47-65	105	62	22	13	1	2
	66-98	85	67	18	14	0	0
Income:	Under $20,000	129	65	15	17	1	2
	$20,000 to $40,000	178	54	27	19	1	0
	$40,000 to $60,000	101	58	25	16	1	0
	$60,000 or more	70	44	28	23	2	3
Education:	High School or Less	248	61	18	19	1	1
	Some College	113	51	25	22	2	0
	College Graduate	187	53	27	16	2	2
Marital Status:	Married	325	56	24	17	2	1
	Not Married	224	57	20	21	1	1
Have Kids Under 18:	Yes	225	53	26	18	2	1
	No	322	59	20	19	1	1
Ethnicity:	White	405	52	24	22	2	1
	Black	75	76	10	10	0	4
	Hispanic	44	63	23	13	0	0
Region:	Northeast	116	51	25	22	2	0
	South	127	66	14	18	2	1
	Central	227	55	26	16	1	1
	West	79	55	22	21	1	1
Community Type:	Urban	305	58	20	19	1	2
	Suburban	62	48	27	23	1	1
	Rural	180	56	25	17	2	0
Voter Registration:	Not Registered	91	52	21	20	3	4
	Reg. Democrat	199	57	24	18	1	1
	Reg. Republican	147	59	22	18	1	0
	Reg. Independent	81	53	19	24	3	2
Denominational Affiliation:	Protestant	238	60	23	16	1	0
	Catholic	168	45	30	22	0	2
	Baptist	64	71	25	4	0	0
	Mainline Protestant	108	54	23	22	1	0
Churched:	Yes	443	61	23	14	1	1
	No	93	34	25	36	3	2
Born Again:	Yes	245	73	19	7	0	1
	No	306	43	25	28	3	1
	Evangelical	68	98	1	1	0	0

Do you find that you generally rely upon prayer as a last resort, when things are pretty serious, or as a regular part of your life, regardless of your circumstances?

		N	Last Resort	Regularly	Varies	Don't Know
Total Responding		551	11%	82%	5%	2%
Gender:	Male	248	13	80	4	2
	Female	303	10	83	5	2
Age:	18 to 27	105	8	88	2	1
	28-46	206	14	74	8	3
	47-65	105	10	84	4	1
	66-98	85	9	91	0	0
Income:	Under $20,000	129	11	85	4	1
	$20,000 to $40,000	178	13	81	5	1
	$40,000 to $60,000	101	10	84	5	1
	$60,000 or more	70	14	84	1	1
Education:	High School or Less	248	12	83	3	2
	Some College	113	13	79	6	2
	College Graduate	187	9	82	6	2
Marital Status:	Married	325	10	83	4	3
	Not Married	224	13	81	6	1
Have Kids Under 18:	Yes	225	11	80	4	4
	No	322	11	83	5	1
Ethnicity:	White	405	13	80	6	2
	Black	75	5	90	0	6
	Hispanic	44	14	83	3	0
Region:	Northeast	116	8	86	5	2
	South	127	7	84	7	2
	Central	227	13	81	3	2
	West	79	19	75	4	2
Community Type:	Urban	305	12	82	4	2
	Suburban	62	17	77	5	1
	Rural	180	9	82	6	3
Voter Registration:	Not Registered	91	16	74	8	2
	Reg. Democrat	199	11	84	3	2
	Reg. Republican	147	10	85	4	2
	Reg. Independent	81	8	85	6	2
Denominational Affiliation:	Protestant	238	11	84	4	1
	Catholic	168	12	83	4	2
	Baptist	64	15	83	2	0
	Mainline Protestant	108	8	84	8	0
Churched:	Yes	443	8	86	4	1
	No	93	24	63	9	4
Born Again:	Yes	245	8	88	3	1
	No	306	14	77	6	3
	Evangelical	68	2	98	0	0

TABLE 133 303

Overall, how satisfied are you with the quality of your prayer life? Are you completely satisfied, usually satisfied, sometimes satisfied, sometimes dissatisfied, or completely dissatisfied?

		N	Completely Satisfied	Usually Satisfied	Sometimes Satisfied, Sometimes Dissatisfied	Usually Dissatisfied	Completely Dissatisfied	Don't Know
Total Responding		551	26%	43%	25%	2%	0%	4%
Gender:	Male	248	28	43	24	3	0	3
	Female	303	25	43	26	1	0	5
Age:	18 to 27	105	25	46	28	1	0	1
	28 to 46	206	24	41	29	1	0	4
	47 to 65	105	27	51	20	0	2	1
	66 to 98	85	40	33	15	1	0	10
Income:	Under $20,000	129	37	41	15	3	1	3
	$20,000 to $40,000	178	26	41	29	1	0	3
	$40,000 to $60,000	101	15	52	30	1	1	2
	$60,000 or more	70	20	48	26	3	0	3
Education:	High School or Less	248	31	42	22	1	0	4
	Some College	113	19	44	30	4	0	3
	College Graduate	187	25	44	25	1	1	4
Marital Status:	Married	325	23	45	25	2	0	4
	Not Married	224	30	40	24	2	0	3
Have Kids Under 18:	Yes	225	26	46	23	2	0	3
	No	322	26	41	26	1	1	5
Ethnicity:	White	405	23	46	24	2	0	5
	Black	75	35	39	24	0	0	2
	Hispanic	44	45	23	32	0	0	0
Region:	Northeast	116	23	49	24	2	0	2
	South	127	31	36	27	2	0	4
	Central	227	27	42	25	2	1	4
	West	79	23	46	24	2	0	6
Community Type:	Urban	305	26	45	22	1	0	6
	Suburban	62	25	31	40	4	0	0
	Rural	180	26	45	25	2	0	2
Voter Registration:	Not Registered	91	23	45	25	4	1	3
	Democrat	199	33	43	22	1	0	1
	Republican	147	25	45	25	2	1	2
	Independent	81	20	42	28	2	0	8
Denominational Affiliation:	Protestant	238	22	47	25	1	0	5
	Catholic	168	26	44	22	3	1	4
	Baptist	64	25	37	32	0	0	6
	Mainline Protestant	108	21	53	23	0	0	3
Churched:	Yes	443	26	46	23	2	0	3
	No	93	23	35	34	3	0	5
Born Again	Yes	245	26	46	26	1	0	2
	No	306	27	41	24	3	1	5
	Evangelical	68	30	38	29	1	0	2

TABLE 134

In the November election for president, did you vote for Bill Clinton, George Bush, Ross Perot, or not vote?

		N	Bill Clinton	George Bush	Ross Perot	Other	Did Not Vote	Don't Know
Total Responding		993	37%	31%	13%	1%	8%	10%
Gender:	Male	455	35	30	14	1	9	11
	Female	539	39	32	12	0	7	10
Age:	18 to 27	136	32	29	13	0	18	7
	28 to 46	365	36	33	13	0	9	9
	47 to 65	230	40	31	15	0	4	9
	66 to 98	187	37	30	12	1	5	15
Income:	Under $20,000	219	45	23	9	0	15	8
	$20,000 to $40,000	315	40	32	12	1	7	8
	$40,000 to $60,000	184	28	40	20	0	3	8
	$60,000 or more	148	37	35	15	1	7	5
Education:	High School or Less	416	37	30	11	0	11	10
	Some College	221	37	33	14	1	8	7
	College Graduate	355	38	32	14	0	3	12
Marital Status:	Married	592	35	33	14	0	5	11
	Not Married	401	40	28	11	1	11	9
Have Kids Under 18:	Yes	376	35	32	12	0	10	10
	No	617	39	31	13	1	6	11
Ethnicity:	White	771	32	36	15	1	6	10
	Black	119	72	5	0	0	15	9
	Hispanic	66	43	27	10	0	7	13
Region:	Northeast	208	38	29	13	1	8	12
	South	211	33	36	9	0	14	8
	Central	403	38	32	15	0	4	11
	West	171	41	26	13	2	9	9
Community Type:	Urban	517	41	28	10	0	10	11
	Suburban	145	32	37	18	1	6	7
	Rural	326	34	34	15	1	5	11
Voter Registration:	Not Registered	0	0	0	0	0	0	0
	Democrat	395	64	10	8	0	9	8
	Republican	315	12	67	12	0	3	6
	Independent	208	31	23	22	2	12	10
Denominational Affiliation:	Protestant	437	33	40	12	0	3	11
	Catholic	277	39	30	16	1	7	7
	Baptist	108	36	44	10	0	3	7
	Mainline Protestant	180	36	37	13	0	4	10
Churched:	Yes	753	37	34	12	1	7	10
	No	213	40	24	19	1	9	8
Born Again	Yes	419	35	39	9	0	7	11
	No	575	39	26	16	1	8	10
	Evangelical	119	17	63	7	0	7	6

TABLE 135 305

Are you registered to vote at your current address? Are you registered as a Democrat, a Republican, or as an Independent?

		N	Not Registered	Registered Democrat	Registered Republican	Registered Independent	Registered Other Party	Don't Know
Total Responding		1205	18%	33%	26%	17%	1%	5%
Gender:	Male	577	21	30	26	18	1	4
	Female	628	14	36	26	16	1	7
Age:	18 to 27	212	36	24	17	17	0	6
	28 to 46	453	19	30	26	20	1	4
	47 to 65	250	8	37	35	16	0	5
	66 to 98	201	7	39	28	17	1	7
Income:	Under $20,000	274	20	38	21	15	0	6
	$20,000 to $40,000	391	19	34	24	18	1	4
	$40,000 to $60,000	212	13	31	33	20	0	3
	$60,000 or more	166	11	29	35	21	0	4
Education:	High School or Less	532	22	36	21	16	1	4
	Some College	262	16	30	29	19	0	7
	College Graduate	403	12	32	32	18	1	6
Marital Status:	Married	689	14	30	30	19	1	6
	Not Married	512	22	36	21	16	1	5
Have Kids Under 18:	Yes	468	20	31	27	17	1	5
	No	731	16	34	26	17	1	6
Ethnicity:	White	903	15	28	32	19	1	5
	Black	150	21	60	4	9	0	6
	Hispanic	90	26	47	16	6	0	5
Region:	Northeast	264	21	32	26	18	0	3
	South	263	20	32	26	17	1	5
	Central	481	16	32	24	19	1	7
	West	197	13	37	30	12	1	7
Community Type:	Urban	638	19	35	23	15	1	7
	Suburban	169	14	23	33	26	1	2
	Rural	385	15	34	29	17	0	4
Voter Registration:	Not Registered	206	100	0	0	0	0	0
	Democrat	395	0	100	0	0	0	0
	Republican	315	0	0	100	0	0	0
	Independent	208	0	0	0	100	0	0
Denominational Affiliation:	Protestant	494	12	29	38	15	1	5
	Catholic	343	19	37	22	18	1	4
	Baptist	122	12	38	30	15	1	5
	Mainline Protestant	204	12	29	38	16	1	5
Churched:	Yes	902	16	33	28	16	1	5
	No	270	21	30	21	22	1	6
Born Again	Yes	477	12	33	34	14	1	6
	No	728	21	33	21	19	1	5
	Evangelical	130	8	24	49	14	1	4

Barna Research Group
L i m i t e d

You may have wondered, *Who is this Barna Research Group?* Let me briefly answer that question and suggest other ways we might help you.

I organized the Barna Research Group in 1984. At that stage, the vision was to create a state-of-the-art marketing research company geared to help Christian ministries. It was a large dream for such a small fish. I began working out of a spare bedroom in our tiny home. But God has His ways of working miracles. In my first month in business, the research director from the Disney Channel called and asked if I would be interested in conducting some research for them. It did not take me long to figure out an appropriate answer. For seven years, we served the considerable research needs of the Disney Channel. Along the way we got to do work for well-known organizations such as Visa, First Interstate, the U.S. Army, J. Walter Thompson, C.A.R.E. and others. It was the ability to build a base of such clients that allowed us to expand our staff, facilities and capabilities to fulfill the original goal.

During the 9 years we have been serving ministries, we have had the honor of working with more than 200 Christian organizations. Some of the names are familiar: Billy Graham, World Vision, Focus on the Family, Youth for Christ, Thomas Nelson Publishers, CBN, Trinity Broadcasting, American Bible Society, Willow Creek Community Church, the Salvation Army, Fuller Theological Seminary, Dallas Theological Seminary, Compassion International and so forth. Others are not as well known, but no less significant in God's work. It has been a great thrill to work with God's people, for His purposes, providing a wide variety of research services.

In order to satisfy our vision—"to provide current, accurate and practical marketing information in manageable pieces to Christian ministries so that they may make more timely and intelligent decisions for ministry"—we have increasingly sought alternative methods of communicating our research to ministries that might profit from such knowledge. Toward that end, we publish books and reports; produce a quarterly newsletter, *Ministry Currents,* to help church leaders remain abreast of the latest trends; conduct intensive seminars for pastors and church leaders ("Understanding Ministry in a Changing Culture"); have produced audiotapes describing some of our research findings; and we continue to provide customized research services for ministries.

One of the most effective means of conveying information to ministries is through the books and reports we produce. Following is a partial listing of some of the written documents currently available from Barna Research.

Books (by George Barna)

Today's Pastors, Regal Books, 1993
The Future of the American Family, Moody Press, 1993.
The Invisible Generation: Baby Busters, Barna Research Books, 1992.
The Power of Vision, Regal Books, 1992.
The Barna Report 1992-93, Regal Books, 1992.
A Step-by-Step Guide to Church Marketing, Regal Books, 1992.
Finding a Church You Can Call Home, Regal Books, 1992.
User Friendly Churches, Regal Books, 1991.
What Americans Believe, Regal Books, 1991.
The Frog in the Kettle, Regal Books, 1990.

Reports

Unmarried America, 1993.
Seniors and the Christian Faith, 1993.
Never on a Sunday: The Challenge of the Unchurched, 1991.
Today's Teens: A Generation in Transition, 1991.
Born Again: A Look at Christians in America, 1990.

Only God knows what the future will bring for our company. We anticipate developing videotapes of some of our public presentations; a radio series; seminars designed for the laity; and diagnostic tools for churches, such as our "User Friendly Inventory." Other books and reports are already in development on topics such as: how to revive a dying church; new insights on ministry to the unchurched; reshaping ministry to address the growing skepticism of the public; and understanding the African-American community and the role of the Church in that people group.

If you would like further information about any of these resources, or regarding primary research needs you have, please feel free to contact us at P.O. Box 4152, Glendale, CA 91222-0152. You may reach us by telephone at 818-241-9300, or by fax at 818-246-7684.